Please remember that this is a library book,
and that it belongs only temporarily to each
person who uses it. Be considerate. Do
not write in this, or any, library book.

The Ones Who Got Away

The Ones Who Got Away

Women Who Left Abusive Partners

by Ginny NiCarthy

The Seal Press

Cover design by Rachel da Silva and Laurie Becharas.
Composition by The Typeworks, Vancouver, B.C.
Printed in the United States of America.

10 9 8 7 6 5 4 3 2 1

First edition, September 1987.

Library of Congress Cataloging-in-Publication Data
NiCarthy, Ginny.
    The ones who got away.
    (New leaf series)
    Bibliography: p.
    1. Abused women--United States.   2. Abused wives--
United States.   I. Title.
HV6626.N56   1987   362.8'3   87-20470
ISBN 0-931188-49-0

Seal Press
P.O. Box 13
Seattle, Washington 98111

ACKNOWLEDGMENTS

The women who allowed me to interview them have my gratitude, respect and admiration. I am awed by their willingness to open up old wounds in the hope it will spare other women the terror and pain they have endured. The interviews were laced with tension, tears and even laughter, and I'm privileged to have come close to each one of these women for a few hours.

The directors of several YWCA's and shelters were invaluable in recruiting women to interview and lending me space in which to work. I will not name those women or their organizations because I want to protect the names of the cities in which I conducted the interviews. Vickie Boyd, Danny Lazares, Addei Fuller and Seattle Counseling Service helped me find particular women to interview. Vickie Boyd was most generous in allowing me to use her transcription of an interview she conducted, so that when I interviewed the same woman she didn't have to answer upsetting questions a second time. I appreciate Marcia Kelley's interviewing of formerly battered women in Scotland, and the willingness of those women to share their stories. Although editorial considerations precluded their use in this volume, they expanded my understanding of the cross-cultural similarities among battered women. I thank George Parks for generously sharing his library on romantic love.

Karen Murphy whizzed through tapes, transcribing them at top speed, when I was overcommitted and rushed. Rosalie Sable patiently typed endless drafts of many interviews and was always supportive and a joy to work with.

Anonymous comments, sometimes in extremely thoughtful detail, came from shelter residents and staff. I appreciate the time those women gave, even when some of them were in the midst of crisis themselves. Thank you to Ruth Ann Howell of Catherine Booth House and Mary Pontarolo of New Beginnings for arranging to let me leave the manuscripts at the shelters.

I started this book in 1981 and many friends have bravely stifled their yawns as they listened to me talk about its progress or lack thereof. They went far beyond tolerance and actively exhorted me to keep at it and get it done. For this I'm especially grateful to Karen Bosley, Sandra Coffman, Ruth Crow, Naomi Gottlieb, Dan Kelleher and Jullee Rosanoff. Sandra and Naomi read early and later drafts and made valuable suggestions. Ruth Goodman and Nora Wood each made helpful comments. Sue Davidson turned her always excellent critical eye on the manuscript and helped point me in a fruitful direction. Her faith in my ability to write has been an important impetus to keep going for many years. Barbara Hart made numerous astute judgments about aspects of several chapters. Her thoughtful reading from a strong battered women's rights perspective is especially appreciated.

Faith Conlon's editorial judgment, attention to detail and patience with my imperfections made some otherwise tedious stages of the process a pleasure to deal with. Her sensitivity to nuances of language enabled me to write with more precision than otherwise would have been possible. Barbara Wilson helped me wrestle with conceptual and organizational problems, adding—as usual—dollops of wisdom and humor. The combination of her intelligent criticism and persistent faith in the book played a major role in its successful completion.

Finally, it is a privilege to work with a press that is feminist, that adheres to high standards of every aspect of its work, and whose political and ethical code makes it possible to trust their motives in all decisions that we struggle over. These qualities in our publishing "marriage," make the association more rewarding each year.

Dedicated
to
The ones who didn't get away: the women
whose bodies or spirits were destroyed by
abusive partners.
and
The movement workers who are striving
to end violence against women.

TABLE OF CONTENTS

Widowed after ten wonderful years of marriage, Edith was a single mother of four for several years. Then she married a man who battered her. She has a rewarding career as a nurse, and though she would still rather be "somebody's wife and mother," there are some aspects of living alone that she likes.

The daughter of first-generation Chinese parents, Lou met a black man at a university and was harassed by members of the Chinese community when she lived with him. Frequent beatings and emotional abuse didn't stop her from succeeding at her work as a store manager. It was her work that ultimately "saved her."

As a union organizer, Kate was strong, resourceful and courageous, yet she endured punishment by her left-wing husband, for ideas that he considered "politically incorrect." She is white. After five years of planning, Kate left her husband and now works to help other women in a shelter.

Abused by her psychiatrist father, Sandy is a white singer who was married to a painter who battered her. She's a feminist who writes, sings, composes music and studies Jungian psychology.

Persuaded by her Native American husband that she was "just a dumb Indian" who could never manage without him, Gloria left him after many years of battering and now supports and cares for three of her four teenaged children on her wage as a bookkeeper. She has learned she's not so "dumb" after all.

Although her husband kicked her in the head, which resulted in epilepsy, that didn't deter this white twenty-year old from divorcing him and establishing an independent life.

She's being trained for a technical job that will enable her to support her two children.

A white woman, married as a teenager to a controlling man twice her age, it took her ten years to leave. Then, her involvement with a violent black man and her debilitating health problems nearly destroyed her. She has a satisfying life with a loving husband and a challenging job.

For the first time in her life May was away from the familiarity of Chinatown and having a difficult time with her college classes. Her boyfriend kept her from being lonely, but tried to mold her into a different kind of person and periodically he hit her. Not until long after she had left did she realize she had been abused. Now she counsels other battered Asian women.

As a college student this white woman was severely disabled by polio and rescued by a medical student, who married her and then beat her. Six children and many years later, still seriously affected by her illness, she left him, and has no regrets.

In and out of hospitals with manic-depressive illness, this white woman knew she would never get custody of her four children from her Latino husband, who knew "all the important people." After a suicide attempt she resolved to leave without the children and is certain now it was best for all of them.

After several years of working as a prostitute and being beaten by her pimp, Hillary has a graduate degree, writes poetry and works in the domestic violence movement. She is white and is now a lesbian.

As a teenager isolated in the South from her Native Alaskan family, Lisa was at the mercy of her abusive first husband, a white man. She escaped, but was soon involved in a second marriage to another white man, who beat her. She is now married to a man who treats her well.

Married in the 1940s, this white woman was loyal to her mentally ill, abusive husband for nearly thirty years. She almost got away to pursue her painting career once, but returned because her husband was ill. He killed himself, and now in her early sixties, she is still trying to put her life together.

At eighteen, after being flattered into marriage to an adoring young man, Janine was beaten. She sometimes believed her destiny was to be beaten as her mother had been. She was afraid to risk alienation from her Latino community by divorce. But friends and family stood by her and her baby.

Joan is a white woman who was about to leave her abusive husband of almost twenty years, but when he kidapped her son she returned. A male therapist, subtly seductive, both helped and hindered her. The next time she left, it was with her son and a restraining order. She's learned to be independent and to enjoy life.

This brief relationship would have been even shorter if Sue hadn't returned to her boyfriend after he attempted suicide. When he flaunted another relationship, it was clear she couldn't rescue him and she left to begin a new life. Sue is white.

A black woman, Maddie was pregnant and married at sixteen. She's a medical records clerk, who is beginning to enjoy her single life and two children after ten years of abuse.

Educated, sophisticated, from a stable white middle-class family, Jane married twice because of social pressure for a conventional life. The second time she was battered. Now she is content to be single.

An "undocumented" woman, from South America, Lucia stayed with her husband, who sponsored her, until she obtained her "green card." She has had unexpected support from her Latin relatives.

A white fifty-year old grandmother of nine, Margaret killed her husband in self-defense. Her conviction for second degree murder was successfully appealed. She is married to a man who is not violent and they enjoy a quiet life together.

A "nice Jewish girl," and an athlete, Ruth was intrigued by what she perceived as the exotic aspects of a black woman who experimented with drugs and was sexually exciting. Although at one point she was certain her will had been broken, she managed to leave and is now involved with the movement against woman battering.

Terry was born in Taiwan and at eighteen came to the United States where she and her mother worked in a Chinatown sweatshop. A brief marriage to an assaultive man ended in divorce and now she volunteers at a service for battered Asian women. Though some old friends have rejected her, she is making new friends and looks forward to a good life, single or married.

Abused as a child by her schizophrenic mother, this white

woman sees herself as having learned to be a victim at an early age. She is manic-depressive, but now feels stable and has begun to take up the activities she left when she met her abusive boyfriend.

Amanda was an enthusiastic college student thrilled to be chosen by a Big Man On Campus, but after just a few months was drained by his abuse and left him. She's a white recovering alcoholic who has a happy relationship with another man.

A Native American woman, Hope left numerous times but was afraid to stay away. When she did get away, with the help of shelter personnel, she worked three jobs to support herself and her child. When she was disabled by arthritis, her ex-husband won custody. With the help of her supportive new husband she is working at getting it back.

Nicole is a black woman who lost her only support, her mother, at the age of ten. Emotionally abused by the man she married as a teenager, she struggled economically to support her two children. She was physically abused by another man, and is now excited about a future in women's studies and ethnic studies.

A highly paid white medical administrator working on her Ph.D., Jennifer knew she couldn't give the necessary attention to her career if she didn't get out of her abusive relationship. Distance helped. She is one of the few women who has been able to remain friends with the man who battered her.

With an eighth grade education, this white woman was convinced she was "too dumb" to do anything. When she left her husband she surprised herself with her competency and was promoted several times at two successive jobs.

The Ones Who Got Away

The Women, the Book and Research About Battering

In 1981, while writing *Getting Free: A Handbook for Women in Abusive Relationships*, I talked with women who had left the partners who battered them. I was moved by their determination to overcome fear, dependency, hopelessness and overwhelming practical obstacles to freedom. I knew there were hundreds of untold stories that could help other women change their lives, and I began to look for them and record interviews for this book.

HOW THE STORIES CAN HELP

My main purpose in publishing these edited interviews is to provide a forum for formerly battered women to inspire other women by relating their struggles, setbacks, triumphs and continuing challenges. If you feel afraid, controlled, helpless or trapped in your relationship with your partner, or if you've just separated and are wondering what to do next, the stories these women tell of their lives can give you a fresh perspective on your own situation. Their courage can inspire you to make dramatic changes and, perhaps, to save your life. If you've already started a new life, free of violence, but your budget is strained, your ex-partner is harassing you, the children are difficult and your washing machine just broke down, these stories will remind you of why it's all worth it and will help you keep in mind that you can endure, that you can create a new and safe life if you give yourself time.

If you're a therapist or a friend of a woman who's battered,

I hope the women's experiences with people who helped and hindered them will point to a way you can support and encourage the woman you know to decide what she wants to do and then to act on it. Chapter 34 spells out advice from the women in this book to other women and the final chapter summarizes aspects of the women's lives that may be useful to anyone who wants to help a battered woman.

The book is about women who left, because that is the only choice for most battered women who are determined to be safe. The entire time the women written about in this book were trying to understand their lovers, seeing counselors, conferring with ministers, listening to family members' advice, trying to be better cooks and housekeepers, learning to distract and calm and nurture and forgive so that they wouldn't be beaten—every moment of that time, they were risking their lives.

Some of their partners seemed intent on killing them, and the women got away just in time. Others apparently didn't want to murder, but placed the women they loved in life-threatening danger. Each time the abusers unleashed their violence they risked misjudging the amount of force they used; some did permanent damage that may not have been intended. Some of the women who are missing from these pages are those who were killed or so severely maimed that they cannot speak for themselves. Many hundreds of women are killed by their partners each year[1] and countless numbers of women are permanently disabled by their injuries. The mental and emotional damage is incalculable. The women interviewed for this book decided they were no longer willing to risk their lives, their health or their emotional stability. Some of them made their decisions just in time to save their lives and they hope their stories will help other women leave in time to minimize the damage from abuse.

A GROUP IN PRINT

Since the beginning of the battered women's movement in the mid-seventies, women have learned there is nothing as helpful to them as a group of women who have been in situations that are similar to their own. The group can be in a shelter or at a community center, it can be a formal arrangement with a professional leader or just three women trading stories at the laundromat. Prior to the late 1970s women at the laundromat would rarely admit to each other that they were battered, but now many battered women are confiding in each other during office and factory coffee breaks, at university sororities, at neighborhood coffee klatches and church socials. If you've been battered and you want to know how other women were able to leave dangerous partners and stay away, *The Ones Who Got Away* is intended to serve as a kind of a group for you.

A full understanding of the circumstances of each woman's decision to stay away from her abusive partner can only be seen in the context of her life. It has been my intention to go beyond statistics, to enable the women to describe the complex fabric of their thoughts, feelings, social situations and values. There is almost nothing in print that tells how women dealt with the many problems they faced after they left abusive partners. How the women maintained the courage to remain safe and free is an important part of their stories and will, I hope, give strength to those of you who have left and are feeling unsure of how long you can sustain enough will power to stay away, or how you can handle continuing harassment.

The chapters in this book each contain a woman's story and are purposely arranged to emphasize the wide range of class, race, age, experience, character and personality types. If you've been battered, you might first look for someone like yourself. To make it a little easier to find those women you can identify with, I have summarized each story in the table of contents. However, after you've read about the women who seem most like you in age, class, sexual preference or ethnicity, I hope you'll read the other stories too.

You may be surprised to find, for instance, that even though you have little money or have traditional beliefs about marriage, you share certain experiences or attitudes with a professional, middle-class woman or one who has a different way of life. If you're a rural white woman you might find that a woman of color or an urban white woman has an extended family that is something like yours. Those are the kinds of connections that are made in groups and shelters for battered women, where women of all sorts come together and help each other change their lives.

OVERCOMING OBSTACLES

If you're being abused you may not be able to imagine yourself managing an independent life. You might believe you can't end your relationship because your partner has made you feel helpless or because you have no marketable job skills, little self-confidence or limited education and experience in taking care of yourself. You may believe you're abused because you've always been emotionally and financially dependent or have low self-esteem and there's no hope of changing the pattern. As you read the stories you'll find examples of women who also felt that way, but who surprised themselves with their own strength and were able to leave abusive partners when it became clear it was necessary. Once they were in a safe place they were able to gradually rebuild their lives. Some of them are self-sufficient and emotionally secure for the first time in their lives.

It may surprise you that some of the women in the book were relatively helpless within the relationship, yet are strong, capable women who held responsible positions during the period they were being battered. Perhaps you are one of those women yourself, or you're a feminist, a lesbian or for some other reason you don't think of yourself as a traditional woman. You might believe there is something especially "wrong" with you, because you are not "that" kind of woman and yet you've been abused. These stories will help you understand the variety of ways that strong and nontraditional women can become involved with dangerous partners.

If you're a woman of color, a lesbian, a member of a conservative religious group or there are other circumstances that limit your freedom to reach out to the larger society, you may feel that the special obstacles to making a new life are too great to overcome. You might also feel that's true if you're an older woman, an undocumented worker, an overseas army wife, a disabled woman, a refugee, the wife of a prominent politician—or in numerous other situations. You won't find a woman here whose life is just like yours, but many had special difficulties in leaving their partners.

IS LEAVING THE ONLY OPTION?

Even if you clearly state to your partner that violence is not acceptable, your decision not to leave is likely to be interpreted by the abuser as a message that the battering is not so bad after all and that it's alright to control you by whatever means necessary. That's because battering is not about losing control of one's temper; it's about gaining control of you and using violence, threats and demeaning emotional abuse to do it. It's true that a few abusers do decide they want to change and are willing to do the hard work to ensure that they can follow through on their intentions.[2] But there are few success stories and as long as you are willing to stay, there is little incentive for your partner to change.

It's hard to change a well-established habit that is physically, emotionally and socially embedded in behavior toward a partner. Those who are willing to do the long-term, disciplined work to change usually need to be shocked into it by "hitting bottom." For some abusers intervention by the law represents that bottom; for others it's the loss of the partner or a serious threat of that loss. For many, nothing at all will bring about change because the abuser is determined to control the partner and is willing to use violence to do it.

Neither researchers nor therapists know very much about couples in which a violent person is able to change while living with the abused partner. The little we know indicates there are several steps necessary for most people to stop violent, controlling behavior for a significant length of time.[3] If you're not yet willing to give up on the relationship, you may want to try one last series of actions. If nothing else, taking these steps may help you face the fact that your partner is unwilling to give up control as well as the violence. If he or she isn't willing to follow through with the steps outlined, if you aren't willing to be separated while your partner goes through the steps, or if they don't result in the kind of relationship you want, perhaps you'll decide there's nothing left for you to try except to leave.

A PROGRAM TO END VIOLENCE AND CONTROL

For you and your partner:
1. Police intervention and prosecution for the crime of assault.
2. Separation for as long as it takes for your partner to stop the violence, control and emotional abuse. This will take at least six months and possibly years.
3. If you have children, legal temporary custody and child support arrangements that maximize safety for you and the children.

For your partner:
1. Attendance at a group for people who batter.
2. Group or individual therapy which might cover these problem areas: sexism and sex-roles, violence and fear, emotional abuse, anger management, intimacy, assertion, jealousy, childhood abuse, addiction, emotional awareness, sexuality, abandonment, parenting, self-esteem, addiction, relaxation, communication.
3. Drug or alcohol treatment if appropriate.
4. Commitment to ongoing therapy or support group for as long as necessary—perhaps for life.

For you:
1. Participation in support group.
2. Development of a friendship network, independent of your partner's.
3. Development of an independent means of financial support.
4. Classes or therapy to help with parenting skills if appropriate, and time to repair any damage that may have been done to your relationship to your children.
5. Classes in assertion training and communication, or therapy for you if appropriate.

For both of you:
    1. After at least several months of the above program, couple counseling which includes contracts outlining agreed upon behavior.
    2. Development of a plan to monitor potentially abusive behavior.

As you read the stories in this book you'll see that many of the women tried some aspects of the program outlined above. But in most instances either the abusers didn't cooperate for long, the abused woman only tried one of the steps, or she didn't stay separated long enough nor insist that her partner adhere to the agreements. Many of the women's lives were in jeopardy for a long time before they fully realized the danger—and when they left, it was too late to find out if a program would work.

You are the only person who can make the decision to stay or leave. It is my hope that as you read these stories you'll become more aware of how much danger you're in while you continue to be involved with a violent partner. Reading about women who thought they couldn't leave dangerous partners and yet ultimately did get away may help you to understand your own choices better.

THE WOMEN WHO GOT AWAY

This is not a large study, nor were the women I interviewed chosen on a random basis, so the stories presented here are not representative of any other populations. These women speak only for themselves. In 1981 I began interviewing women who had successfully left violent men and who had been away for at least a year. Some of them were former clients and their friends. Some came to me in response to a flyer I sent to professionals. Even though I didn't try to reach a random or a national sample, I did want some geographic distribution, so I advertised in daily newspapers in three Western cities and interviewed several women in each, as well as a few on the East Coast, ultimately including women in seven states. They lived in both urban and rural areas. In some cities I asked shelter workers to help me locate women of certain ethnic groups.

I had made the decision, in 1982, when I began the book, not to include lesbians, because the subject of lesbian battering was still mostly in the closet, even though it was being talked about in a few small circles. By the time I neared completion of the book in 1986 it was clear that the subject was "out." It had also become evident that lesbians who are battered find it even more difficult than heterosexual women to get help. They are often made to feel invisible in discussions with women in the battered women's movement or when they initiate the subject with lesbian counselors or in lesbian communities. Battered lesbians need models of freedom from violence at least as much as heterosexual women do, so it became out of the question to finish the book without including some of their stories.

THE INTERVIEWS

Each woman was asked the same questions about her life before, during and after the battering. The women were encouraged to take as long as they wanted to answer a basic question such as "What was your life like before you met your partner?" and usually would incorporate most of the sub-questions in their answers. Sub-questions included "How did you feel about yourself?," "What was your occupation?," "Did you have friends?," etc. They were asked to describe their expectations of the relationship with the person who battered them, as well as the violence and emotional abuse. They were asked why they stayed and left and what people helped them to change their lives. They were also asked whether they had ever thought of killing their partners. Most interviews took between three and four hours. All but two were done in one sitting. Two were conducted over the telephone, others took place in my office, shelter offices and women's homes.

I interviewed forty-one women and reluctantly have used

only thirty-three stories. In a few instances I had to omit interviews because of technical difficulties with the tapes. I had to make difficult decisions because there was too much material to publish in one book, so I chose the stories of the women who illustrated a variety of experiences. I was sorry to have to omit some of the rich, emotionally moving stories, and to cut others to manageable length; however, all of the women interviewed contributed to the chapter on advice to women (Chapter 34), and all have helped me to broaden my perspective on the complexity of this subject.

I selected the aspects of each story that illustrated the woman's background, her lifestyle, personality and character as well as how she felt about herself before, during and after the battering. I also used material that would make clear the extent of the abuse, and what enabled each woman to leave and stay away.

Although a few of the women were willing to use their real names, some of them were still in potential danger even after many years. For their protection pseudonyms have been used for all names, locations have been changed and other identifying characteristics of the women have been disguised or altered.

As I organized the book I found myself continually trying to put the stories into categories, such as religious women, women who stayed because of their children, women who worked outside the home, women who were persuaded by professionals to stay, and so on. But the women refused to stay in their categories. Many could fit into several of the proposed sections, many had numerous reasons for staying and leaving—so where did they "belong?" I ultimately held to my original position that each woman is unique and finally I arranged the interviews to emphasize exactly that.

WHAT THE RESEARCH TELLS US

We still don't know much about what characteristics or situations, if any, are typical or common among women who are abused. The research does tentatively indicate some trends, but they are by no means definitive and are sometimes contradictory. Nevertheless, it may be helpful to compare them with the situations described in the book.

Many of the women I interviewed were emotionally abused as children. It seems clear that emotional abuse is widespread in families, but we have no statistics with which to make comparisons. About two-thirds of the women were physically abused by their parents, which is a higher proportion than most researchers (but not all) find in surveys of women who were battered.[4]

Lenore Walker found in her study of 435 battered women that forty-eight percent had been sexually molested as children, many by relatives.[5] This is hardly surprising, when we consider the large number of women in the general population who have been sexually molested. Diana Russell, in a random sample of 930 women, found that thirty-eight percent had experienced at least one incident of sexual abuse before they were eighteen.[6]

Only Hillary, Chris and Nicole told me they had been sexually molested by family members, but others may have survived incest and chosen not to tell me about it. I asked each woman if she had been abused by other people, not specifically whether she had had sexual acts forced upon her as a child. There may also have been experiences that wouldn't fit into most definitions of molestation, but were traumatizing or frightening. Such experiences were described without the women identifying them as sexual abuse.

In addition to the large numbers of women who have been molested as children by trusted adults, virtually all women have been subjected to "indecent exposure" and have experienced demeaning, frightening and humiliating sexual harassment, verbal assaults or attempts at exploitation as children and adults. Many women discount the impact of such experiences because they occur so often. Yet for some children and women those events are as disturbing as physical molestation is to others. We have no way, yet, of isolating these events in the lives of each woman and determining whether it will make her particularly vulnerable to later abuse. We do know that some of the women, such as Melissa and Lou, were subjected to experiences by their partners that were similar to their childhood or teen sexual abuse. The repetitive aspect of the experiences may have exacerbated the trauma and made them less able to free themselves from their partners.

Many people believe that women who have been battered are living impoverished or otherwise marginal lives. Statistics vary widely on this question, but it is clear that battering crosses all class, race, lifestyle and religious lines. It is not yet known whether it is more prevalent in some groups than in others. Many studies have been conducted among shelter populations, where the residents tend to have fewer economic resources than average, which adds to the impression that a disproportionate number of poor women are battered.

It is commonly thought that women who are battered become involved in one violent relationship after another. Mildred Pagelow found in her sample of 350 battered women that seventeen percent had been battered by a previous boyfriend or husband.[7] But research has barely touched on this question, and my impression from counseling hundreds of women who have been battered is that only a small minority are caught in that pattern. Very few of the women in this book had more than one physically abusive relationship, although several women were subjected to emotional abuse by more than one partner. Many were able to recognize damaging relationships more and more quickly and to leave them at an early point.

Almost two-fifths of the women in this book were involved with alcoholic partners, which is close to the forty to sixty percent than has been found in most studies.[8] Although there is clearly an association between drinking patterns and battering, so far no definite causal relationship has been established. Some abusive people use their drinking as an excuse to batter and battered women who believe it's the alcohol that causes battering absolve the abusive partner of responsibility for the violence. They would be safer if they insisted that the abuser take responsibility for ending the drinking as well as the battering. The women can also remind themselves and the abusers that many alcoholics don't batter and much violence takes place without consumption of alcohol.

An abused woman can refuse to see her alcoholic partner until there is a clear indication that the abuser has completely stopped drinking. Even then, that is not a guarantee that the violence will end, or that sobriety will be dependable. Madlyn's husband stopped both drinking and battering for a year, but then he resumed both.

THE VALUE AND LIMITATIONS OF RESEARCH

Quantitative research has been important in establishing that battering is widespread. However, because it focuses mainly on information that can be counted and measured, it doesn't help us understand the context of battering.[9] It doesn't tell us about the complexities of feelings, thoughts, moral imperatives and conflicts that each woman experiences as she tries to decide the best way to react to her situation. Nor does it explain the political context of battering.

Feminist research has made a major contribution to our understanding of the political nature of male battering of women, which had been previously seen as only an individual problem. Men who batter are each responsible for their choices of how to behave, yet they are also playing out traditional masculine roles practiced for hundreds of generations and reinforced by all of our institutions. Feminists have helped us see that men who batter do not simply "lose their cool." They are not "sick."[10]

There are a few exceptions and some of the men described in the interviews were apparently mentally ill. However, many mentally ill men and women are not violent, and mental illness, like alcoholism, can be used as an excuse to control. It is difficult for most women to leave partners who are ill or disabled in any way, but those who are determined to remain safe must ultimately decide that they are not the appropriate people to act as therapist or doctor. The mentally ill person must seek help from a professional. In some instances medicine or therapy may aid a person who is committed to stop the violence and who does not insist on controlling the partner.

WHY DO ABUSED WOMEN STAY?

Since social agencies began to recognize that battering is a pervasive social problem, the question most frequently asked by researchers and the public is, "Why do they stay?" Unfortunately, very few social scientists have investigated the more important questions: "Why do men batter?"; "Why do women leave?"; "What helps them stay away?"; "What can be done to help women be safe?" In recent years it has become apparent that researchers need to ask the additional questions: "Why do lesbians and gay men batter their intimate partners?" and "How can they be helped to be safe?"

The question "Why does she stay?" implies that women who are battered don't ever leave their partners. The testimonies of the women interviewed for this book, as well as the experiences of thousands of others, indicate otherwise. Battered women do leave, some after many years, some after a few months and others after the first time they are hit. Lenore Walker has noted that the couples in her study stayed together an average of six years, which is the same as the average length of marriage of all people in the U.S.[11] The question might more appropriately be phrased "Why don't they leave sooner?"

For about ten years sociologists and psychologists have tried to find out why women stay with violent men, but their conclusions are varied and far from definitive. They include sexism, fear, helplessness, brainwashing, guilt, addictive love, childhood bonding through negative and positive reinforcement, religious beliefs, traditional ideas about loyalty, duty and the role of nurturer, lack of resources, and hope for change.[12] None of those phrases explains very much, since they encompass many different aspects of each of the reasons stated.

For instance, fear may indicate the immediate threat of being killed, which Lynn and several other women in this book experienced. But it may also include such fears as Sue's that she would feel responsible if her boyfriend killed himself. It may mean something quite specific such as Lucia's fear of not getting her "green card" and facing possible deportation, or Ruth's fear of her family being told she was a lesbian before she was ready to come out to them.

Guilt may include feelings of obligation that are based on traditional ideas about women's roles, religious beliefs, deeply imbedded unconscious assumptions or individual ethics. Lack of resources may imply having no job, no money and no place to live, or it might mean having no one available to help clarify options. Hope for change could mean that the abusive partner's promises to change are believed, or that the woman hopes she can change herself enough to prevent the abuse. Jennifer, Kate and other women interviewed for this book tried to take on the role of psychiatrist. This was a particularly compelling role for women whose partners were alcoholic, mentally ill or who had had difficult childhoods.

The list of reasons women stay with abusive partners is long, and as you will find in the stories that follow, the above categories are not the entire answer. Some of the explanations are based on social and political concepts and some imply purely individual, psychological reactions. Though feminists and others sometimes try to separate these factors, they are so intertwined as to be virtually inseparable. An individual woman's lack of money or marketable job skills, for instance, is intimately tied to the politics of unequal distribution of resources to women and men. Since all of the beliefs any of us has are influenced by institutions, and all of our institutions have been established on a sexist foundation, we may not be able to determine where the social-political rationales differ from the individual dynamics. Certainly the patriarchal political and economic system we live under has tremendous weight in guiding the forms that violence takes, yet we don't know why people are differentially socialized. Why, for instance, do some men not batter, and why do some lesbians batter, even though both patterns are counter to male and female conditioning?

Battered women reported, in Pagelow's study, that after the first assault they stayed because they hoped for change, and because of the lack of alternatives. After more assaults their major reasons for staying were fear and helplessness.[13] All of those reasons were common, along with others, to the women I interviewed. Yet, when certain things happened

—fear of being killed if she stayed, the batterer's interest in a new woman, the battered woman's interest in a new man, and many others—those reasons dissipated. After she leaves, the reasons a woman gives for having stayed as long as she did may be very different from what she had thought when she was still in the relationship. Some women have said they can't leave because they love their partner, yet after they left they realized it was dependency that kept them with the partner, not love. If forced to give one or two responses to a question, women will pick out the most important reason for staying, but in telling stories, they give different reasons for different periods in their lives; they change their minds about the "real" reason even as they are talking and often contradict themselves. Anyone who has talked with a woman who's been battered (or who remembers her own process of making a difficult decision) will recall a shifting list of reasons for doing one thing and then the other.

"But I love him, I can't abandon him" may be the first response to a question about leaving. A few moments later the same woman may say that the children need a father, that she's afraid she'll lose her community support if she leaves, that she'll be killed, that she can never support herself or the children adequately; she may also say that the partner might change if she can just figure out how to do exactly what is demanded of her. She might believe there are no better partners out there for her and be afraid she can't emotionally survive on her own. On some days she may believe some or none or all of these factors are important and true; on other days she may be sure of the opposite. If she overcomes all those obstacles, she may seek advice and then decide to stay because of what a lawyer, minister or counselor advises. Many women deny or minimize the danger because they have overriding reasons for taking the risk.

For example, Madlyn had multiple reasons for staying, with different priorities at certain stages of her life. She said of herself in the period before she married, "At gut level I knew it was serious but I just put it out of my mind." She also recognized something: "After the first time he hit me it seemed like he gained some kind of power." Her religious beliefs helped to further her denial. "Coming from a religious family I felt that God would not let anything like that happen to me." She had a "storybook" idea of what her life with George would be like. When she was hit three months after the wedding, she felt it would be too shameful to leave so soon, it would disgrace her parents and herself and she had an obligation to stay "till death do you part."

Madlyn also felt guilty and believed she must be doing something to deserve the punishment. When George gave her flowers she believed he was making an effort and would change. Most of these feelings and beliefs were reinforced by her psychiatrist, her minister and George's boss. She thought her children needed a father. At some point she was so depressed she "had no will." The "real" reason she stayed is open to question.

Few researchers have even asked questions about lesbian battering. There is every reason to suppose lesbians have all the reasons for staying mentioned above and more.[14] If they seek support outside the relationship, many lesbians face the necessity of "coming out" as lesbians and as battered women at the same time. Some feel humiliated by the disparity between the positive image of lesbians as strong, independent women, and their picture of "helpless victims" who are abused. They may be reluctant to view violence as anything but a purely heterosexual problem.

Some lesbians' social circles are confined to the same people who are friends of her partner and in some lesbian communities there is little or no support for the lesbian who is battered. Many of the services available to heterosexual women do not serve lesbians, or the personnel are too biased or untrained in how to help lesbians to serve them well.

ADDICTIVE LOVE, SEX-ROLE SOCIALIZATION AND RISK-TAKING

Many people believe there is something peculiar, flawed or "crazy" about women who don't immediately leave and stay away from partners who have assaulted and tried to control them. Many popular books imply that "women who love too much" or who are "codependent" become involved with partners who mistreat them as a result of faulty adult character traits or individual childhood experiences in nuclear families.[15] The authors of these books focus on deficiencies of individual women without taking into account centuries of female socialization. The most striking aspect of women's dependency is how it has endured throughout history, supported by legal and institutional proscriptions against economic or political independence from men. Women's dependency on men is our sociopolitical legacy of sexism, not an individual sickness.

All people in Western Civilization have been taught to be addicted to romantic love, but women, especially, are socialized to believe they are only half a person without an intimate partner—until recent years, usually assumed to be a man. U.S. popular songs of any decade in this century illustrate the phenomenon, as well as the idea that true love is painful, demands sacrifice and makes one feel crazy, sick, intoxicated or drugged. This doesn't imply that people who are addicted to love crave suffering. They desire the good times, romance, excitement, periodic nurturing or sense of security, and hope this time it will be different, that the bad times won't follow. Some people settle for the pain, accepting the fact that it is the price of rewards.

Like many other women, some women who've been battered confuse addictive love with emotional and economic dependency, nurturing love or filial obligation. "I can't leave because I love him" may refer to any one of those factors or more likely a combination of them. This confusion is the result of centuries of history that rest on the shoulders of women and weigh them down with ideas of how they should feel about intimate partners, children and family. Messages given to women about how they should care for their loved ones further compound the problem by equating how they should feel with how they should act. "If I love my partner, I can't leave." "If I love myself or act to please myself, that means I'm selfish and not a real woman."

Centuries of women's economic dependency on men cannot be lightly dismissed and the pattern persists as a norm for many people, despite the knowledge that most women are employed outside the home. This traditional idea endures because most women with children still can't earn enough to supply more than the family's bare survival necessities at best. If a woman finds a man who will take care of a woman economically, she may talk herself into thinking he is important to her emotionally.

Just as some people learn society's desirable lessons easily or with difficulty, some learn the lessons of addiction more thoroughly than others. To say that some battered women are addicted to their abusive partners is not to say there's anything unique about them that differs from other women. The thing that differentiates them from other women is that they are at risk of serious physical and emotional damage from the abusive partners they love.

When a woman is addicted she finds that she continues to indulge her habit or arrange to be with the person in spite of the knowledge that the long term effects (at least) will be damaging and will leave her feeling depressed, guilty or angry at herself. As time goes on she derives less and less pleasure from the habit and more grief in between the "highs." Or the "highs" may not even be experienced any more. Other aspects of the woman's life diminish in importance: she sees less of friends, becomes less involved in work, is anxious to leave activities she used to enjoy because she wants to go home to listen for the telephone.

When a woman has those experiences, it doesn't mean that she's *physically* addicted. Although some people believe that addictions are by definition, physiological, others make a persuasive case that addictions are learned. Stanton Peele, in *Love and Addiction*, describes how certain classes, racial and age groups learn to be addicted to particular drugs long before they even try them. Alan Marlott and Judith Gordon, in *Relapse Prevention*, state their view that addictive behavior is an "overlearned habit." They recognize that social factors are involved in learning an addictive habit as well as in maintaining it.[16]

Most people view addictive love in quite a different light from other addictions, especially when considering women's relationships. Until recent years it has been acceptable for women to give up almost all other obligations and pleasures to devote themselves to their families or their partners. If a woman's world becomes constricted and she feels truly alive only when she is devoting herself to others' pleasure, convenience, comfort or growth, that is still viewed by many people as an admirable trait. It is not labeled as "addiction" and she is rewarded by social approval for this condition, whereas other unrestrained habits are disdained. (Addiction to work, for men, is often accepted as normal or even admirable.) Many women are still given mixed messages of approval for sticking by violent partners and scorn for putting up with the abuse. When women do decide to leave abusive partners, they can't be sure what their reception will be among friends and relatives. They risk social standing and other relationships, as well as, perhaps, their sense of identity. To disrupt a home and family remains a choice that threatens many women's basic values. To avoid making such a decision they minimize the danger or persuade themselves they will have time to get out before the risk becomes lethal.

HOME AND FAMILY: UNIVERSAL VALUES

In certain situations men as well as women are reluctant to leave their homes, their loved ones, their countries. We have examples of people taking life-threatening risks to avoid giving up the people or place that represents home to them. Some Jews didn't leave Germany during the rise of the Nazi regime because they felt an obligation to stay and change the situation, because they hoped things would improve or denied the possibility that they personally would be victimized. Or their resources were too slim to affect a move. Some planned to leave, but waited too long. Many were willing to risk their lives rather than face the loss of home, with all that the word implies. There are numerous examples of such reactions in other countries.

Yuri Orlov, a Soviet physicist and human rights campaigner, was sentenced to seven years in a labor camp where the beatings he endured resulted in pervasive weakness and the temporary loss of his peripheral vision. But according to his wife, "He never wanted to emigrate. He is a Russian. He loves this land and you know he still believes it can be improved."[17] Others who sought freedom by emigrating from the Soviet Union to the U. S. returned to their homeland a few years later. One of them put a common feeling succinctly in saying "East or West, home is best."[18] People have had similar reasons for staying or rebuilding year after year in flood and forest fire areas, at the foot of volcanoes or in other dangerous places. Although experts warn against building in such areas, they are often ignored or attended to only during the crisis period.

At the height of danger many people resolve to leave the familiarity of home and seek safety in a new place, yet when the immediate threat subsides many decide to stay put. A sociologist surveyed 3500 Southern Californians following a warning that shifting ground "might presage a major earthquake" and found that the "people at greatest risk for being hurt in an earthquake appear to show the greatest denial of the threat." He also discovered that fear peaked when a seismic threat was publicized, but soon afterward the sense of urgency dissipated.[19] Women, too, are afraid and plan to leave when the threat is greatest or when their awareness of it is heightened by a recent beating. If it isn't repeated soon again, time and their wish to minimize the danger helps them forget the urgency.

BALANCING REWARDS, DUTY AND RISKS

Some women stay because they "can't afford to leave," just as some miners, soldiers and others work in dangerous occupations because they can't afford to quit. U.S. citizens employed in Lebanon stay there at the risk of abduction by terrorists, reluctant to quit jobs that pay better than anything available to them in the United States.[20]

Women are sometimes brainwashed by abusers in ways similar to the methods used to control prisoners of war and kidnapping victims.[21] They have a particularly difficult time determining their reasons for staying in a dangerous situation, and may not be sure until long after they've left just why they stayed as long as they did.

Soldiers rush into battle because of patriotism or to protect their buddies. Some police officers choose to work in dangerous neighborhoods and fire fighters volunteer because "someone must do it" and because they care about their communities. Women have been conditioned to believe that their community is their family and "family" may simply mean partner. Their duty is to be of use and to help others.

Although Gwen believes now that it was not her duty to stay with "a psychotic who had no conscience," at the time she interpreted her responsibility differently, and she still has moments of doubt. "I'd always been very devout," she recalls, "and when I took my vows, I felt that I had to abide by them. I had to do what I felt was right within me, and that probably kept me with him, especially after I came home and found that Jonathan couldn't move his arm and needed care . . . I did go that extra mile with him and if there's a God, He knows that I was really in there doing all that I could do under those circumstances." The ethic of caretaking is very strongly implanted in most women and, unfortunately, doesn't always allow for taking care of oneself.

Women who are battered are not so different from anyone else. As you read the interviews you will see the wide variety of reasons the women gave for staying, as well as the similarities. The shortest answer to the question "Why do they stay?" is something like "All of the above."

More importantly, the stories related here describe how and why the women left and how they were able to stay away. Their lives seem to be made up of very similar stuff; yet they're woven into quite individual fabrics. The similarities are in the courage that emerged from despair and terror. The telling of these stories did not mitigate the pain each woman endured, but it is made bearable by their capacity to inspire other women who, in their turn, will get away from abusive partners. And their success will encourage still others—and others and others.

CHAPTER 1

Madlyn

Madlyn grew up in the midst of a very loving, religious family. She was an independent, headstrong little girl from at least the age of five, when she frightened her mother by disappearing to play with friends on the way home from kindergarten each day. Her youth was spent enjoying "outdoorsy" and athletic activities in a small suburban town, where she treasured the freedom of going barefoot in summer. She made plenty of friends and had a good time in school, while performing well in her classes. From the first grade she was involved in theater. In sixth grade she wrote a play, chose the actors, made the costumes and put on the production.

She continued her theatrical activities in junior and senior high school and was challenged and excited by her senior radio class, which built a small transmitter and broadcast a weekly program. She was also third-page editor of the high school paper, earned good grades and was active in Girls' League and Pep Club. Madlyn's friends were the "girls who didn't," the ones who were not sexually open with boys. She had male friends, but she didn't date much until she was a senior.

As a child and adolescent Madlyn felt good about herself, with one exception. Her breasts developed in sixth grade and by the time she was in high school they were unusually large and she was subjected to teasing by teenaged boys. After high school graduation her first venture away from the security of her small town home took her to a large West Coast university, where she was subjected to further humiliation.

I remember walking downtown and a bunch of boys hanging out in a fraternity were making ribald remarks, yelling "Pig! Pig!" and "Sooey! Sooey!" (a call for pigs). "Look at the tits on her!" and "Let's get her!" I just cringed. It was very demeaning to my self-concept. It just laid me out. I was devastated. I could hardly get through there and when I got back to the dorm I cried and didn't go out for the rest of the weekend. So I didn't want to go out with boys, because I knew they would be too sexually advanced for me and I couldn't handle it.

Madlyn retreated from the large, impersonal, frightening university to her home town for more classes and soon she began work for a newspaper. She liked her work as a cub reporter and did well. She was serious about a career in journalism and not interested in marriage. There were few women writing national news columns at that time, and she dreamed of "wowing the newspaper world" with her abilities. "I was very good" she says. "I have a facility for writing and I could get it down fast. I knew I could do what I wanted to do, and in order to advance myself, I did things on my own. I didn't wait for things to come to me, I went out and made them happen."

When she met George, Madlyn was attracted by his eagerness to be successful; it matched her own ambitions. He hadn't graduated from high school, but he was very intelligent and got on well with people. He began his career in insurance as a claims agent and was quickly promoted. Both he and Madlyn were impressed with the fact that by the time he was twenty-three he was a successful insurance broker. She admired his ingenuity and cleverness and the fact that even though he didn't have a high school degree, he was well respected by his co-workers and was invited to social occasions at the company president's house. He was definitely going places. But on the way there was trouble.

Though most of the time George drank beer, one night at a party he drank eveything in sight. He got drunk quickly and I watched his personality change. He talked in a hateful tone about his work, his mother, his sister—everybody! He'd never done that before and I was astonished. I just couldn't believe what was happening. It was like Dr. Jekyll and Mr. Hyde. I was just stunned. He started smashing windows, put a fist through one of them and kicked a fence down. Later, he wouldn't talk about it, because he said he didn't remember anything. Then he was fine again—for a while.

Before we were married there were several more violent episodes whenever he drank hard liquor. We finally did talk about it, and I said "You know, you really do change personality," and he said, "That's the Indian blood in me." (His mother was about one-sixteenth Indian.) The stupidity of it is that I didn't make any demands of him not to drink, because he said he was going to drink no matter what I said. He said it only happened once in a while and that was true.

At gut level I knew it was serious but I just put it out of my mind. We were making plans and I wanted to get married. I was twenty-one, living at home and there were remarks about "Madlyn's an old maid," so I was feeling pressured. When George came along I thought I really loved him and that we were well-matched.

Before we were married he never lashed out at me, never called me any names or verbally, physically or emotionally abused me. He was always considerate, opening doors, bringing me flowers and presents. I thought all that was a part of love and I was into the romance. I envisioned myself working, then having a baby, settling down at home and being a perfect little mother. I pictured myself as the wife of a very prominent insurance broker and entertaining with the right china and the right silverware and a wonderful house and my own car, and being in society. I had this little storybook of my life. We'd grow old together and there'd be no problems. He would listen to me and I would listen to him, and we'd be loving and kind to each other forever.

George was married at fifteen and divorced after five years, a few months before I met him. His sister told me he had beaten his first wife, and I just sat there stunned. George said, "But she was such a bad woman. She ran around on me and she deserved it." I left and later he told me, "You're not like that, that's why I never hit you." Well, that was music to my ears. I knew I wasn't a bad woman and I knew that would never happen in our marriage. Our love would save the day. Also, coming from a religious family I felt that God would not let anything like that happen to me. Aaaaaaagh! It's really sick to think that way.

So we were married in a beautiful church ceremony and went off to a wonderful honeymoon. We came back and set up housekeeping in a nice little apartment, and George was making enough money so I could be home and play wife for a while. We were married three months before I was hit. We were supposed to go somewhere that night and he came home late, very drunk, very belligerent. I was arguing back and he told me to shut up and I said, "I'm not going to shut up. We were supposed to be somewhere tonight and you came home drunk and I had to call these friends to say we couldn't make it and I really don't like it. I think you're being irresponsible." And I probably said a few thousand other things.

The argument got very heated and he just doubled up his fist and hit me in the stomach before I even knew what was happening. It was so quick! I fell over on the bed and couldn't move. He hit me again and the fear was unbelievable. I think I sort of tripped out. I remember getting into the car and crying and screaming—the next day the landlord asked us to move—and I drove around for a long time.

I was confused and hurt. The hurt was deep. How could someone who says he loves me hit me? George wouldn't talk to me about it. He was very defensive. I couldn't be very loving and I felt that I'd been terribly deceived, but I didn't know what to do with it. "I'm married. I have to be married for the rest of my life. I was married in church. God says "till death do you part." There hadn't ever been a divorce in my family on either side. How could I shame everybody, shame myself? How could I leave this man after three months? What would my friends think? What would my parents think? I thought about myself, but I thought more about what other people would think than about how I could be healthy. I was just scared shitless of being married and divorced so quickly at twenty-one. I felt I was supposed to stay with this man no matter what.

I'd always read that the first year of marriage is the roughest. I said, "Okay, for the first year it's going to be rough and then it's going to get better," even though in my gut I knew it would happen again. I was walking on eggshells. "Do not do anything that will upset him." The emotional game that I played was hard on me, trying never to upset him, never to make him angry and never expressing my feelings for fear of upsetting him. I was always doing what he wanted, always submitting sexually.

I also felt guilty. He said he wouldn't hit me because I wasn't a bad person, but then he did. What was this thing I had done? I could never find it, but there must be something really bad. You don't go around hitting people for no good reason. I didn't know that it was something within him.

After he beat the shit out of me the first time he was kind and apologetic. The next day when the presents and the flowers came I just felt that he meant every word he said. At that time I felt that if a man sent flowers to a woman it was very special. I would think, "He really is going to be okay. He really cares for me. He really is making an effort." He couldn't say enough of the good things, the compliments. I just lapped it up. My self-concept had been hurt so badly by being beaten that I needed someone to pump me up and he knew exactly how to do it.

Madlyn sought help from her minister and was told, "You must not be a very good wife, a very submissive wife. You must not be doing what God wants you to do." He read the Bible to her and scolded her for "talking back" to her husband. She felt guilty and became more depressed. At an earlier period she and George had settled in a town several hundred miles from their families, a move that Madlyn hoped would improve the marriage. Then she thought a baby would help, so they adopted a baby boy. She went back to work and was successful in her journalism career. George was made an assistant vice-president of his company; he was becoming involved in the community, and was gaining status. For a few months things were better.

George was well liked by his employers, but he started drinking heavily and missed work, sometimes arriving at the office smelling of alcohol or even showing up drunk. Finally his boss spoke to him and after discovering there were marital problems, recommended a psychiatrist. But George wouldn't go, so Madlyn did. The psychiatrist wanted to know what she was doing to provoke the violence, and once again her guilt increased. Looking back, Madlyn characterizes herself at that time as still young and rather immature and confused. She had been happy until she was married and then, she says, "Everyone said I was wrong. 'You're not cooking his meals right, you're not washing his socks right.'" Madlyn says she was a good wife and housekeeper because she was afraid. She saw the psychiatrist for six months but gained nothing from it. The violence continued.

One night George was drinking. He had hit me a couple of times and I was getting my son Joey, who was about eight months old, ready to leave, just to go to a motel for the night. I was trying to very inconspicuously pack Joey's stuff and leave very quietly. George was sitting in front of the television polishing his guns.

He caught me going out the door, and said, "Stop, or I'll shoot you both." Believe me, I thought that he would. He said, "Close the door and come back in the house," and he told me to sit down. I sat down. He said, "You're not going anywhere" in a very calm, deathly quiet voice. That frightened me even more. I fed Joey and put him back to bed and George followed me around with the gun while I did these things and then he made me sit in a chair until the early hours of the morning. He sat holding the gun and watching television and now and then he'd say something very derogatory. I was scared to death. Finally he fell asleep and I took Joey and left.

Once more George persuaded me to go back. This time he stopped drinking for a year and for a year he worked at being a human being. He didn't verbally abuse me or try to use his power against me. I took a six-month leave from my job; we bought and remodeled a house with three acres in the country, and then we both wanted another child. We were given a one-month old girl. That was a mistake. George immediately started drinking again, and the violence started again and we separated—this time for a month, which was the longest.

Then his boss came to talk to me and said, "Madlyn, are you sure you're doing the right thing? Give him another chance. George and I have talked, and he has told me he'll stop drinking and he's promised to get help this time." This was a beautiful man, very kind, very loving and altruistic. I said, "Okay."

George came home for about two months and was fine. Then he started drinking again, and the knives came out. He would hold a knife to my throat or he would stand in front of me with the blade pointed at my throat and be verbally abusive. Then he would throw the knife down and start hitting and kicking me. One night when our second adopted child was only about four or five months old he slapped her and threw her on the floor. That was it. I took both the children and called my attorney the next day. I said, "I want back in the house. I want George out. I want a restraining order."

There was a pattern. First it was hands, then it was guns, then knives, and I knew if I didn't leave, the three of us would not be alive one day. No matter how much shame my divorce brought on my parents, no matter how guilty I felt, there were these two children who deserved a hell of a lot better than what was given them. I called the social worker and said, "I'm leaving George and I don't know what you want to do about this baby. I want to keep her, but I don't know if you'll let me." So they came and took her away.

I just can't believe that I took it for five years, but I did. I've never felt intense hate for anybody as much as I felt for him. It grew slowly until at the end I would get physically ill when I thought about him and I'd want to throw up, I hated him so badly. I couldn't stand his touch, I couldn't stand to look at him because of what had happened—because of what I allowed to happen to myself.

I used to think about doing something to his car, so he would have an accident and be killed. And I'd go to the grocery store and stand in front of the poisons—rat poisons, strychnine—I'd look at them for a long time and contemplate giving him just a little bit at a time. But I was afraid somebody would do an autopsy and find he was riddled with strychnine and I'd be thrown in jail. If I could have found a drug that would have never shown up, I bet I would have done something to him, because I hated him.

After the first time he hit me it seemed like he gained some kind of power. He didn't have to be nicey-nice any more. Even when he was sober, he could be a shit-ass if he wanted to. During the first few years of our marriage when he was sober he wasn't physically abusive, but he was emotionally. "I don't love you. You're a cunt, a bitch." I didn't grow up around those words and to me they were very offensive. I was crushed.

I still don't understand why I continually went back, and I hated myself for it, so I didn't think anyone else could like me, could love me. When we were separated he would call. "I miss you. I care about you." The words would always get to me. I used to believe in words. I would think "Okay, it's going to be better." In my gut I knew it wasn't going to, but I couldn't stop myself.

I think that I was so depressed that I had absolutely no will. At this point all the independent feelings that I'd ever had—the headstrong girl and all that—had gone. And of course having a child was an extra responsibility. "How am I going to care for this child? This child needs a father. This child could have had two loving parents somewhere else, and we adopted him. What a responsibility that is."

I used to think women who were divorced were the lowest form of life and I didn't want to be like that. Already I felt like the lowest form of life on the inside, so on the outside I had to present this facade that I was a wonderful wife and a wonderful mother and that we were the ideal couple of the year.

For the first nine months after leaving George, Madlyn felt a sense of release, but she was also very lonely and depressed. She lived in a trailer on her parents' property and was surprised and gratified that they were so supportive, but it wasn't enough to counter her loneliness. Madlyn didn't make friends, though she did go out with men with whom she was sexually "promiscuous."

And still there was fear. George called in the middle of the night, threatening her with statements like "I'm going to get you, you bitch." Madlyn would hang up immediately but the words stayed with her. At other times he threatened to take Joey away or to kill her. She was afraid that if he had a chance he would do one or the other. Madlyn would wake up in the middle of the night crying and would pace up and down the little trailer until the fear diminished. She never left Joey alone, and never went anywhere that first year without apprehensively looking over her shoulder.

The second year after she left, Madlyn moved to a larger city and embarked on a frenetic round of activity, working two jobs, bar-hopping with other women and picking up men. She was afraid of loneliness and of raising her difficult, demanding child by herself. She knew she wasn't emotionally capable of giving him what he needed and couldn't be a stable, nurturing mother. To avoid that responsibility she left him with babysitters much of the time, which she now says "was horrible for him."

Then Madlyn met Ben. She watched carefully and determined that he was a good man, family-oriented, with no violence in his background and no interest even in arguing. When he did begin to get angry he would leave, rather than take it out on her. She was seduced by the fact that Ben was the opposite of George. She wanted someone to take care of her, and he wanted someone to take care of. They went together for a year and then were married, but within six months, Madlyn knew Ben was not the right man for her after all.

When Madlyn learned that her mother had cancer and she turned to Ben for support, she found that he was unable to give it to her. Still more loss and sadness came Madlyn's way. Her father died of a heart attack, and nine months later her mother died of cancer. Although she and Ben cared for each other, she did not want to live without the emotional support she was finally able to ask for, and she left him. They remain friends, sharing custody of Joey, to whom Ben remains devoted.

Madlyn's newspaper work had been "most exciting for the ego" and had included feature stories and a regular column; she enjoyed being a public figure and having her name recognized. But she had had enough. She decided on a complete switch of careers and took counseling classes, which prepared her to work with children. Working, taking care of Joey and going to classes kept her mind occupied, and she allowed herself little time to grieve for her losses. Her relationships and social life usually took place in groups, with little opportunity for intimacy.

As graduation approached and Madlyn was faced with the cessation of her frenetic schedule, feelings she had denied caught up with her. She became extremely frightened and couldn't eat or sleep. For about three months she spent much of her time crying. In addition, she began having serious problems with Joey, who was nine years old and becoming physically violent toward her and people at school. He frightened her by kicking holes in walls and throwing things. Madlyn and Joey went to family therapy to get help in creating the structure she knew he needed but that she hadn't been able to provide. After three months Joey was able to stop therapy, but she continued for several years.

For two years, she said nothing to her therapist about having been abused. During that time she had a physically satisfying relationship with Brad, but it lacked emotional depth.

Brad frequently broke his promises and sometimes stayed out all night or became suddenly cold and withdrawn. He was rarely affectionate in public, but behind closed doors he was "so good, so different from George," that Madlyn was confused. Brad was sexually giving, and she wanted that so badly that she thought the emotional satisfaction would follow. After a two year relationship with him, she talked about him to her therapist, who shocked her by saying, "You're acting just like an abused wife."

She was stunned when he said that. She was dismayed that after ten years she was still "not out of it," even though she wasn't being physically abused. After two months she was able to tell Brad she didn't want to see him any more.

Even though she had grown up in a loving, caring family, Madlyn feels she somehow missed learning how to form a relationship. Looking back, she sees that at twenty-one she was beginning to gain independence. "But then," she says, "I went into what I thought I should be, depending on someone else, instead of developing my own consciousness, my own capabilities and strengths. I wish I had been stronger."

Counseling children is wonderful and I'm also learning that I am very creative, and that in spite of all the things that have happened, I'm a very happy woman, much happier every year. The most significant thing for me, out of all those pleasures, is that I'm learning to ask for what I want as a woman. I've learned that I love being a woman. I like my emotions and being able to express myself. I like my shape. I love being who I am. That's very unexpected, because for so long I thought I was such a terrible person. I'm a capable, loving woman, and I can give and receive well. That's a wonderful feeling. I have supportive, nurturing relationships with women and friendships with strong women and men.

I never even thought about forgiving George until the last few years. When the time was right, it helped to meditate and think about what I wanted for myself and for everybody else. Why hate someone who is sick? Why spend any energy at all in hating him? Or even thinking about him. Finally, one day I said out loud, "I forgive you, George. I forgive you and I forgive myself." And it just vanished. It had taken me a long time to like myself, and mostly I was forgiving myself.

CHAPTER 2

Maria

With the help of shelter staff, Maria packed three small knapsacks, one for each child, and left her Spanish-speaking native land to seek safety in the U.S.

My father is an elementary school teacher and my mother is a housewife. I went ten years to school. Since I was fifteen my mother and my sister and I did cosmetology together in a shop my father started. I didn't work full time, but women came in for special occasions, holidays. There were occasional disagreements in the family, but there was no violence. My mother and father were Catholics then and later changed to another religion. I didn't change. Catholic, Lutheran, it's okay with me.

Arturo is the man I married. I was twenty-two and he was nine years older. He had moved away to go to school. There was a good relationship with his family and my family and he came back from school to see my brother and sister. He took me out to dance and to the theater. We went out two months. It was fast. For me, it wasn't love, it was a flash, but he loved me a lot. Then his family didn't like me to be involved with him, because they wanted him to be with a professional woman. But I got married about two months after we were going out together. After that his family never talked to me or my family or to him, even though I worked on it. It was terrible. A lot of pressure and disagreeing. When my first one was born, his mother started to talk again.

At first, before we were married, he treated me okay, but as soon as we got married he changed. He changed all of my image. He said, "I don't like the tint in your hair, and don't wear any makeup." He didn't want me to wear pants or shorts. He didn't like me to work. He started drinking and it was a terrible life. For twenty-two years I hoped he would change.

He was jealous for no reason and when we had been married a month he took me by the arms and shook me, and I ran into the closet and cried. Then he came in and took me out and hugged me and kissed me, but I didn't like that. He said he would never do it again. I went to my family and said I wanted to leave and go home, but they said, "No!" There was no place to go. He did that every week.

He usually shook me and sometimes he put me on the bed and put his knee on my back and bent my back. My daughter saw that when she was eleven. It hurt my back for about six months. I saw the doctor for therapy. There were no good times, because he didn't like anything I did. Nothing was okay, nothing. He called me every hour from work to ask what I was doing, to give assignments for the children and to tell me what to do. He worked at a good job in a physics lab, but I didn't know how much he made. He controlled all the money and controlled all in the house. He made all the decisions. He didn't like people in the house. I had one or two neighbor friends and they knew my life. They said to leave, but my family still said I should stay.

I wanted a future for my kids. I think about that, about my separation. How am I going to live? I know I need money, I need housing, I need everything. I have nothing. I decided to continue my studies. I was about thirty then, and my children were in school. I went to classes in the morning and I finished my GED. I didn't tell my husband, but my brother and my father knew, and they said, "Okay, that's your decision." My brother told my husband I was taking classes and he was very angry and shouted, "You don't know nothing."

I wanted to go to the university to study more and

Arturo went to the director of the university and said, "You can't take my wife into this university because she can't do good work in this institution. She doesn't know enough." And the director said, "Yes, she can." I start to study and there is lots of disagreeing. He decided okay, continue your studies, but he is going with me to the university, and sits next to me for three years.

I was afraid, but I wanted to separate, and he was thinking that I was planning it. He is thinking I have another man, so he changes his work so he can be working at night and can stay with me at the university. I went every morning and he went with me every day for three years and sit next to me. I can't talk with nobody.

He stopped drinking but he started taking pills. He said I should stay in the home, not talk to nobody, not go to the store. He would drive fast when he was angry or hit the children on the head with his knuckles. It was a lot of pressure for the kids. He wanted sex every day, I don't know why. I didn't say yes or no. If I said no he would say I had another man.

After I finished my three years of university the pressure on my heart was more. He said I changed in the university. I'm the same person, but I study and I know more. I study psychology and everything. I opened my ears and got ideas. It was a good experience for me. He said, "I'm going to kill you," and I'm afraid. He has explosives in the house and he says, "I'm going to put a bomb in the university." I tell him, "Okay! Set the bomb. That's okay!" But I think if I stay I don't know what I'm going to do. I telephoned the shelter and they said I should leave. I know if I go somewhere the chances are good he's going to find me, because his sister is a social worker and knows all the people in the shelters and all the institutions. She says, "You need to wait, because you have nothing to do for work." If I went to the shelter, she would know and tell my husband.

But the woman at the shelter helped me go. I don't care where I'm going, I just close my eyes. I wait for the opportunity and he went to take a computer course and couldn't call me all day. That was the opportunity for me. My mother and father wanted to stop this situation. They know a lot of women in abuse now. They saw a man kill a woman, and they're afraid of my situation.

I had little knapsacks for each of the kids, and I called my mother and my sister and they say okay and they bring me money and a neighbor calls a taxi for me. My sister brought a suitcase with something in it, not much. I didn't care where I was going.

I don't remember how I thought. I closed my eyes. My children didn't want to go. It was a terrible change. My big boy cried. The other two were all right. The woman from the Lutheran church took me to the shelter in the United States. I don't know nothing. I stayed for three and a half months. The regular time is twenty-eight days, but my situation is different. I didn't speak any English. I studied English in my classes, but only reading and writing. I could read it and understand it, but I couldn't speak it. No one at the shelter spoke Spanish. A Mexican woman at another shelter called on the telephone and I talked to her. But my kids learned so fast, English. They were thirteen, eleven and ten. They went to school. They say they feel good in this country. They like the peace, the tranquility.

I felt terrible. I was an automaton. This is my body, I walk, but I don't know nothing. I talked to my family sometimes and they say I need to stay here. The welfare office say I need to go back to my country. They say they can't help me. I don't know why. It is a mistake. I decide I'm going to stay in this country, I don't care about nothing!

I don't go back! I don't care! Harriet was the president of the shelter. She say, "You need to move to another shelter" and all of the other women say, "You can't make her leave." I say I don't go to low income house. I don't like it! I need a house, but no low income. Harriet's grandmother had a house and they repaired the house for me and put everything in it. I paid two hundred and fifty a month for the rent. That's okay, it's a house. They pay the telephone. I live there two years, then they sell the house, and I move two months ago.

Now I pay three-fifty for two bedrooms. That's okay. I have everything. They give me a television. I don't think about going back. It's occured to me, but I need to finish my studies first.

It took Maria two months to arrange for public assistance. She had to get letters from the shelter, from her lawyer and the the community college where she took English lessons, to prove that she was in need and not still tied to her husband. She has no immediate plans for a divorce, because she is afraid if she files, her husband will find out where she is.

Maria took a course in computer English for three quarters. She began studying in a bilingual class, but her advisors thought it was too limited for her and advanced her to a regular class with native English-speaking people. She did well in reading the basic English text, but she says she needs to practice speaking. She will go back to school after a summer break and make a point of finding opportunities to practice speaking English. She is working as a medical service volunteer and has finished volunteer training at the shelter that housed her.

Maria has met many new American and Latin friends. She speaks English to a neighbor who is such a good friend that she calls Maria her daughter. She hopes to go back to her native land some day, but it will not be until she has a profession and until she has reason to know she will be safe. Her children are emphatic about wanting to stay in the United States.

It's horrible to leave, but people have to do it. I waited a long time, and I stay here because it's best for my kids. The men never change. They need to think about the best life for the children. They are the future men. It's hard for every woman, but the Latin woman is another object for a man and they don't have higher education. My first year was hard. The shelter helped me a lot. I think they love my kids. They say my kids capture their hearts. My kids are so sweet, they melt the heart.

My difficulties are with the money, now. From welfare I get five hundred and twenty-one a month and coupons worth a hundred and fifty for food. It's not too much, but my children are very happy. They like everything. They say, "I know English now." They love English and don't want to study in Spanish. I don't care what kind of work I do. I like social work, shelter work and computer, too. I hope I can go to the university and finish there. I like my life now. I have peace. I can do everything I like to do. I have friends. My kids are very happy. I go wherever I like to go. Everything changed for the better. It is a good life.

CHAPTER 3

Barb

Barb grew up in the small Western town of Sundown, a lively child who enjoyed the security of a close-knit family. Her mother recalls that she was a determined little girl who would persist at a task until she succeeded. She was close to her parents and other family members and she experienced no abuse until she met Mel.

I was eighteen or nineteen when I met Mel. I was going to school in Mexico, busy putting myself through college and enjoying everything. I had no thought about getting married or involved in a relationship. I had too many things to do to even consider a relationship or a marriage until I was thirty or so. I worked full time, went to college full time and took dance classes, so I was pretty active and eager about life.

Mel and I started going out and when I moved to Phoenix he came down and visited for a while. We started getting serious about each other and were going to get married, and then the next thing he called me and said he was joining the army. I continued with what I was doing and he went to Viet Nam. Before he left he was more communicative. He was gone a year and when he came back it was always me that was talking, and he wasn't. If it was anything in depth, it was about me, and if it came close to him or how he felt, it got diverted in another direction.

The first time he hit me was three or four weeks after

he came home. We were shouting at each other and it was like a quick slap. I was really shocked. We talked about it and decided it was just his readjusting from Viet Nam, where he had been head of heavy artillery. He was still irate over being told what to do by people he didn't respect, and the tone in my voice was something he could strike back at.

On our honeymoon I couldn't hold his hand, because he still had the feeling that he didn't want anybody or anything touching him in case he'd have to duck, run or hide. We spent a strange night with a gun by the bed. But I thought if I could get him to see what he was doing, we could solve the problem.

I had this blind optimism that love would solve everything and that given time it would just all go away. We never had arguments over anything. I had gone away to college and it was very clearly defined that I wouldn't get married unless he would live in Phoenix for a year so I could finish school. Then we would move back to Sundown and he would go into a partnership in his dad's boating supply store.

I finished school and we moved back to Sundown and everything was going along real great, everything I had planned. I was twenty-five or twenty-six and I had a job that had benefits that allowed us both to travel. His dad was opening another store and Mel was going to manage it, and we had a lot of friends. It was a fairy tale come true. We figured by the time we'd been married five or six years we would see about having children.

We did a lot of hiking, swimming, canoeing and rafting. Going out to dinner was always special and fun. I liked owning a house, taking care of it and interior decorating and he liked working in the yard. He always said that he was extremely happy with his family—his one wife and his one cat. We both had ideas about an equal relationship, but as I look back now, it wasn't like that.

Five weeks into the marriage he hit me. My family always had this big thing about birthdays, so I assumed he should have the same feelings. But on my birthday I visited his grandmother, while he went to the football game and went out with the guys. He picked me up and I was expounding on how hurt I was, and nagging on and on, and he started getting really, really angry. I stopped the car and said, "Get out and walk home," because I can't stand arguments. We weren't far from home. He says, "No, I'm not going to do that." We got in front of the apartment and he said he wasn't going to get out so I did, and started walking down the driveway. He came after me and threw me back in the car and there was a lot of violence. My brain clicked and said, "If you don't quit fighting, you're going to die." I just went limp, it was instinctual, and as soon as I did, the blows stopped.

He helped me up and we walked into the apartment, and he was really concerned. He got a washrag and started dabbing at my face. He said, "You have some blood on your cheek. How did you get that?" I said, "You don't know?" He said "No", but then he cleaned it up and said "Yeah, I do." I think he knew then. I said, "Do you want to get the marriage annulled, or what, because I don't want to live like this." He said, "No, I just need some time. It won't happen again." And it didn't happen for quite a while.

Mel and Barb tried a few sessions of counseling, but neither thought it was helpful. There were arguments about whether Mel should start his own business, since he was under pressure working for his father. Then it became obvious that Mel was involved with other women, and at first Barb didn't complain, for fear of upsetting him. But toward the end of their marriage, as the number of his affairs increased, she sometimes took risks by confronting him, trying to shock him into realizing what he was doing to her.

One night, in a rage for no discernible reason, Mel picked Barb up, threw her and then pinned her against the wall and choked her. He said, "There's a gun in the drawer. Why don't you use it? You'll be doing us both a favor." She knew then that she would have to get out. The decision had been made even though she didn't know how she would live with it. After that point she was never tempted to change her mind. She moved to a large city several hundred miles away.

I did the right thing. I took it as long as it could, and then I left. I never had a second's worth of "Oh, gosh, if I'd stayed, maybe if I'd tried . . . " I got out at the last possible second. I'm still in love with the person I married. The person I thought I married died in Viet Nam, I'm sure. I know he killed three men at one time and I know this bothers him. He's never talked about it since the first three days he was home. I was an extension of himself and he hated himself, so if he could drive me away, if he could hurt me, he was getting back at himself.

I found that during the marriage I had compromised myself away. I was a dance major and always involved in dance. He didn't like it. He said I could do it, but there was no support and I would choreograph something and he'd never come to see it, so I stopped doing it. I wanted to see some of the plays at a summer festival, but he didn't want to see them and he always worried about something happening with me driving. After six years of this you start thinking, "Maybe I'm incapable of driving ten miles."

It was two years before Barb was able to recall any of the beatings. Two events triggered her memory. At a party a man making his way through a crowded room accidentally nudged her against the wall. A few weeks later a man she was dating leaned forward to give her a peck on the cheek and she leaned back and felt the back of her head against the wall. Both times she felt panicky without knowing why. She began to have nightmares, but was unable to recall them. Gradually it became clear that she was dreaming of being pinned on a bed, unable to move, with a figure looming over her. Until close to the end of the relationship, she hadn't allowed herself to be aware of her fear when Mel was beating her, but the nightmares told her she had been terrified before.

After seeing a television program about battering and reading a book about women who were battered, Barb decided she had better go to a group for abused women. Listening to other women's experiences helped her remember her own. The group backed her up in overcoming her panic whenever Mel called. She didn't want to talk to him, but she wanted to be able to answer her phone and hear his voice without feeling terror.

In retrospect Barb believes she had looked to Mel for emotional security and felt that if he wasn't there she "wasn't anybody." She hadn't wanted to be taken care of, but she had wanted to feel taken care of. Now she is surprised to realize that she was stronger than Mel. Paradoxically, she sees a kind of arrogance in her previous attitude.

You think you can do anything. I remember thinking, when Mel had me pinned on the bed, "He's not going to hit me. I can stop him from hitting me. I won't let this happen." I was determined to make the marriage work, but you can't do it by yourself, I found out. It was a hard pill to swallow. I hate it when I hit a brick wall of life, something I can't change.

After I left I went through a couple of weeks deciding I wanted to get away from the whole thing and thought I should become a drunk. Well, I can't drink, so it didn't work too well. I tried it for a couple of days and then one Saturday morning about eleven o'clock I was drinking Scotch and I looked in the mirror and I had black circles under my eyes and I looked like I was sixty-five years old. I said, "Nope, no more. You're going to do something with your life." That doesn't mean I didn't scream and yell and cry a lot, but I just decided that I wasn't going to look in the mirror and see that face again.

That was a month after I left. The helplessness of "what do you do?" and not knowing. When you don't have a pattern of having to have his six o'clock dinner ready, or of going home to work in the garden and have a barbeque with friends, when all of a sudden it's gone, your purpose for the day is gone. You're not having friends over for dinner, so you don't have to go to the grocery store, and you didn't have dinner so you don't have any dishes to wash. It's real basic. There's a sense

of security in those patterns. To this day, the hardest
hours are between five and seven.

I went through a period when I didn't want to go out
or do anything. I had "failure" stamped on my forehead
and a friend called one day and said, "I'm going to meet
you at six o'clock at the Hilton dining room and we're
going to sit and have a beer." I said, "No. I'm not going
to do that. I just want to go home." But I went and he
walked in the door and that was the push I needed at the
time—to be able to walk into a semi-social place and to
know that everybody didn't stare at me when I walked
in, didn't know what a terrible person I was because I
was now getting a divorce. Then I met a couple of gals
who were roommates and they loved to go swimming
and do river sports, so I went camping and swimming
with them. I felt good that I could do it. You know,
women can go camping by themselves.

When Mel left I didn't jog for about six months. Then
I started out one morning and I hadn't gone a mile when
I got really tired. All of a sudden it just dawned on me,
this is just like life, right now. I won't let being tired
stop me. I would say, "Nothing can stop me. No one can
stop me," and I'd just keep running and laughing. The
tireder I'd get the more I'd say it, and it helped me to
determine that all I had to do was put one foot down,
and pretty soon I'd be a block closer to home. I'd say, "If
I can make it through this day, I'll be one day better
off."

I never looked at anything beyond the next hour, because it would scare me to death if I did. I would wake
up in the morning, put my feet on the floor and say,
"Walk to the bathroom, take a shower, brush your hair,"
talk to myself the whole time. Maybe that helps out with
loneliness, because you've got a big conversation going
there. No matter how alone I feel, it's much better than
waiting for him to come home, or wondering what I'm
going to do if he doesn't come home.

Now I travel all over the world. I just changed my job
a month ago. For the previous two years I was working
for a Hawaii tour operator as a wholesaler and sales

rep. I worked out of my apartment and then about a month ago I started working for a cruise company, so I have an office and a real secretary. My salary is fifteen hundred a month and all my gas and a company car and a good incentive program. I travel a couple of weeks a month to California and Oregon. I like people, and I certainly couldn't do a nine-to-five anymore or work at a desk.

Eventually I'll probably go into a marketing company of my own. I'd like to start my own company and have as an account one cruise line, one Hawaii line and one small airline. That's a ways down the road, but I know people that are starting companies now, that would like me as partner in a few years. By then I should be a cruise expert.

CHAPTER 4

Lynn

When Lynn was six years old her mother divorced her father and took Lynn and her brother to a new home fifteen hundred miles away. Aside from one unrewarding visit to her father when she was in eighth grade, Lynn never heard from him until she was in her mid-twenties. The knowledge that he kept in touch with her brother made his neglect especially hurtful. But the move to the new city had some positive results. For a time the family lived with her mother's parents, with whom Lynn formed a close relationship, and when they later settled into their own house, Lynn had the opportunity of being close to her matriarchal great-grandmother, who lived just around the corner and who became an important figure in her life.

When Lynn was in fifth grade her mother married Harry. That put a stop to the good times Lynn had had at the family and neighborhood get-togethers, because Harry was so verbally abusive and hypercritical of everyone that there were no more parties. Lynn's mother worked as a teacher's aide, was a community activist and believed in equal rights for women, yet she waited on her new husband "hand and foot." Lynn was not intimidated by him and was an outspoken child "who had opinions on everything."

Lynn began her education in a desegregated California school and became aware of racism for the first time after she moved. In third grade she was bused to a school in which she and her brother, Mike, and the children of one other family were the only black students. Her mother tried to move to a new neighborhood, so the children wouldn't have to take the bus to school, but when she found a suitable apartment, "they didn't want any blacks moving into the neighborhood."

As a child Lynn didn't start fights, but she defended other children who were picked on, including her brother who was frequently teased for being fat and who wouldn't fight back. She recalls her attitude as one of "I'm not going to take any shit off of anybody." On one occasion a white boy called her a "black bitch" and she "leaped across the room right on top of him and before I knew it we were just going at it." When Lynn's mother heard about it from the teacher she said, "I don't blame Lynn. I would have knocked his block off too." She had always told the children, "Don't fight, but if somebody hits you, hit them back."

Lynn was subjected to sexual harassment and attempted molestation by men in the street and elsewhere. When she reached adolescence white men came into her neighborhood and insinuated that since she was black she must be a prostitute. As she grew older there were more and more streets she was reluctant to walk on alone.

Lynn attended a large public high school that was racially mixed, but "Black children came in one side and the white kids came in on the other side and even when school was out people left by those same entrances and we didn't even eat together." Lynn rarely dated and was not much interested in boys. She was on the track and volleyball teams, won awards on the speech team, was involved in a church group and was president of the honor society. Nevertheless by her senior year she had become bored with school and she had accumulated enough credits so that she could leave at eleven o'clock for a job.

Lynn went to a college at which she knew all forty of the black students and met Don, a musician who introduced her to classical music and soon became her very close friend. She also began to date her first boyfriend, who was jealous of Don, but Lynn stood up to him, saying, "Look, Don is a friend of mine and there is nothing sexual going on with him and if you can't accept that, then that's too bad." Her first real love was an acting student, whom she dated in her sophomore year. When he transferred to a school in California, they agreed not to attempt a long distance romance.

Lynn also moved to another city to complete work on a teaching degree. She found a job as teacher's aide and enjoyed her colleagues, but she didn't socialize with them outside of work and she began to feel something was missing. She was not developing black friendships and when she met Warren she thought he was just a nice person who would fill that gap, but soon he became more to her. "He appeared to be quiet, kind of shy. That quality attracted me. The 'little boy' type, but he seemed self-sufficient and giving," she says. He often invited her to his home where he lived with his mother and she was treated as part of the extended family. To her surprise she began to like the idea of settling down with one person, though not necessarily to be married. Friends and relatives were getting married and she wanted to have somebody, too, though she thought Warren had some problems to resolve first.

We would have arguments that went on and on and on, and I would be the one who was getting loud. I'd say, "What the fuck are you talking about?" And he'd say, "You don't have to cuss." "Well, okay, excuse me." But then he would just keep verbally harassing me, asking me about my past boyfriends, wanting to know anyone I'd ever screwed. He would just wear me down until I'd tell him. And I'd say I didn't want to talk about it anymore, and why didn't he just leave.

The first time he hit me we were arguing about something. I think I told him I wanted to go to bed 'cause I was tired of arguing with him, I wanted him to leave. He punched me and drew back real fast. I just started screaming, "I can't believe you've done this" and screaming for him to get out. He said, "If you give me a hundred dollars I'll leave." I said I didn't have a hundred dollars, but I wrote him a check and he left. I called the bank and they put a hold on it.

One night he started punching me and I don't know how I got away from him. I got off the bed and I had this big vase that was sitting on the window sill. It was a real heavy thing and I was going to hit him with it if he came near me. But I was too scared to hit him because I thought, "Oh my God, if I hit him hard he's gonna really beat me up bad, and I don't want to have to go to the hospital." I kind of hit him a little bit with it but it wasn't really hard. Somehow his lip got cut and it started bleeding and he said, "You've done it now," and I got really scared and I was screaming. I was down on the floor on my knees praying he would stop and he said, "Yeah, you better pray, you better pray that I don't kill you."

He beat me up and then he forced me to have sex with him. I got up the next day and went to school, but I couldn't even hardly move. He dropped me off at school and I couldn't even hardly walk. I sat in class for a little while and I got up and then I called my girlfriend. She came over and stayed with me.

His mother called me about four days later and asked me what happened because I hadn't come over, and then she puts Warren on the phone. He said he was sorry and all this other crap. And then I think he comes over and we talk and I asked him if he beats up on women all the time. He said he had and that's why he couldn't keep a relationship. He said he never really had a girlfriend and I said, "Well I don't go for that kind of stuff." He said, "My mother really likes you, and my family really likes you. You really made something of yourself and I want to help you. I know you're not the type that likes to be beat up on and I'm sorry."

Sherry, my girlfriend, she and her boyfriend had gotten into a couple of scraps and I'd said, "Sherry, you got to leave him because you know once they do it they're going to do it again." And boy, did I eat my words. Warren was just standing there and feeling so pitiful and I think that's when he started telling me things about how his mother used to get beat up by men and then I felt like, "I can change him. I can rescue him. He's had a hard life and people just don't love him enough and they don't understand him." After that I was real careful not to make him angry. I was busy trying to prove that I wasn't better than him. He didn't beat me up like that for quite a while. He would hit me or slap me, but there was no extreme battering incident.

One time we were arguing about something and he slapped me. I went into the bathroom and started crying and then I came out to the kitchen and I got a knife. I told him not to be hitting me. We got into a struggle and he was trying to get the knife away from me and rolling around on the floor and he couldn't get it away from me. I was just threatening him, but he had picked up something too and I said, "You put that down and I'll put this down," so that's what happened.

After the first time there were little things every two or three months. The next big incident was before I moved in with him. I was living in the dorms, but school was out and he was going to help me move. He says, "Lynn, I want you to move in with me," and I said, "Warren, we talked about that. No, I can't do that." He kept on and on.

I could see him getting excited and upset and I tried everything I knew to calm him down. I felt if he wanted to calm down, he could have. I kept saying, "Okay Warren, I want to call a time out. I gotta get out of here." I was really afraid he was going to beat me up real bad. I felt he was going to kill me. There was something in the way he was looking at me, something in his eyes. I just saw myself dead.

When I finally said, "No," directly, that's when he all of a sudden just jumped over and started hitting me on my head. It was so fast, just wham, wham, wham, wham, like that. I was on the couch trying to cover up and he just stopped and went into the kitchen and got a glass of water and threw it on me, and said, "You'd better cool down."

He beat me up real bad and I didn't even get up and go to school that day. That morning he asked me to move in with him again and I agreed. I felt like I **had** to. I was too scared. I didn't want to get beat up any more. I just looked at him and said, "Okay," and I just wrote him a check for the deposit. He always stayed and we always had to talk about what happened. It was like a twelve hour thing. I'd be up all night and he always wanted to have sex afterwards.

Then it got worse. He was on my back every day when we first moved in. Sexually, I felt drained all the time and a lot of the fights and arguments would be over that. I'd be tired and Warren would want to have sex two or three times a day. I would say "No, I don't want to" and then it would turn into this long discussion about "Who are you seeing?" So I got to a point where I would just give in, instead of being harassed for the next five hours.

I gave him every chance that I could give him. He agreed to go to counseling, which we did, but he didn't change. I pressed charges and he went to batterer's group, but he still didn't change. Then I stopped protecting him and being so secretive about what was happening. Even though we were back together, I pressed charges again. His family didn't like it, but I didn't care any more. And he still threatened me. I kept saying, "Okay, Lynn, if he does it again you're going to have to leave."

I knew I should leave, but I was too scared that he was going to shoot me. He had chased me with a gun one night. Where could I go? I had school friends, but I didn't want them to know about it. Janet was the only person that knew. I couldn't see myself protecting myself.

I had been saying, "All I gotta do is wait it out 'til I'm through with school." Finally, I felt "No, I can't stay any more. I can't, because by me staying, I'm just saying 'Yeah, it's okay.'" I realized that he wasn't really going to change. He didn't care about me. And I was too scared to even be around him. So I left.

This time, I knew what he was capable of. I knew if I left, I had to leave him for good, no matter what. This time I knew he would be calling me and following me. Because of the gun incident, the danger was more real to me. Also, he had told me that he stayed over in this vacant building next door, waiting for me all night, and that persistence scared the shit out of me.

Sometimes I used to just watch him sleep and I'd wonder if I could just take something and hit him over the head, just bash his head in, or get him killed by someone. After I had left, I was getting angry about him. I started getting angry about everything. I wanted to go over and kill him, to blow his house up. I'm glad I didn't because I could have been one of those women who wound up in jail for manslaughter. I just kept talking to myself about how I was justified to be angry toward him about everything that had happened, but that I have to take some responsibility for things too. I'd have to report to my counselor and say, "I burned down his house and killed four members of his family today!"

Lynn had only one good friend in the area to support her after she left, but she got direct help and emotional support from a legal project for abused women and was referred from there to a counselor. Regular contact with those two knowledgable, supportive women helped her to stay away by giving her someone to be accountable to when it was hard just to get through the day without contacting Warren. A woman she hardly knew gave Lynn a trained guard dog, who provided a sense of security and control as well as devoted company.

Fear was the principle motive for not going back to Warren. When Lynn felt she was in danger of becoming less fearful, she wrote lists of the terrifying things Warren had done and she read them "over and over and over, instead of listening to him brainwashing me." "I think," she says, "my saving grace was that this time I just did not listen to him. All the other times I had talked to him and listened to what he had to say." One of Lynn's regrets is that she didn't go to a shelter. At that time she didn't recognize the importance of talking with other women and she resisted being with women who were battered because she thought, "I'm not as bad off as them. I'm not really a battered woman." Reading books about other women in situations similar to hers helped her see she was not alone.

Lynn has a need to help people, so she said to herself, "Instead of trying to help Warren and endangering myself, why not help myself and other women?" She became a co-leader of a group for black women who are abused. Participating in the movement against battering has been extremely useful to her. She feels strongly that all women need to talk to each other, and that black women who have been battered have many common issues and can find it especially rewarding to share their stories with each other.

Our families have been split up so much that it's like you're supposed to stay, you're supposed to try to hold the family together and work. Black women have always been in the role of helping and caring, supposed to take care of everybody else, clean people's houses and watch their kids and everything else. It's like we're not supposed to do anything good for ourselves. Blacks are already isolated out of the mainstream and battering adds more isolation. In the black community you don't put your business out in the street. You can handle it. You don't want white people to know that you're having some of the same problems that they're having.

The police? My God, that's the ultimate enemy! Don't call the police over here, they'll probably beat you up, drag your man off and throw him in jail for three hundred years. But, Ann, at the legal service agency, thought it was important to call them and follow through, for myself and because it's going to help other women in the long run. And I knew he wasn't going to jail. He was just going to have to go to counseling.

I always kind of thought he'd tell the whole world I sent him to jail, abused him, that I was the evil person, but Warren didn't do all the things he threatened to do. He didn't kill me or my family.

Sometimes I feel lonely and want male companionship. I call my friend and we go out doing things that we want to do. We go hear music and if no one asks me to dance I'm not going to worry about it. Three of us might get up and dance, whereas, before, that was more of a symbol of failure. We hear jazz, we see plays. If I

wouldn't have left Warren, I woudn't have known Mary-
beth or Chrystal or Marge or Sarah or Audrey, I
wouldn't have known any of these black women. I'm
feeling really good about that.

There are certain places I won't go, even after a year,
because the odds of running into him are fairly high. But
I'm not running like a fugitive, I don't feel in danger. I
feel like I had been in a prison or somebody was brainwashing me or torturing me to death. I don't have to answer to anybody. I don't have to listen to anybody if I
don't want to. I can just go home and go to my room and
close my door. And if I fail at anything it's because of *me*
and not because I got beat up the night before or that
Warren kept me up all night. All of a sudden I'm free to
do whatever I want to do.

CHAPTER 5

Allie

Allie grew up in a conservative Midwest town, the second child of six in a Catholic family. Her father managed a gas station and later owned a small auto parts shop. He "closed off" from the family and "had a relationship with the television set," as Allie remembers him. "He'd get home and the TV would go on, he'd have three or four beers at dinner and a drink beforehand and be asleep in his chair by eight o'clock." During the day her mother cared for the house and children and in the evenings Allie's parents often went to the neighborhood tavern, leaving the two older sisters in charge of the younger children. Allie was the major caretaker, the one who always remembered to get birthday presents for the others and who always did what she was supposed to do.

My mom, when she was into a heavy drinking phase, she would beat us up. Well, it wasn't really beating us up, though a couple of times she did totally lose control. My father only intervened once, when he had to pull her off me because she was strangling me. I remember being woken up at night when they came home from the tavern, because we hadn't cleaned up the house the right way. The door would open and immediately there would be a diatribe. I was scared, knowing I was going to get it, knowing I didn't do it right, that I was lazy and if I'd had it all together I'd have gotten it done. My mom would start hitting on us and we'd go down and clean up the house.

I paid for my tuition in high school by working in a hospital kitchen after school and weekends. I was a good student until I got angry, but then I said, "I'm not going to do what I need to do to get an A any more; I'm going to get a B and get by." A lot of anger was toward the Catholic school system. When I went away to college I had nightmares for two years about Catholic school and about working in the hospital, which were both real oppressive.

I met Jane the first day of our freshman year of high school and until that time I always thought I was heterosexual. It was first love and there was a real romantic aspect to it. In the morning we'd go in my garage and kiss and then ride our bikes to school. She gave me a card every day and there were flowers too. After the first time we slept together, the first thing I did was call our priest from the Catholic Family Movement. I told him what was going on and he said "Well, you have two choices. You can either stop now and never go back or you can go on and know that people won't accept you for it." I was just amazed. He wasn't giving me explicit permission, but...

I said to myself I wasn't a lesbian. I was just in love with a woman. Once Jane and I were in bed talking and we said, "We ...are ...not ...that." The word caught in the back of my mouth and I couldn't get it out. Then I convinced myself that since she wasn't attracted to men and I was, that she was a lesbian and I wasn't. I did a lot of dancing around that. It was a "sin" and it was "unnatural" and I was the scum of the earth. It was such a horrible thing I was doing. I had always thought there was something wrong with me, and being a lesbian at that time in that environment compounded it.

I'm a "recovering Catholic," but I was lucky that I went to the Catholic school where there were a lot of middle-class kids, who assumed they would go to college and I took on some of that. When I graduated I was offered a full-time job in the hospital and there was a lot of pressure from my family to take it, rather than going on to school. My mother said it was safe, it was security, it was close to home and if I ever got sick I had wonderful medical care.

Allie turned down the job and pursued her studies on the West Coast, while Jane went to the local college. Allie had noticed, when she chose a nontraditional college, that it had a Gay Students' Coalition, but it took several months for her to gain the courage to join it. She immersed herself in class assignments and continued to work with Camp Fire Girls, as she had in high school. She didn't make friends, because all of her emotional attention was still directed toward Jane. They wrote and talked on the telephone about feminism and other political issues important to each of them during their first year on the two campuses. The next year Jane joined Allie and they began living together for the first time.

During their high school years Allie had sometimes been shaken, slapped or pulled by Jane, and while she had tried to protect herself, she didn't fight back. She thought it was a sign that Jane really loved her, but she also believed that if only she could "get it together" the violence would stop. After they moved in together Jane beat Allie with her fists as often as once a month. For a long time Allie didn't see it as battering; it was just a part of the relationship in which they "were having a fight."

Allie had come out as a lesbian and became active in campus organizations; for the first time in her life she had a large number of friends. She was "going through incredible changes, developing the ability to think and be creative, increasing self esteem, being with people and knowing (she) was a likable person." The trend continued throughout her four years as a student and by the time she graduated she was on the board of directors of the Associated Students and was a coordinator for the Gay Students' Coalition.

While Allie was achieving important goals on the campus, at home Jane knew exactly how to make her feel low about herself. She judged everything Allie did on a scale of one to ten, and Allie never quite measured up, whether in the meals she cooked, her appearance, or any other activity. Jane was a highly sexual person and Allie's role was to please her. When they lived next to a freeway Jane took a notion one night that

Allie should dance naked on the lanai. Allie complied, even though it was humiliating, because "that's what she wanted and that's what turned her on." Allie dressed in skirts and low cut blouses, always wore make-up and long hair in an effort to please Jane. Although they both worked part-time, Jane controlled all their money. Allie didn't talk to anyone about their "butch-femme" relationship, because she knew her friends would disapprove. Being in the "femme" role was "another shame issue," which made her feel she was "horrible."

When I tried to get help I encountered homophobia. I called a hotline and I would not mention the gender at first, and if they would say "he" I would just continue saying "he." Jane might as well have been a "he," so, why not? Other times they would kind of clam up a bit after I mentioned it was a woman. I knew that the rhythm was broken, that something had shifted. I would sense the change in how they were perceiving me and I just got off the phone. I was angry and hurt and I felt invalidated. One night I was wandering around and I needed a place to stay for the night. I had to go back and be with Jane because there wasn't any such place.

Jane had always been clear that she was not at all attracted to men, but Allie sometimes was, and she had told Jane, when they separated to go to college, that she felt a need to explore that aspect of her sexuality. She did have sex with two men and found it to be pleasant, but she continued to be more emotionally drawn to women and didn't want anything to do with the men after she had sex with them. After she told Jane what she had done, Jane, in a rage, beat her up. Two years later, still seething with jealousy, Jane insisted that Allie tell her exactly what had happened when she was with the men. Allie believed Jane when she said she could deal with what had occurred if she knew all the details. and hoping the truth would end the beatings, she began to tell Jane all.

I felt safe, because the sun was shining. It was daylight and nothing could happen. I think I told her I had oral sex with one man, and she started to attack me. I remember her fist coming at me so fast! It wasn't only a few hits. She wouldn't stop. I remember wishing I could just fall into the floor, wanting to be invisible, wanting it to stop. I thought I was going to die.

Earlier, I had told my next door neighbor that I was scared, so when I screamed she came right over. I ran to her apartment and locked the door. After a couple of hours Jane left the house and I went back. Everything of mine, including my pictures, was torn up.

A few months earlier Allie had told Jane that she was going to work in a children's camp for the summer and had held to her decision in spite of Jane's angry protests. She is not sure why she was adamant about leaving for the summer. "I think," she says, "it was probably the same part of me that was able to have a lesbian relationship in a Catholic school, the part of me that wants to get what I want to get."

There was no more violence during the two-month period they continued to live together, and though Allie was glad to leave for camp, they were still very much a couple and planned to continue living together when Allie returned. While she was at camp she sent all of her paychecks to Jane to deposit in their joint account. She also had deposited the money from some redeemed bonds her parents had saved for her and had left the car her father had given her with Jane.

At the end of the summer when Allie returned, she found that Jane didn't have a job, had spent all their money and had been using Allie's car to escort her new girlfriend around town. The new girlfriend, Rachel, had been Allie's best friend. Allie tried hard not to admit to herself that she was jealous, and the more jealous she became, the more she "tried to please everybody" and play "earth mother," saying to Jane, in effect, "You go do what you need to do to take care of yourself." In retrospect she believes she was saying, "You can come back to me and walk all over me."

Jane lived with Rachel because her apartment was bigger than Allie's, but she continued to bang on Allie's door when she wanted something or when Rachel threw her out, and she helped herself to Allie's things, including her car. Allie was beginning to set some limits and even pulled the spark plugs

from her car, so Jane couldn't take it. The physical violence
had subsided, but the emotional abuse continued. Allie and
Jane went briefly to counseling and Allie saw a counselor on
her own, who told her she was "just like a battered wife." She
wasn't ready to hear that yet and discontinued the therapy,
but she was changing.

I had come back from camp in September of '79. In
November of '80 I was going through a box of cards I'd
saved since we got together in high school, and I
thought, "I don't want to be in this relationship any
more. I don't want to be here." I went through the stuff
and called her and said, "This isn't working the way it
used to." I told her I didn't feel safe, that I didn't want to
see her and that the relationship was over. She was very
loving and warm and she agreed that it was over.

I felt a lot of sadness, letting go of the dream, the fantasy that we would be able to work things out. I had always thought that if I somehow did it right she would
come back. But I was letting go, letting the grief come
through that this relationship was over. I·moved back to
the Midwest where I found a graduate program. I enjoy
learning and used that time to heal. After six months I
worked in a camp for the summer and after that I was
really finished.

After that phone call we would just meet and have
sex, and sleeping alone was hard. I don't know if it was
my addiction, or her addiction and my being caught up
in pleasing her. The way I had grown up, I was sexual to
get validation, but now I go through long periods when
I'm not sexual and it's perfectly okay with me.

The break-up happened the quarter I was graduating.
I had just taken my own power away, and was having difficulty finishing my school work. Suddenly I blanked out
on the whole outline of my senior thesis, after all the
work I had been doing. And I knew that if she was there
she could tell me what I was going to write. I know now
it was probably because I discussed with her how I was
going to put things together but I didn't take any credit
for that. It was real hard not to have that support, say-

ing, "You can do it." It was hard not to call her, to not
want to go back to her. I sometimes would end up calling her anyway.

Jane hadn't allowed me to go out to eat, so I would
take myself out to eat and go somewhere real nice. That
was something that was totally for *me*. But it was hard to
take care of myself, because I didn't want to, like I didn't
deserve it. It was hard to say, "You deserve it." There
was this feeling that was like an unsatisfied wanting. I
read *Fat Is a Feminist Issue*, which talked about choice
and compulsive eating, an ongoing issue for me. It talks
about really wanting food rather than just eating it and
that had ramifications through all parts of my life. I
thought, "Do I really want that?" I'd never asked myself
that. I always thought I should want what I'm supposed
to want.

The incredible aloneness would ebb and flow, but it
lasted nine months. I wanted someone to be intimate
with, but at first I didn't try. I still worked at camps in
the summer, drove a school bus and enrolled in graduate classes at night. Workaholism is one of my "drugs."
Then I went to an event at the Lesbian Counseling Center and I was so scared. I didn't want to go, but I
thought, "Well you want to meet new people," so I went
and I sat there. I didn't have an overwhelmingly wonderful time, but I knew I had to come back the next
week and I did it.

With some people in the lesbian community I would
say, "I'm dealing with having been abused" and it was
the blank stare that I would get, or the frozen smile.
Like, "Okay, she thinks she's been battered. This
doesn't happen here." They would gloss over it, not taking it seriously. During the intake at the lesbian counseling service after I said I was abused they just went on
to the next question. Later I saw that in my record they
had put quotes around "abused." I saw another therapist
and when I said I'd been abused, she said to me, "And
when you were supposedly abused . . . " Other people
were real supportive and would say, "You know, there
just aren't any resources for you." I think people do be-

lieve me now, but I project onto people that I won't be believed. That's my own stuff, but there were so many times when I wasn't believed.

There were good times too, and Allie gradually learned that it was a joy to be appreciated by people and that she didn't owe it to them to please them. She was surprised and delighted when she cooked dinner for a friend and the friend said, "Thank you." In 1983 Allie began a relationship with Lonnie. They decided to be monogamous and Allie explained to Jane that their occasional sexual meetings would have to stop. Jane flatly refused to accept it, and when it became clear that Allie was serious and not to be moved, Jane refused to speak to her. "Once I'm with a woman," she said, "she's mine forever." Allie would still like to be Jane's friend, but realizes it's impossible.

I'm real happy these days. I'm looking lots more at codependency on substances or situations. In my case it's my work that's the consuming thing in my life. My job before this was full-time at an adolescent treatment center where most of the patients were on a closed ward and had anger control problems. It's a closed space, with lots of yelling. I've had my life threatened a number of times—at one point I was kicked in the head and had a concussion—had desks and chairs thrown at me and it was a process for me of learning to fight back in a healthy way, not trying to kill that person but to try to restrain them.

In my relationship with Lonnie we're both committed to growing and I'm so cautious about abuse that I project onto Lonnie things that Jane would have done. She may do some of the same things but her intent is different and that's the key, to me, of knowing whether its abusive. And we have a commitment to talking it out. It's different in this relationship because I'm here because I want to be. If anything started—and I don't think it would—I know I could get out of it and that I'd take care of myself first. That's real different.

I'm keeping up my contacts with other people, not

getting myself isolated. I've done a lot of work on myself through therapy and reading, looking at my family background, at the abuse that was there, and the substance abuse. It's a sense of knowing who I am in the world, of seeing myself as totally separate from anyone else at the same time as that I'm connected to everyone else, not necessarily to just one person.

CHAPTER 6

Edith

I grew up in a small town that was run by the church.
If you were out after midnight you were no good. People
wouldn't talk to you. You couldn't wear red shoes, have
pierced ears or dye your hair, or you were a lady of the
night. The church didn't believe in lipstick or dancing or
movies, but I did go to movies and dances, because my
folks were broadminded.

My dad was very good to me except when he was in a
bad mood, which wasn't often. I never saw him hit my
mother, but he was a wife abuser. I saw him chase her
and heard him say things that made her cry. He had
been gassed in World War II and was badly burned. He
had a heart condition from then on, and we lived very
meagerly on a government pension. I couldn't belong to
Camp Fire Girls because it was fifty cents a year for
dues. I vowed that my children would never be in that
spot.

My mother was very, very submissive, one of those
people who couldn't make up her mind. She babysat and
took in laundry. I was doing other people's shirts at the
age of ten; I always baked bread and I worked in a grocery store after school for seventy-five dollars a month. I
worked six days a week and when I wasn't in school I
worked ten or twelve hours a day, whatever it took. It
was in the days when you called into the store and the
man put it up and delivered it. I had that job for nine
months until the owner's son came back from the service

and my boss said, "Will you train him to do your job?" I went home and cried and said I had to quit, but my mother said, "No. We're not made of that kind of stuff. You will go down and you will train him and you will do your best, and then when you leave you'll have a clear conscience." So that's what I did.

I've known since I was ten years old what I wanted out of life. I didn't know how to get it then and I still don't know how to get it. I have always wanted to be someone's wife and someone's mother. I got married at twenty and just sheer luck, Russian roulette, I married the right man. We had four children, all planned, and I was happy. I had what I wanted. We had planned what direction we wanted our lives to go, how to finance different things, what kind of an insurance program we wanted, where we wanted to live, how long I was going to work—all this, before we ever got married. He wanted to drop his plan to go to school in favor of getting married, but I said, "I'd love to be your wife, but I won't marry you unless you go to school." So he went to school for the first year we were married. I quit work when I was five months pregnant, saying I'd go back to work when my kids got hungry, thinking that I was going to forever be a housewife.

My husband, Tom, was a very intelligent, very kind man. I'm a much better person for having been married to him, but I guess God needed him more than I did, because he was killed in an auto accident when he was thirty years old. My children were two, four, six and seven at the time. I got social security of a little less than two hundred a month. We did all the fun things that were free. I can tell you everywhere to go in this city that costs nothing. I'm an expert on how to make potato soup four hundred ways.

My daughter didn't have the use of one leg when she was born, and the doctor said the worst it could be was that she'd spend her life in a wheel chair, and the best was that exercises and braces would do it. I elected to have her go to ballet, rather than to physical therapy, but since you can't send one child and not the other, they all went. I made costumes for entire classes, trading it for my kids' lessons.

I had a lot of rules, I was a very strict mother. Everybody went to bed by seven, because my tolerance for children is absolutely marvelous all day long, but at eight o'clock I want everyone who is not six feet tall in bed. Everybody learned to cook and do dishes and when you're nine you learn to iron and do your own clothes. God put mothers and fathers on earth not to do for the children, but to teach them to be independent. I was everyone's room mother and took cookies to everything.

I went to school to become a licensed practical nurse, so I elected to put the children into a private school and we were gone for eleven hours every day. Every night I had to pack lunches and do the laundry. I've never seen giving up as an option, which is no doubt why I stayed so long with the wife beater.

Edith was "properly" introduced to Jack by a neighbor, and was sympathetic toward him because he had lost two of his four children in a fire and was raising the other two alone. He was the best date she ever had. He "never said anything cross," was good to her and to her children, and the only sign of trouble before they were married was that he once slapped his daughter.

They met in January, were married in August and the first time Jack beat Edith was a week after their honeymoon. "The minute you say 'I do,'" Edith says, "it is Dr. Jekyll and Mr. Hyde". Almost anything could trigger Jack's temper. Although he was not an alcoholic, one of the beatings did occur when he came home late, after a night of drinking with his boss. He walked in the door, passed right by the dinner that was waiting in the oven, and went directly to Edith, who "woke up seeing stars", her head "beaten from one side to the other." She was subjected to battering as often as twice a month and afterwards he would say he was sorry and be "just as sweet and soft as butter." There was sexual abuse, as well, which included Jack's efforts to coerce her into participating in "kinky sex." On one occasion he displayed his rage by pulling out her pubic hair and stuffing it in her mouth.

The emotional abuse took the form of sexual innuendos and assaults on Edith's self-esteem. He would say, "If you were worth as much as I am, they'd pay you more" and criticize almost everything she did. Edith questioned whether she was at fault, and thought she was such a "low creature" that she "belonged under the rug." But then she would think she could "fix things," and throughout the eight years of her marriage she kept trying.

Two months after the wedding Edith had asked Jack to see a counselor, but he declined. Three years later she told his doctor what was happening and he spoke to Jack, but Jack said he was leaving her and that everything would be all right. He did leave for four months, but came back on Saturday nights. The children were pressuring her to be either truly married or definitely separated, so she decided she had better stay married. She was also concerned, during the separation, that he might carry out his threats of suicide.

After a severe beating, Edith woke up one morning and thought, "God didn't mean for this man to kill me." She saw an attorney who referred her to a counselor, but when she told the counselor what Jack was doing to her, he said she was responsible for it. The counselor and her minister both said, "Don't put those kids through a divorce," advice which corroborated everything she had heard or read about the negative impact of divorce on children. Meanwhile she tried to appease Jack by going out dancing when he wanted to, drinking coffee with him when she'd have preferred helping her children run the tractor on their farm, talking to him about their problems. She tried to do exactly what he asked, to be sure she wasn't in some way egging him on. When he was violent, she attempted to get away, but he was faster than she was. She called the police, but they said the only thing they could do was to take her into protective custody—which was exactly what Jack, a reserve police officer himself, had predicted. She is sure she would have left much sooner had there been a shelter available to her.

At times Jack would say he wasn't going to be violent any

more and Edith believed him, because she wanted it to be true. "Marriage," she recalls saying to herself, "is the biggest, the most important thing we do in our lives and I can't have made that big a mistake." Finally the thin thread of hope snapped.

I suppose it had been coming. He had been complaining about my working nights and I had quit. I was home for a week with no job and nothing changed, nothing was better. We went out New Year's Eve to dinner and everything was just great and then he wanted to stop at a topless bar which wasn't my dish of tea at all. So I said, "If you want to stop, I will, but it's not the sort of thing I like."

He pulled up to the parking lot and there were some guys coming down the street and he said, "When you see those guys, what do you think?" I said, "They don't do anything for me. Nothing." "When you see guys do you ever wish you could go to bed with them?" I said, "No!" He pursued it and I said, "Bag it! I don't want to talk about that sort of thing. That's enough." We went into the bar and the conversation didn't get any better.

The next morning I got up to take his daughter to work. I got a glass of water from the kitchen sink and he knocked the glass out of my hand into the sink, and it broke. I looked at him and I said, "Why don't you take her, I'm tired this morning." And while he was gone I left.

He was so insistent that I had to have desires for other fellows that I couldn't tolerate it. Some things are sacred. Whether it was just the breaking point or whether I was just ready to say, "Hey, look, I'm going not to be killed," I don't know.

When I applied for the divorce he applied for family counseling. I thought, "Okay, no one is going to say I didn't do all I could." We went. That was the nicest thing I ever did. The counselor said the most healthy thing I ever did was to file for divorce. He pointed out I have an education and can take care of myself, that I knew I could do it because I had done it before.

I said the thing that bothered me most was how it was going to affect my son, who was the only child at home. The counselor said, "Have you asked him?" And I said, "No. Isn't that strange?" And when I did ask, he said, "Well, Mom, you're still my mom, you'll always be there... " So I'd wasted an awful lot of muddling through that this was going to be hard on a child—a child who certainly had a fairer picture of it than I did.

It took about three months to get a good job, and then I got into nursing school. I felt that if I went to school and gave it my best shot that would keep me from being an overload on my kids' lives. I took between eighteen and twenty-three credits and worked full time that first six months and I didn't care if I lived through it or not. When I look back I realize I made all the preparations you make for suicide. I sold my home, the jewelry that was of any value I gave to the child I wanted to have it, I had my will made, I had everything stored. I wasn't saying, "I'm going to kill myself." I just didn't care if it happened.'

One of the hardest things was to learn to do things on my own, even though for several years I had gone to work and come home and baled hay and cooked for the family. The kids and I had done nearly everything, but I had felt there was someone there to share it. It's all in the head.

The divorce was a big shock. I hadn't expected to lose thirty thousand dollars in the settlement. Besides that, when we married, Jack owed six or seven thousand dollars, a lot of which I paid, just because I was too embarrassed to admit that he was that poor a manager. Until I married him I didn't know what it was like to get pink slips from people to whom you'd owed money for years.

I'm lonely at night, because when I come home from work I can't say, "What happened to me today?" You don't talk to walls. They're not good company, where before I always had the kids to talk to. They are warm and cuddly, they care if you come and go, and someone would notice if you were dead before the odor got next door. People say I must be going through the empty nest syndrome. I think the depression I feel now is as much age-oriented as anything else. I'm fifty-four and I'm not bouncing back the way I did when I was younger. I have always been resilient, and I'm not that way, now.

But nothing is all bad or all good. There are pleasures in being alone. If you get up in the middle of the night nobody says, "What are you doing out of bed?" and you can go have your cup of tea and think your thoughts. When you get off work if you're very tired you can sit and collect your thoughts and you don't ever have to watch somebody else's TV program. I also discovered that it was all right if I sing with the radio or the TV. Nobody else is listening. And any woman alone has more money than any woman married even though the income is triple that of a single woman. The difference between men and boys is the price of their toys. But they don't *all* think they should have these toys. That's one thing about having a good marriage first, you know that it isn't everybody. You don't have to hate all men.

I have a rewarding job, doing home health nursing and I make between eight sixty-three and nine eighty-one an hour, depending on the shift. That just does my ego so much good because somebody thinks I'm worth that much. I certainly have a much better feeling of self-worth than I had with Jack.

I take classes and go to singles dances (but not when I'm feeling lonely because they make me more lonely), I sew for my grandchildren, make afghans, go to garage sales, go out for cocktails and conversation with girls at work. Most of my days off are spent with my kids and grandchildren, of which I have six. When an extra day comes along I can take it and enjoy it now. I go for a ride and look at tulips. I went to Sea View one day last spring and stopped along the way and walked on the beach all by myself and enjoyed it. I haven't done that type of thing before. I'm a person who wants to grow and wants to go, and if it gets to be dull or routine I'll look for something different.

CHAPTER 7

Lou

Lou's parents immigrated to the United States from China during World War II. Her mother was devastated by the dramatic contrast between her upper-class, sheltered life in China and her poverty in this alien country. Lou was her first-born child and a great disappointment because she was merely a female. Lou has three younger brothers.

Lou's father worked seven days a week from early morning until late at night. Her mother stayed at home with the children until they started school, when she began working as a sewing machine operator, sometimes two shifts a day. She kept a close watch on Lou, who usually kept to herself, trying to avoid her mother's anger and surveillance. Lou did not date at all because of her mother's disapproval and suspicion.

I never felt happy as a child. I always wanted to leave home. I wasn't allowed to laugh, so every time my mother saw my teeth I was in for it. She talked a lot about sending me back to China and reminded me that "they don't like girl babies in China." My father favored me and I think that made my mother real upset. We didn't share anything as a family.

My mother would keep track of my periods in a notebook; she didn't understand that there was such a thing as an irregular period. So each time I went forty days or so she would think I was pregnant and would say things like, "You slut, who did you sleep with?"

It got so out of hand that she laid me down on the bed to see if I was still a virgin. She spread me open and there was this excruciating pain, and she said "Does this hurt? Does this hurt?" I didn't understand that it's supposed to hurt if you've never had sex, and I said, "No, it doesn't hurt." I didn't realize until years later that she got from that that I had had sex. I was thirteen.

Lou was depressed and always daydreaming. She was a good student and respected by others, but she felt that her life was incomplete and that she was missing the opportunity to explore and make her own mistakes. In high school she worked at a department store, in a restaurant and as a secretary, saving every penny for college. Her overriding passion was to leave home. She managed to get a scholarship and grants, which, along with her two thousand dollars in savings, enabled her to put a down payment on a dormitory room and pay the fees at the local university.

Right up to the day Lou left, her mother refused to believe she was moving. She told her daughter she could never come back, but she didn't stop trying to control her. She sent Lou's father to the dormitory to check on her and one evening when Lou was out for the evening her father called the police. Lou moved into an apartment for more privacy, but even there her father continued to spy on her. In her sophomore year of college Lou dated several men, including a Chinese student whom she took to her parents' home. Her mother treated him rudely, complained that he was too short and predicted Lou would have unacceptably short children with him, though there had been no talk of the possibility of marriage.

Lou chose not to introduce any other men to her mother, though she did tell her about Barry, a black man she had begun to date. He was a few years older than Lou and seemed to be a man of the world. In addition, she was able to laugh with him—at last she could "show her teeth" without fear of punishment.

Barry represented a lot of things I never had. I was able to confide in him my feelings about my mother, and he wasn't happy with his mother, so we were able to cry on each others' shoulders. I hadn't had a lot of experience with men and I just needed to share my feelings with somebody else. It was not love, but at the time I thought it was.

After a summer trip away from Barry she moved in with him and soon they decided to marry. Her mother refused to meet him and would not believe her daughter would marry someone who was not Chinese. She sent members of the Chinese community to Lou and Barry's apartment to go through Lou's papers, checkbooks and other possessions in order to find out if she was involved in drugs. On one occasion her father climbed through an open window and startled the couple making love. "He wouldn't knock on the door, but climbed up to see if I was really doing it. And I was. He was forced to come in and meet Barry, and told us it was wrong of us to marry different races. I suggested he get to know Barry, but he said no."

A few nights before the wedding the doctor who had delivered Lou was sent to her apartment by her mother. He arrived at three in the morning to deliver a lecture about her responsibilities. "You've got the community against you," he said, "and your mother is depressed and you're destroying her. Your whole family is in an uproar about this and you're going to be looked down upon and no one is going to accept you." When he had left, Lou's father came with more entreaties not to go through with the marriage. He cried and told her she was destroying him.

Lou expected marriage to be "something out of a fairy tale," and was confident that she and Barry would be able to resolve the few problems that would arise. Barry's mother and most of his friends didn't accept her, but he had so little involvement with his family that it didn't seem of great importance.

Barry had worked in sales as well as other jobs. He and Lou painted apartments in exchange for rent, so most of the money Lou earned working in a drug store was available for his gambling, which became his full-time occupation once they were married. He sometimes "made it big," but he would usually lose his winnings the next day. Lou didn't resent his gambling and thought "the woman should be subservient to the man." She believed, "If you loved somebody, you would do just about anything for him." Since she was working, she should provide for him. She never challenged him about going back to work.

Barry considered himself a very special, creative person who shouldn't take an ordinary job. He wasn't like the rest, therefore I shouldn't judge him like I judged other people. He said things like, "I've never gone this long without hitting anybody," or "You're the first woman I've never felt like hitting." I was in love and I overlooked a lot of things. We dated for two years without any incidents of anger. It made me feel good. He had turned around for the better, just because I loved him.

He started getting involved in drugs and gambling and he never took me out as he had in the beginning. I think he was a little bit ashamed of me, because I wasn't a polished, sophisticated woman like he was used to. But what attracted him to me in the first place was that I was naive. I was very trusting of him and made him feel real good. And those same qualities he came to resent.

He accused me of going out with others and would say, "Let me see your underpants, they've got secretions. I'd better have someone check this out, because they're not mine." Just real demeaning things. There was a little bit of shoving and pushing, but I didn't think too much about that.

We were at a friend's house and on the way home he slapped me. That was the first time I got hurt. I said, "What was that for?" He said, "You should really go to finishing school. I don't like the way you acted. And you should start using eye makeup." He tried to drive us off the road and that scared the hell out of me. When we got home he blackened both my eyes and grabbed my hair. My face was all bloody and swollen and I was screaming and he kept banging my head into the wall.

The next day he said, "I'm so sorry that I did this to you, and I'll never do it again," just sweeter than you'd

ever want to see, so of course I said, "I'll take you back
and we'll work things out." When he beat me I would do
my best to pretend it didn't happen or didn't hurt and of
course that didn't help. I just got hit harder until he did
get a reaction and usually he did get it, because he is six
foot two and I'm only five foot one. I'd cry and I'd mope,
but usually not for very long. I'd just pretend it didn't
happen and wash up and go about my business.

Ensuing incidents of violence were similar to the first one.
Barry usually bruised Lou where it wouldn't show. He
whipped her with a belt and a few times he punched her in
the mouth. In the beginning the violence occured every two
months or so, but gradually it increased to every other week
and escalated in severity. Lou became pregnant and Barry
threatened to "beat it out" of her, insisting that the baby
wasn't his and that he didn't want a mixed-race baby. She got
an abortion. His attitude toward her pregnancy was the most
severe of many emotional blows.

Lou believes that Barry is schizophrenic and that there
were signs of it even at the beginning of the relationship. He
accused her of "messing with his head, controlling his mind,
doing things when he was asleep."

I'd wake up in the middle of the night with him beating me and I'd say, "What are you doing?" and he'd say,
"You're fucking with my mind while I'm asleep." In the
first part of our marriage he beat me because he was
ashamed of me, in the last part it was because I was
"controlling his mind." I went to see a psychiatrist. He
said, "Lady, your problem is that you *think* you have a
problem. Your *husband* needs to see me." That was the
first time I thought it was something he was doing rather
than what I was doing. I was shocked because I had expected him, and wanted him, to tell me I was kind of
screwy and these were the things I had better do to get
myself fixed, so we could have a good marriage. After I
saw him I started to think maybe it's not all me and
those thoughts came more and more often.

Eventually, Barry said he wanted a divorce, and at first Lou resisted, still hoping he might change. Finally she gave in and they were divorced, but for the next three years Barry continued to live with her as if they were still married. He left dozens of times and stayed away longer and longer, but each time he would return and apologize. He persuaded her he needed her, promised never to mistreat her again and that he would get help. His insistence that if she loved him she would take him back triggered Lou's guilt feelings. She had convinced herself that she loved him and his apologies were sweet and believable, so she let him come back each time. She never really thought of leaving herself. She didn't like "failing" and didn't want to prove her mother right. She thought if she just worked harder at the relationship, she could make it work.

Barry choked Lou to the point that she was unconscious and when she came to he said, "Oh, I thought you had died." Then Lou realized that if she stayed he would eventually kill her. Shortly after that she moved out and agreed to pay his rent until he got on his feet. He stayed away four or five months, and then broke into her home. She was able to get him to leave, but soon after that he called and said he had had a stroke and needed someone to take care of him.

Lou's immediate response was to say she would do it, but she called him back to say she wouldn't. She agreed to give him two thousand dollars and to pay the twenty-five thousand dollars they had borrowed and charged, on the condition that she would not hear from him at all. Even though she had a job that paid well, it took her five years to pay off the bills. Early in life she had learned to save, so she was even able during this period to buy a house.

Barry stuck to his bargain most of the time, but occasionally he did ask about her at the store she worked in. Once she forced herself to speak to him briefly, rather than risk a scene. She told him there was nothing to discuss and and he agreed to leave. She was finally free of the fear that he would cause a commotion or talk to her colleagues about their marriage.

I had friends and they would try to get me to ask for help, or offer a shoulder to cry on, but I didn't let them help like they wanted to. It was real hard financially, but my career was going well and I could pay my bills. My job kept me sane. I had to work to get paid.

If I could do it over I would have left at the point of the divorce, but I came out a lot stronger than I went in. And the things I saw happen in street life opened my eyes. I don't judge people as harshly as I would have in the past. Not seeing my mother for nine years opened my eyes to a lot of things about her. I always thought I could change her, but now I take her as she is. I went to see her and she acted like nine years never happened and started bossing me around like I was living at home. I invited her to my house, but she wouldn't come. My mother did undergo lots of stress with the community, but I told her people can't make you ashamed of me, only you can do that. She chose to go along with what they said about me. I'm more a part of the Chinese community ·than I ever was before.

I love to garden and I knit, make rugs, crochet and embroider. I don't just dabble, I really do them. I still volunteer at the shelter and I'm into aerobics and running and I got a lot heavier into real estate. I have my own store to manage and last year I earned forty-one thousand dollars plus a six thousand dollar bonus. I bought a condo in Hawaii with my brother and a triplex and some houses. I can't believe it. Within the last three years I feel like I'm standing on my own two feet financially.

I was married in October. On our first date we went running at 5:30 a.m. The second date he helped me dig up my garden. It's real different from a guy trying to wine and dine, because from the beginning we shared in each others lives. I never thought I'd get married again. I enjoyed living alone and was doing real well. But I haven't had to give up anything, because he encourages me to keep doing everything. I like to cook and I do it.

He's handy around the house and he does all that, and sometimes he washes the clothes and sometimes I do. I was shocked. I didn't expect to find anyone like that.

CHAPTER 8

Kate

Kate grew up in an Italian ghetto in an Eastern city, sharing a thirteen room house with her "very poor" family—her parents, four siblings, grandparents and an uncle. Her father worked in a shoe factory and her mother stayed at home. Kate remembers her mother "just sitting" for a year or two, while suffering from agoraphobia; she also had two "nervous breakdowns." Kate immersed herself in art classes and spent time with friends. She was a bright, outspoken, rebellious child who achieved high marks in school, defended the underdog and had no fear of authority.

At thirteen, embarrassed about her family's poverty, she began to identify herself with the hippies, who made it seem acceptable not to be well-dressed. She fought with her mother over her interest in boys and was distressed by her mother's habit of listening in on her telephone calls. When she was fifteen she ran away to California with a boy, became a "flower child," experimented with drugs and was on the fringe of political protests. When she returned to the East she didn't want to return to high school. She had only completed two and a half years of course work, but because she had been an honor student and had taken extra credit courses she was given a diploma. She did continued her study of art.

At seventeen she was living with another young man. He was involved in the anti-war movement and through him Kate began to develop a serious interest in politics. She began to distance herself from drugs, became interested in workplace organizing, and joined a study group. Her self-confidence was enhanced by support from students and other middle-class political workers who appreciated her because she was a working-class woman. Her studies helped her see that she had choices, and she felt good about choosing factory employment in order to organize workers.

Kate worked at the factory for five years, the first year getting to know people and the second year organizing a study group. She was brought together with other political workers, including Joe, a somewhat older man, who had been a tenant organizer. "I was totally infatuated," Kate says, "and attracted to him. He was a genuine proletarian and I felt he was someone like me."

Almost from the beginning, however, they disagreed. Joe continually argued with workers, who then began to avoid him, but Kate was friendly and successful in getting people out to meetings. This difference was a source of criticism and tension throughout the entire relationship. But Kate knew she wanted more than an organizing relationship with him.

> My first impressions of Joe was, "This is the person who's got the most pain of anybody I've ever met," and that really attracted me to him, because I felt like I could help him, get through to him.

Kate expected that they would be involved in the factory organizing for a long time, but suddenly Joe left his job. She went after him and questioned him about why he had quit. He said "it was all the boss's fault," nobody could understand what he was trying to do and "everybody was dishonest and reactionary." Kate interpreted the situation very differently and was disappointed that they wouldn't be working together any more, but she continued to see him and the relationship grew.

A couple of months later she moved in with him. She often wasn't sure about the right thing to do and one of the things she valued about Joe was his certainty that things were either wrong or right. Kate says she wasn't in love with him, but it was important that they respected each other politically and that she wouldn't be so lonely doing the work. In other relationships she had felt torn between her partners' needs and her desire to spend a great deal of time at her political work.

Now she expected to be free of that conflict. She had been in and out of several relationships and she said to herself, "Okay, this is the end. Joe is going to be the one. I'm really going to make a commitment and I'm really going to work on this."

The violence started soon after we moved in together. The first time, he was trying to degrade me and ripped my nightgown off me and scratched me from under my ear lobe all the way down my chest. I remember it as an act of violence, but also as an act of making me vulnerable. It had nothing to do with sex. Then I go to work the next day and I have these scars on me and I said, "A cat scratched me," but people knew. Violence was all around. One woman had been shot in the leg by her boyfriend.

The union contract was coming up and I had done a lot of work to get a strong core of people who made agreements and we had a lot of meetings with bureaucrats. Joe kept insulting these people that I had come to respect and depend on. He was saying, "You're a sellout" and getting more and more upset that they weren't ready to make a revolution in six months. I would say, "You left after six months and I stayed and I know these people better than you do."

The night before a strike we were having one of these arguments and he punched me and I got a nice black eye. The next day was the union meeting for the contract and they were offering a real bad wage and benefit package and I got up and just started to read the salaries of the union hierarchy, which were like sixty thousand dollars. That was enough to incite people not to vote and to walk out of the meeting. The wild-cat strike started then and I made a speech, and I was out on the street talking to these truck drivers in these big trucks that were delivering supplies, jumping up on the cab and telling them there was a strike, and seeing these big trucks pull away saying they wouldn't break our picket line.

I think Joe was very threatened by my independence, my being able to do the work, my having something besides my relationship with him. Sometimes he would come home and he had had a fight with somebody and I would say, "Maybe if you had put it this way the person would see it," and he would just go bananas, would say that I was sticking up for the reactionary, that I was politically incorrect and that he was correct. Then he would start with the violence.

He would do real animalistic things like coming really close to my face and gnashing his teeth like he was going to bite me, and he did bite me a couple of times. I didn't like the violence, but I was used to crisis and I was used to being around a person who was emotionally unstable. I would slap him in the face or push him away and once I went after him with a knife and put a scar on his arm. I didn't think there was anything wrong, because I was fighting back. If I'd thought it through I would have said, "This is nuts. He could kill me." He was a weightlifter and did real heavy work at his job, and he'd been a professional boxer, so he wouldn't even blink. In fact, one time he knocked me out on purpose, because I was hysterical. We were both five-ten, but I weighed a hundred and forty-five and he weighed two ten.

Kate's friends advised her to tell him to stop hitting her or she would leave, but she knew he would walk out if she said that, just as he had walked out on one job after another. She tried to curb what she said, but she couldn't always do it, and his rage came so fast that she often had no idea what had triggered it. Kate sees herself as a person who knew how to get information and how to go after resources, and she is amazed now that she didn't know anything about shelters.

After Kate and Joe had lived together for about three years, she became pregnant and they were married. He kicked her once during the pregnancy, and she left. He apologized, she returned, and the rest of her pregnancy was free of violence. She had a caesarean section and the violence started again almost as soon as she came home from the hospital.

If the baby woke up and Kate couldn't stop her from crying, Joe would scream at her, "You're not doing your job with the baby," which would upset the baby even more. One night Kate cowered in the corner of a room with the light off, holding the baby and hoping Joe wouldn't see them. He was "on a rampage," breaking things in the kitchen, and she ran into the kitchen and called a hotline. But Joe grabbed the phone and, after telling the hotline worker there was no problem, he pulled it out of the wall. It was then she began to make plans to leave. One night he pulled the baby out of her arms. "If it was between him and me," she says, "it was fine, but I could see this child was going to get hurt, so I started saying, 'The violence has got to stop or I'm leaving.'"

Kate felt strongly that a mother needs to be at home during the first two years of the baby's life, but Joe never kept a job for long and he began to call her a leech and a parasite, and insisted she get a job. She worked as a waitress at night and took care of the baby during the day. Joe did the childcare at night, and Kate did the paper work for Joe's G. I. benefits, so he could go to school during the day. She made it her major business to take care of him and "make him well."

Kate went to a meeting about family violence, and picked up a pamphlet about groups for men who batter. She notes, now, that she was still focusing on caring for him and had not gotten any information about shelter for herself. She told Joe he would have to get help or she would leave, and he agreed to go to a group for men who batter. During the year and a half he attended the group Joe stopped the direct violence against Kate, but the emotional abuse, including threats, continued. On one occasion he threw a dish over her head, which broke a light bulb, the glass shattering onto Kate and the baby. At the time she didn't consider such incidents direct violence.

The men's group encouraged Joe to go to couples counseling with Kate, which she was reluctant to do, because she was seeing a therapist she trusted, and they couldn't afford both. But she let herself be talked into couples counseling. Joe verbally abused her even during the therapy sessions, throwing things at her and pounding the floor with chairs. Kate says the counselor was afraid of him. He taught Kate "how to handle Joe's emotional illness" by techniques like calling his name over and over until "he would come back down to earth." She is certain the counselor kept them in the relationship for an extra four years.

Meanwhile, at the men's group, "he was such a model person," Kate says, "that he was training to lead groups. He was political, articulate, he had all the right jargon and he was confronting these guys on their violence right and left. This is the period when he was wearing this as a badge. 'Well, I've battered, I've hit my wife and I wouldn't do it again.' Kate spoke to a counselor from the group once, but she felt it wasn't safe to tell him everything.

Kate left many times for short periods. Once she pulled her daughter on a sled through a snow storm for five miles, seeking sanctuary at her parents' house. Joe followed her and smashed the door in. When he hit her mother Kate decided she had better go home with him.

In hindsight Kate sees that Joe has a deep hatred of women, but when she was with him, she was fooled. "He never," she says, "made chauvinist remarks about women's bodies, didn't read *Playboy*, and he had the terminology of respect for women, because he had the exposure to the Left."

After my daughter was born his seeing things in black and white became very oppressive. With a child I felt everything should be very open, the kid should experience different things. The last couple of years I spent most of my time out of my house. I gained a lot of weight, I became very depressed, then I started becoming totally neurotic about cleaning the house. I made all my daughter's clothes, I made his shirts, I crocheted. I think my world was closing more and more in on me and him and the apartment and the baby and I just couldn't cope with other things. He would call me at work and harass me and people would see it.

I got hired as administrator at the feminist cooperative daycare center where my daughter was, and this was when I started getting a lot of support around being a strong person and having skills. Working there the last two years enabled me to get strong enough to separate from him. In the last five years I had made my life separate. I set up childcare, I had a job. That was my goal; to relieve me from ways of depending on him, so I didn't need him.

Kate met a woman who lived in a cooperative house, and arranged to move there with Joe. She had found a place she could afford on her salary and she was surrounded by nine supportive people. A month later she asked Joe to leave. It had taken her five years from the time she began to plan it.

I wasn't staying with him because I thought I couldn't live without him, but because I didn't want him to give up the struggle to work it out together. But I got to the point where I didn't care about his pain and anger and confusion any more. I don't think there was a week that went by in the last five years that I didn't think about killing him. And by the time I wasn't caring whether we were together or not, he was beginning to be less violent. That was sad. But throughout the separation I saw how quickly he regressed back to being his violent self and that made me see that it would just take some incident and it would start all over again.

Kate hired a lawyer who was a politically compatible person, and a "nice guy," but who had no experience with people who batter. He kept persuading her he would be able to reach an agreement and that Joe's behavior was simply a temporary aberration, so she wouldn't need a restraining order. Joe pushed Kate down the stairs at the daycare center where she worked, and told people there he was going to kill her. Still, the lawyer refused to believe that that was his characteristic behavior.

Joe wanted legal custody of their child, so that he could have the decision-making power, but he finally agreed to let Kate have it. The day before the agreement was to be signed, he changed his mind. Kate felt as if he would never let her go, that he wanted custody, not of her daughter, but of her. Finally she called a hotline and was referred to another lawyer, who said, "All this negotiation has got to stop." Kate stopped talking to Joe, let her lawyer talk to his lawyer, and got herself a restraining order. Two and a half years after the separation, the papers have been signed, she has custody of her daughter, and Joe's visitation is spelled out in detail so that he knows he is not permitted to go near Kate. Kate had detailed protection written into the court order so that even when Joe picks up or drops off their daughter, he is restrained from going up Kate's stairs or ringing her bell.

Kate says she stayed with Joe during the last four years partly because of his sporadic work patterns, which put them in a position of poverty.

We owed everybody and didn't have any resources. I guess I didn't think it out. It amazes me that it's just me and my daughter, and just me supporting us, and now I have all this extra money and a car and money in the bank and no bills. What happened? Obviously he was a big drain, but he had me convinced that it wasn't him, it was me. I don't think I could have done it if I hadn't moved into this communal house and surrounded myself with enough people to feel safe to do it. And being around other people that treated me as a valuable person made me say, "Wait a minute, I'm not the slob that he's saying I am."

I had spent those pretty formative years—twenty to thirty-two—with him and I wasn't the person I was before. After I left, I couldn't focus. I could walk through various menial tasks, but if I had to do any creative thinking I couldn't do it. I almost lost my job. It was like an aftershock, the intensity of the relationship for so many years, and then all of a sudden being alone. I didn't know where I was or who I was.

We got evicted from our house and I found an apartment in my old neighborhood, which felt good. My mother lives down the street, my sister lives a block away. I saw a flyer for a job at the shelter and I got hired for it. I felt like if I could cash in on all those years of hell with him, then it was a good thing. I came in as a direct service advocate and I had a lot of organizing skills and we developed this job which is called staff coordinator, so I moved into that. I coordinate the volunteer pool and I mediate any staff conflict.

Right now I have everything I want, except he's still there, in the same city. I'm not in crisis, but until you get far enough away that you don't have any contact at all, you just don't feel in control. Working in the shelter movement will enable me to move somewhere else, because there are shelters everywhere.

I have a job I want to do and I bring in enough money that I can save. After I left I got involved in theater for a while and then I took a lot of classes. I'm still interested in men and I'd like to do things that would help me meet other people. The shelter takes a lot of my energy and so does my daughter, but things are so much easier. I have enough money to have choices. I don't have to worry about what I'm wearing or what I'm eating We can just do what we want and not be called names. I can go and see any movie I want and not be criticized for being politically incorrect.

CHAPTER 9

Sandy

Sandy remembers the childhood message she and her sister heard from her father as: "You girls are a bunch of useless morons and my boys with the penises are just terrific." She has thought a great deal about the abusive actions of her father, her ex-husband and other men toward women and she explains it as men's fear of "the enormous variousness and creativity and flexibility of which women are capable." It is that fear, she believes, that keeps men "knocking down women's self-esteem." Sandy's father was a psychiatrist and a brutally violent man who beat her mother and emotionally and physically abused Sandy and her sister.

Sandy's musical ability was an important source of strength as an adult and was evident as a child, but her father devalued it. Fortunately Sandy trusted her teacher's assessment and music turned out to be her "salvation." She was a singer, but not yet working professionally, when she married Cary, who was a painter. Soon after the marriage he began to batter her, sometimes as often as once or twice a week. Sandy never knew why Cary assaulted her, but he did say to her once, "The worse I feel about myself, the worse I treat you."

On rare occasions, Sandy knew Cary was building to a violent explosion and, wanting to get it over with, would do something to precipitate the incident. Sandy had also learned manipulative patterns from her mother, but she tried hard not to follow them. She remembers that after her father had beaten her mother he would become sexually aroused and her mother would lock herself in the bedroom. She would then demand that her husband get on his knees and say demeaning things before she would let him in. Even though Sandy was repelled by these ploys of her mother, she admits to liking the apologies that followed her husband's beatings. "I think," she says, "there is an awful lot of power, even for the non-battered woman, in making a man just get down and abase himself." Cary's period of atonement often lasted ten days or two weeks, before it began to build into rage again. In spite of the violence, he was sometimes introspective, sensitive and intuitive, qualities which appealed to Sandy.

Initially I would just run away from consideration of the whole problem. I developed migraines and had a lot of accidents, in which I would cut myself and burn myself, minor stuff. I was an emotional acrobat, thinking that if I just pleased him he wouldn't batter me. He would say, "I won't sleep with you, because your hair is too short," so I grew my hair down to here, which looked like shit on somebody my height. I had my mother's model of always trying to please my father. One of the major lessons in my life was that that doesn't work with this guy. He either wouldn't sleep with me, or it was total objectification—he was Mr. Portnoy screwing the piece of liver—or worse. I used to have hemorrhoidal cystitis, very painful, and you are not supposed to have sex. I'd wake up in the middle of the night, and he'd be shoving it in me on a sore urethra.

I went to a wedding of a college friend in Baltimore. The best man and I, a man ten years my junior, put the wedding on. I trusted him, and after the wedding we had a beautiful affair, three days long. That was all it needed to be, because I saw for the first time that a man could be a man without being violent, that tenderness could be involved in sexuality, that there could be wonderful, wonderful things happening between a man and a woman and that, just by contrast, ended any lingering feelings of love I had for Cary.

I don't know why I stayed after that, but I think it was still fear. My self-esteem, from not being allowed to talk to people, was just as low as it has ever been. I was afraid of everything, and I didn't feel well most of the time, which lowered my energy. I just wasn't ready, yet. It was almost as if I was physically paralyzed and I wanted to, but I couldn't. I did leave from time to time, and once I even got an apartment and a job. This city being the small place it is, he came out and found me, and gave me one of his down-on-the-knees apologies, and I went back. The longest I stayed away was a couple of days, so I never had the chance to set up the kind of life I wanted and to get the rewards from it. When I went back I thought everything was going to change. I knew it wouldn't, but he's an enormously persuasive talker.

I fought back for the first time when I was pregnant. I was washing dishes standing against the kitchen sink, and he took me from behind and began slamming my belly against the sink and something snapped. His attempt was unconscious, but it was to get me to miscarry. I had real long fingernails then and I turned around and I raked him down both cheeks. He was scared for a good long time. He only tried it one more time during the pregnancy but the landlord was watching, so just knowing somebody could see stopped him for the duration of the pregnancy. After the baby was born, he took it up again and was very, very violent.

One time he was coming at me and I aimed a solidly placed kick to the testicles, which had him crawling around the floor for approximately two hours. If I could get him in the balls, that would stop him for the moment. But sometimes he got there first and then I'd get it again. And it was contrary to all my mother's little lady training, to just get my foot up there at the right time and let him have it.

The worst physical damage was usually on my breasts, pelvis and face, but when he would throw me against the walls, I really was afraid more than anything of being murdered by him. I was afraid that my neck would be broken or my skull would be smashed. I knew he was not uncivilized enough to pick up a knife, but if he could make it look like and accident...

The worst of the emotional abuse was accepting his opinion of me, his devaluing what I know are my considerable skills. "You're a rotten person, a lousy fuck, a rotten cook, a rotten lover, a rotten musician, you don't know anything."

I didn't have friends, because he was so rude to them if they came to the house, and he would hit me if I went to see them. What I had were his friends, many of them men who were also artists and batterers. If I went to one of their wives I just got a cold shoulder.

He abused my son practically from the day he was born and that was one of the major factors in getting me out. It was done in very subtle ways, but almost as accidents. When Jay was a small baby I asked Cary to change his diapers and he shoved a safety pin through his penis. Yes! "Accident." When he got a little bit older, he'd take him to the park to play ball and somehow Jay would get hit in the head by the ball. It became a pattern.

I began to hear voices. I had begun to see a therapist and he saved me. What I heard was a heartbroken sob, and at first I went to the door and listened and didn't hear anybody sobbing. I called the neighbors. "Is there a new kitten in the neighborhood?" No. Finally I knew it was an internal voice, sobbing. I was very anti-psychiatrist, especially the Freudian stuff, but I'd heard of a Jungian man, and I was absolutely desperate. I went to see him, but for six months I didn't say anything about this weeping child. I was just bullshitting around about the tensions of being a painter's wife, yackety yak. But I was hearing it all the time, when I was alone, in the shower, walking down the street, this sobbing child. My sister had heard voices and was locked up in a Freudian hospital for three years by my father. So it was a big risk, to talk about it.

After six months I said, "Would you think I was crazy if I told you I heard voices?" "Tell me what you hear." There were times when I just sat there and wept and wept and wept and he held me. My self-esteem was coming back, and I don't know if I would have been able to do it without him. He could have been the best theoretician in the world, but it wouldn't have mattered. The important thing was that he loved me.

I was singing in California and Nevada and getting away from Cary for a few days at a time. There was a lot of fear associated with singing, but it's one of the best highs you can get. The first time I sang for an audience of a thousand people I thought I would die, but after I got through the first number, then boom. It was wonderful, and that's what I wanted. Cary is totally unmusical and couldn't stand it. My father put down my music, for years. Right back to the circle of jealousy, again.

The stronger I got, the more my self-esteem developed, the less Cary tended to hit me, so things had been improving between us. He hardly hit me during that last year at all because I was just, "Oh, no, baby, not this lady." Then he came home one day from his therapist and whammed into the house and said, "You dirty whore, why don't you go drag men in off the street? Jay probably isn't even my son." He said this in front of Jay. This is one of those pictures that your heart takes that you wish it hadn't. Jay ran out in the bushes and stood there in his little blue sailor suit, sobbing and I said, "Look, I'm going to take that kid out to pizza, I'm coming back in forty-five minutes and I don't want you in this house when I get back." By which I meant, "Calm down." When we got back forty-five minutes later Cary had moved everything of his out of the house.

He disappeared for ten days. I called a lawyer and he said, "Go down right now and take out half of his savings." I took out ten thousand dollars from a joint account and put it in a separate account and then I filed separation papers.

What I saw with that "you dirty whore, he's not my son" routine was a rebirth of the original form of battering by my father, wiping up the floor with my self-esteem. Cary came back and said, "Gee, I'm sorry honey, I'll walk on my knees," and I said, "No. That's it." And that was it.

I cried a lot. Sometimes I drank a lot. The hangovers were just unbelievable. I did something else, which I didn't know at the time was self-destructive. I slept with a lot of men. I know other women who have done that and we all said the same thing. All right we did it, and it was embarrassing waking up in the morning and saying, "Who are you, and how did you get in my bed?" For a while you think you have to do it, because women tend to link sex and love. I wasn't sleeping around for the sex. I was sleeping around to get held. I found out it didn't do any good.

I didn't miss Cary. He missed me. He called me and said, "Why don't we sleep together?" After two years he came over to the house and said, "I have an idea. Let's get married again." I said, "Fine. Who are you going to marry?" When I was done, I was done. I was never tempted to go back. Just not having to deal with his put-downs liberated me from a lot of things.

I was married briefly, after Cary, and there was no physical abuse, but it was not good. I trusted and gave everything. And then, a week after the marriage he wanted the control. I would like to love, to trust, but I think it would take some kind of hero to understand where I've been. I've been bisexual for years, but you run into relationships with women that have some of the same problems as you have with men. I recently ran into a very charming, lovely young girl, who wanted to manipulate me. But I get smart faster. I had her figured out after three weeks and said, "No. You're just wearing a different gender this time."

In the past couple of years, the few lovers who were capable of sexuality and tenderness, the price has been my autonomy. "Sure, I'd love to hear you play some Mozart, but why don't you fix dinner first?" You get brainwashed from the time you are quite small on the control business. Your place is to clean the toilets, and the man's place is to design the toilets. Being autonomous means having the ego to accept the label "narcissistic," which just means you're taking care of yourself.

There's obviously a pleasure lacking, but I won't play the on-hold woman, just waiting for that phone to ring. Women have to get accustomed to not fear failure and also to handle a certain power that sustains their independence. It is very meaningful to me that I have been able to make the payments on my house for eight years, no matter how hard it was. And it was hard. For me to borrow thirty thousand dollars two years after the divorce—I thought somebody else was doing it.

I felt both excited and terrified by my professional success. I still do, sometimes. I turned the guitar into a concert instrument and I can play Brahms on it. I'm getting fifteen dollars an hour to do what I want to do anyway. I want to look over my shoulder and say "Who?" I used to think I couldn't make it professionally without a man. Now I don't think I can make it with one.

There is a growing pleasure in my relationship with my son. I found nurturing in unexpected places. I have a student whose parents invite me to their parties and love to have me sing. They listen just spellbound and when I really get down they come over and just pick me up and say, "I'm taking you home for dinner." I volunteer in the schools, stimulating interest in literature. For three years I read to six classes, and still one little girl comes up and throws her arms around me. This is where I get some of the things I needed to have. I don't get them from men.

I teach music to adults and children. I make my own music and I love it and I'm terrific at it. For years I couldn't say that, but now when I play, the neighbors knock on the door and say, "Next, would you do so and so?"

I love my friends. I get a lot of mileage out of the good relationships I have, which are principally with women, though a few men. I have work that I love. I still get depressed sometimes but I am willing to go with that. Some of the stuff I went through still makes me sad, and when I need to let it out, I let it out, because that child that cried in me was not for nothing. That child still needs to cry. I have a close friend who has been down some rough roads, and we've said we have learned so damned much from our pain that we wouldn't trade anything for it. All right, it hurt, but I learned a lot from my pain.

damned much from our pain that we wouldn't trade anything for it. All right, it hurt, but I learned a lot from my pain.

CHAPTER 10

Gloria

Gloria spent her first eight years in an Indian community in Alaska. She is the eldest of seven children and both her parents were alcoholics. Her father was a "wife-beater" and when her mother was "too drunk to beat up" he would take out his rage on the children. "He didn't hurt badly," Gloria says, "but would slap me around sometimes so that I would hear ringing in my ears and see flashing lights." As a young child, living on a small island, Gloria learned the "Indian ways" and style of speech.

You just pick up the wrong word and use it a different way. Or you may not complete a sentence. Like saying, "I'll go after," and "after" would hang in the air, and we understood that it meant "Well, I'm not going to go now, I'll go when I feel like it." You've learned Indian ways and then you're kind of dropped into white man's ways, but still have the Indian characteristics.

In the third grade I transferred from my island school to one on the mainland, where even the teacher made fun of the way I talked. She pointed at me and asked me to repeat what I had just said, and I wouldn't because I knew that I was being laughed at, and she would do this just to get me to say something wrong, to be making fun of me. In a spelling bee, the first word she gave me I misspelled and everybody howled their heads off because I spelled it the way it sounded. And actually I didn't know too much when you add it up. But because that hurt so badly I told myself, "I'm going to learn to spell and I'm going to learn to speak."

During the summer I studied hard and didn't play with my sisters or cousins, and we had a houseful because we were living with my grandparents, and two other families were living there as well. Then, in the fourth grade, my very first spelling bee, I was the only one standing after about half an hour, and I wouldn't allow the teacher to let me sit down until I spelled every word. But I proved to myself that I had learned something.

In high school I was going out with a boyfriend who was a high school drop-out and he drank, and his brother had been in jail several times, so my parents thought he was a bad influence and they wanted to get me away from him. They wanted me to get interested on their friend, Hal. Hal tried so hard he scared me at first. I wouldn't go near him because he was twenty-six, almost ten years older than I was, and he was an ex-marine and I heard stories about military men. "They know everything, they've been everywhere." I don't even remember when I began to become attracted to him, because I was so afraid of him. I'm young, naive, I'd never gone all the way like a lot of girls I knew in high school. A lot of them used to talk about it constantly, and it scared me because I knew that with going all the way came getting pregnant.

Somewhere along the line I became attracted to Hal and got pregnant. That's when I dropped out of school. I went through part of my twelfth year, but—the typical pregnant girl story—had to drop out and get married. In 1960 you just didn't stay. Three days after my eighteenth birthday I went to live with Hal on the island and we lived together a few months before we got married. In a way I was trying to get away from my father. I didn't know that Hal was the same.

The first time he beat me was when I came home to the island with the baby. Hal was out hunting when I got there and it's quite a walk from the airplane landing to the house, about equal to eight blocks. And he wasn't there to meet me, which should have given me an indication then just how much he thought of marriage at all. I walked all the way home with the baby and he wasn't there.

Later, he came home and he played with the baby for a while, and I found out he had had a big party while I was in city having the baby. I was hurt that he would even have the party knowing I was in the hospital with his baby. That's when I first got mad at him. Well, in the old tribal ways, the wife does not show any aggression at all, and that was the first time he beat me. I was so *shocked*, so hurt. I just couldn't believe it.

A short time after that beating Gloria found her husband drinking in their living room with some men she considered "winos." She complained about them drinking the beer and wine that had been bought for a housewarming party. Hal became enraged, and gave her cuts on her mouth, two black eyes, a cracked ankle and an arm that felt like it had been jerked out of its socket. There were no doctors on the island at the time.

When Gloria was in the eighth month of her second pregnancy, Hal went off fishing and she went to a beach party given by his sister. She became uncomfortable when the men and women paired off and was relieved when she was able to find a man willing to take her directly home. But when Hal returned and heard stories about the wild party he wouldn't believe she had left it early and that she hadn't been sexually involved with another man—eight months pregnant or not. That was the third time he beat her up.

I had black eyes again and the next day I called my parents and told them for the first time what had happened. My mother had heard stories, but I had always denied them. I don't remember what I thought then. All I know is, over the years I thought that this was the way of life, this is how the husbands are. The wife's supposed to take it. At first I didn't try to leave. Sometimes I would think "Eventually he'll realize what he's doing and he'll stop." And he would. But then he'd get mad at me for making him feel guilty and ashamed of himself and he'd start all over again. Sometimes I would run away from him in the house, but sometimes I'd just sit right through it. What the heck, you know, it doesn't hurt any worse than the last time. The black eyes usually came from backhand slaps. And he'd kick me or throw me on the bed or hit me on the arms or legs or head. He never hit me around the stomach, but he was convinced, after the baby was born, that I was just a sleep-around.

I went to live with my mother in Anchorage and after about a week I was missing Hal terribly. He called and said he couldn't stand it without me. I was so happy to hear from him that I ran down to meet him. The baby was born soon after, and Hal got a job at the local airlines about a week later, so we stayed in Anchorage. I wanted to stay there, because I associated the beating with the environment on the island. Everybody there beat their wives. I used to sport black eyes just like all the other women, bruises on the cheeks and cuts in the head. Women would say, "God, Gloria, if so-and-so did that to me, I'd leave him right now. I'd tell him where to get off." And then I'd find out later that she was in the same boat I was.

Hal used to have one or two beers with the guys after work, maybe once a week, and then pretty soon he wouldn't be just having two beers, he'd be drinking whiskey, until sometimes he'd be so drunk he'd have to call a cab to come home. There were times I'd go looking for him, when he'd be gone so long and I'd get scared, because I didn't want him to come home drunk. He'd beat me when he came home.

During the first, say ten years, of marriage, I kept up with him in drinking. I tried not to, but I did. There were times when I would black out. I would be on my feet and moving but I wouldn't remember. Mom and Dad still do it all the time and us kids spent a lot of our lives with our noses pressed against the window looking for them, waiting for them to come home, and they never did 'til we were all asleep. I don't want my children doing that, and my daughter told me there were nights when they would be sitting in the trailer window, watching for her dad and me to come home, and they'd start crying because one o'clock would go by, two o'clock, and we wouldn't be home. That hurt so, because I remembered how it felt. I felt so terrible.

Somewhere around the tenth or twelfth year, I just plain quit. I would go out with him, but I wouldn't drink, or I would have one drink, but I didn't like the idea of losing myself. I don't know how I quit. I was never addicted to the stuff, never dependent on it. I just decided one day, I've had enough of this and if I went with their dad I would call the children about every half hour just to let them know that Mommy's still thinking of them and she's okay. And then I just plain quit going out.

We'd been married almost twenty years and for the first—God, I would say seventeen years—I kept thinking he would change. I left him an average of three times a year, sometimes more, when he would get mean. There were times when I'd actually think, "This time he's gonna kill me." He'd be hitting me in the same places, but it would seem a bit longer than the last time. I would actually think, "This time I'm going to die." After we were here in Anchorage and I was working, when he would beat me and then pass out, I would gather the girls and we'd take off either to a hotel or to my mother's place or a friend's house. But I never added up our years of marriage and thought, "Well, how many years have we been married and he still hasn't changed?" I never thought about that.

Life was not entirely bleak for Gloria. Her progress at work brought limited, but enjoyable relationships with colleagues and feelings of satisfaction. These rewards did not come without struggle and pain, especially in the early years. When she moved back to Anchorage she was able to get her GED, but she wasn't able to pass a test to qualify as a typist. From January to December she went to a hundred interviews, only to be told the employers wanted someone with experience. She kept looking, encouraged by the man who had helped her get her GED. He had enough faith in her to say he would even create a position for her if she didn't get a job.

After a year of searching, she was called, and she impressed her prospective employer with her telephone voice and manner. She had more confidence in Gloria's potential than Gloria had in herself. "Hal had me believing," she recalls, "that I was just a dumb Indian wife and would never amount to more than that. So when I got the job I went home and I called my mother, I called Hal, I called everybody. I couldn't believe it. I had the job.

Gloria had supportive colleagues on the job and a boss who encouraged her, after a few months, to show more initiative. Gloria wanted more responsibility, but had been waiting to be told what to do. Once it became clear that she was expected to risk trying new tasks, even those she wasn't confident about, she found out she could do many of them. After six months she was given a promotion and another a year later. She has moved up the ladder and is now a bookkeeper, an upgrade she achieved after a year of courses at the community college.

She is matter-of-fact now about her accomplishments. "I started working for the state retirement system, and somebody had to calculate the benefits for employees. It was a very simple mathematical problem, and it was just easier to do on the calculator than by hand, and from there I just learned to be really fast on the calculator, and I decided that I liked that better than being a typist, which includes filing and all these routine, boring jobs." At home Hal was still trying to keep her believing she was "just a dumb Indian wife."

> He'd say things like my eyes were too close together, they're beady, my double chin is now becoming a triple chin, I've gotten too fat around the middle. I have always told myself that I'm not one of the prettier-looking girls, and I'd been conditioned to believe that I'm not all that good-looking, because my dad would always tell me that it was unfortunate I had his eyes or his ears. I still find myself staring at the mirror and the eyes are kind of

small and close together, and the closer I look the worse the ears look. It looks to me like the chin just begins to drop a bit more. But, you know—I never thought of it before right now—even though he always said I was ugly, he was always jealous of the men I worked with. He'd even accuse me of making it in the stockroom or in the lobby.

The worst thing that Hal ever did to me was probably the night he made love to me when we were parked in a car in front of my aunt's house. He was drunk and I didn't want to, I really didn't, but he forced himself on me. I'd never experienced satisfacation during love-making with him, so I didn't care one way or the other, but it seemed immoral to be making love in the car.

A male colleague's greeting to Gloria at the grocery store or her decision to atend a PTA meeting or Tupperware party could trigger Hal's jealousy, so she usually played it safe by staying at home. She tried to appease him by learning his moods, by avoiding male acquaintances, by lying and even teaching her children to lie. The children learned to follow her model of building Hal's ego at every opportunity, something she says she would never do for any man now.

Though she left many times, there were always many reasons for going back to Hal. She missed hearing his voice and felt dependent on him. She had never lived on her own and thought that violence and possessiveness were conditions of marriage. After a beating Hal was often good to her and bought gifts of clothes, a stereo, a tapedeck, a color TV and on one occasion, a car. She was told by friends and family that she could never support four children on her own.

For the first fourteen years of marriage Gloria believed everything Hal said. He told her he had left his first wife because she had been sleeping with someone else, and later Gloria learned his wife had left the first time he beat her. Gloria thought that if she tried to get a divorce, he might take the children and vanish, and she would have nothing. She believed she was "still Hal Baldwin's wife, no matter what. I never thought I could be divorced," she says, "with nothing between us except a name and children. And he'd tell me that no matter where I went he'd find me and kill me." At one point he held a gun to her head.

Six years before she finally left him, Gloria filed for divorce. Hal's lawyer told him she could sue him for everything he had, which caused him to "mellow out." They stayed married and Hal made some significant changes. He drank very little, curbed his jealous outbursts and went out socially with Gloria. But his best friend was killed in a crash and "Hal went into a terrific black depression and started to drink very, very heavily." By the time Gloria got home from work he was slurring his words.

The beatings weren't there, but the feeling was, the feeling of being beaten at the drop of a hat if I said the wrong thing. He called me one night to pick him up at the bar, and on the way home he was shouting at me about something, slamming his fist into the dashboard of the car. I kept thinking, "Pretty soon that fist is going to come this way." In the past year he'd gotten to the point of taking drinks every day. He worked from six in the morning until two-thirty in the afternoon, and by the time I got home from work at five he was drunk, gone and out of it. Hard liquor. He can drink a gallon of V.O. in one week.

This last time he was drunk and he woke up about six in the morning and wanted to make love and I didn't. I know what to agree to when he's talking to me, but I pushed him away and he got mad, so he went down into the kitchen and started drinking. Well, I let him do that for about two hours. So maybe about eight o'clock, eight-thirty, I went downstairs and he wouldn't talk to me. He was watching television and drinking, so I said, "Did you make any coffee?" and he said, "No! If you wanted me to make coffee, why didn't you say something? Or make your own fucking coffee. You just tell me what to do all the time." And I said, "Well, I'm just making conversation."

I made breakfast and he ate, but he continued drinking too. Then he went into the bedroom and I stayed out there with the kids. By then they were up, and real quiet. Nobody would say anything. The kids would look in on their dad, and say, "Well, he's asleep." That didn't last long, he was awake a couple of hours later and then he made his daughters fix his drinks. He wouldn't come out into the kitchen and I could tell he was building himself up to a big mad.

I cooked dinner, and I went in there and told him "Dinner's ready. You want to eat?" He just looked at me, so I repeated the question. He said, "Yes, I'll be out there in about ten minutes." I kept the steaks on the stove, turned down real low. About fifteen minutes later I told my girl to go up and tell her dad that dinner was ready. She came back and said, "Yeah, he knows." Another half hour went by. He finally came out. I served dinner, I put the steaks and everything on the table. He finished his drink, he sat down and cut his steak and he said, "Look at that! You know I don't like my goddamn steaks well done." and he threw the fork and knife on the table. Nobody said anything.

Well, he got up, fixed himself another drink, and went into the bedroom and I started to cry. And I told the girls, real quietly, I said, "I'm going to leave, and you can stay with your father or you can come with me." And they all said, "We're going with you." I said, "Okay, go and get your shoes and jackets. Don't let your dad see you and be quiet about it." I cleared off all the dishes, made it sound like I was going to do the dishes, put them all in the sink, threw all the steaks to the dog, and then the kids and I left. It was February twenty-first and that's when I made up my mind I'm not going to take it any more.

I had always thought every time that happened, I was going to leave. And I would go in the bedroom and take one last look and he would smile at me and say, "Are you still mad at me?" This time I was just sitting there thinking, "This has happened repeatedly, over and over again, and it's going to happen again tomorrow night and Tuesday night and Wednesday night and Thursday night for the rest of my life with that man. He's become a terrific alcoholic. I cannot stop him, and I have to face this every night, even when the children are all married and gone, and what is that worth? I'll be an old, dried-up woman, bitter. I don't want that."

I went to my sister's and she went downtown one night, and called me and said, "Hal's buying me drinks and he's arguing with Mom right now, and you should see the look on his face. Boy is he mad!" I really got scared, so I called the shelter. I had been kind of toying with calling them, but I used to think that I didn't need it. I thought, "I'm older than some of those girls. I'm going to be embarrassed, because, shit, I've been with the guy twenty years, you'd think I'd have known nineteen years ago when to leave." And a lot of the girls there are very young, but what I didn't know was that a lot of women go back, too, so it's the same pattern as mine.

I thought I didn't deserve to be there because Hal hadn't actually abused me, and that's what I thought it was for. Well, I stayed there a month and I called him one morning at work and said, "Now listen, this time I'm getting a divorce. This time I mean it. But I want the house. The kids and I don't like living here. We want to sleep in our own beds. We want to be in our own home." He said, "Okay. good. You can move in as soon as I find a place."

So we were at the shelter just one month and then moved back home, and the following Sunday he called me, and said he hated my guts, just really hated me and never wanted to see me again. I knew he was drunk so I didn't dare say anything for fear he'd come out there. Well, the kids and I got so scared that I packed them up and we went back to the shelter and spent the night.

Then the next morning I called back and I said, "Listen, Hal Baldwin . . . " Well, I called him a couple of names, and this was the first time in twenty years I had ever actually talked back. I told him, "This time I have had a belly full. Everything that has happened to us is not my fault, and you're never going to convince me otherwise ever again. I see differently, now. I've been counseled and I've been told that you're never going to make me feel guilty again. Now, don't ever call me again. I'm getting a restraining order and it'll probably be effective tomorrow morning."

I told the girls, "I'm not going to let you girls rule my life. I've always gone back before because you'd cry and carry on, and you can either go to your dad or you can stay here, and when this all blows over, you'll have us both. But I'm not going to go back because of you."

It is difficult for Gloria to stay away from Hal when the children are sick or need braces, when she's afraid the "maniac" across the street will break in and rape someone and when the washing machine or dishwasher breaks down. However when she was able to fix the dishwasher herself and could give herself credit for being more than "just a dumb Indian wife," Gloria's courage was given a boost.

Loneliness, the lack of a sexual partner, age and depression are important issues. Gloria has lost some friends since her divorce and has not yet made new ones. She reminds herself that "life begins at forty," yet worries that she will never find another man, because she's thirty-eight years old and "before long will be fifty." Nevertheless, she was asked out by a man shortly after she left Hal. Asked about sexual satisfaction now, compared to the past, Gloria's instant laughing answer is "None! This is getting a little too personal," she says, "but I had a dream one night that someone was making love to me and I woke up and actually had a climax in my sleep. I couldn't believe it! I didn't know whether to be embarrassed or what . . . I wish I could remember who it was." There are definitely satisfactions in her current life.

I don't have to be home right at four-thirty after work any more. There are no questions asked. The kids and I drove out to an air show, which Hal would never have let us do, and then we stopped off and had hamburgers, which we'd never been able to do before. The pressure is gone from all of us and the girls are easier. They laugh about a lot of things. I plan to rearrange the house, should I ever get enough money. The kids and I want to go to Disneyland. Next year, or maybe the year after, I plan to take another bookkeeping course, so that I can up my position one or two notches.

I used to envision myself laying on the ground like a murdered woman I saw a picture of once. The fear is still there, but much less than before. I think, "If he shoots me, he shoots me." But I want the children to be a bit more stable, so they can accept any tragedy, should one happen.

I'm more realistic, now, a bit more brutal with myself. I don't fantasize any more. I think I'm even beginning to like myself a little bit more and I'm beginning to find out that's very important. I used to get mad at myself for having allowed the thirty-eight years to go by, being somebody's else and not my own, but I still have thirty-eight more years and that feels kind of good to think about.

CHAPTER 11

Chris

My parents moved around a lot in Lincoln County, which is a bunch of towns of three, four and five hundred people. My dad's a truck driver and my mother was a bookkeeper and a secretary. Now she runs a community action center and works the ranch. My folks divorced mainly because of infidelity, and I never saw my father hit my mother.

My stepfather was only physically abusive a couple of times. He couldn't handle liquor and once he had been out in the garage drinking whiskey with my uncle. I don't know how much they had drank, but he shot a gun off out there and blew a hole in his roof. Then he came in and was shaking me and telling me he was going to kill me. I have scars on my wrists from his fingernails.

He used to be a little sexually aggressive with me. Every morning, to wake us kids up for school, he would come in and feel around. When my mother went to the hospital he had made a pass at me and also at my aunt and a girlfriend. He didn't try to enter me, but it scared me. I didn't know what was going to happen and I was still a virgin. Here this man is supposed to love my mother and he's touching me.

My mother didn't understand why I would run away from home, and she took me to a psychiatrist, but I wouldn't reveal what my step-father had done, and the psychiatrist said I was jealous of her and my stepfather's relationship. I wasn't, but I just wouldn't know what to do.

Finally, instead of running, Chris told her father she wanted to move away from her mother and stepfather and he arranged for her to live with her aunt and uncle for the next year. She "adored" her uncle, the only man she would call a real "father" and her aunt was like a second mother. At the end of that year, when she was fifteen, she moved in with her father. He was not abusive, but allowed her to do whatever she wanted and provided little guidance.

Chris thought school was "dumb," and at sixteen was bored with it. When she met Wes at a concert, she was excited and attracted by this older man of twenty-three and fantasized about living happily ever after with him in a country house full of children. After only a couple of dates they moved in together. Chris thought the relationship would last forever and that "all the bad stuff would go away." For the first two or three months Wes worked as a carpenter and took her "everywhere." The dream she thought was coming true began to turn into a nightmare when Wes was sent to prison for stealing.

Chris continued her high school classes while Wes was in jail. Four months later he was out on probation and Chris felt confident that he wouldn't break the law again and would return to his old self, pampering her as he had before. A month before graduation she dropped out of school to marry him. To her dismay, Wes refused to go back to carpentry; he frequently stayed out late and began to deal drugs. She attributed those changes to his discouragement over not finding work and resentment over being on probation. She did her best to encourage him, telling him he was a "great carpenter," but to no avail.

Wes began to assault Chris a month after they were married. The first time, he knocked her head against the wall and floor because she was too sick to go to a family picnic. Usually he would try to hit her between the eyes and she would try to block him, but she didn't fight back because she couldn't bring herself to hurt him. He always seemed surprised, later, that he had hurt her so badly. Chris felt sorry for him.

After a beating Wes usually wanted to make love, and Chris was afraid, so she would submit. She thought his experiences in jail and the pressure of being on probation—or of being tied down in marriage—upset him so much that he couldn't help hitting her. As she sees it now, she was always looking for an excuse for him. Yet she knew that his rages appeared out of nowhere and had nothing to do with her. "All of a sudden his eyes would change, and I knew he was going to hit me. It was like he would freak out. He did a lot of speed and drank a lot, and I think it altered his mind."

After her daughter was born Wes stayed out more; Chris complained more about it, and he said he hit her because she complained. At a family picnic Chris threw some food away and Wes slapped her to the ground and repeatedly kicked her in the head with his steel-toed boots. Wes' brother told Chris he hadn't tried to stop Wes, because he had tried intervening when Wes had beaten his first wife and had been beaten for it himself.

Three weeks later Chris began to have headaches and grand mal seizures. The kicking had resulted in temporal lobe damage on both sides of her head. At first she tried to deny that she had epilepsy as a result of Wes' treatment because "It sounds so cruel," but opinions from three doctors persuaded her it was so.

Chris was expected to have dinner ready the moment Wes stepped in the door, whether that was at six o'clock in the evening or one in the morning. If it wasn't ready or it had dried out he unleashed his rage. At the very least Chris would have to cook him a second dinner on the nights he was late. He gave her orders and called her names and she complied with his demands "like a dog." She began to ask permission for everything and her fear was increasing. Now she blames herself for becoming so frightened of him and letting him have so much control.

Sometimes when they were away from Wes' family and friends, he used fewer drugs and worked at legitimate jobs, like carpentry or cleaning gutters. Her best memories are of living near a commercial hot spring where Wes rebuilt cabins and she cooked for loggers and ran the general store. They worked hard and the beatings became less frequent. She recalls an exciting sex life, when "the trailer was rocking" three times a day.

Things got worse when Wes began to deal drugs in a serious way. Once he became violent while she was cooking dinner. Chris turned off the gas burners and reached up to block his punch, but he pushed her arm onto the still hot burner, which "sizzled it." Because they lived in the country and because Chris didn't drive, she was isloated and confined to their home. Despite the violence she tried to create a peaceful atmosphere by devoting herself to taking care of the baby, baking bread, making quilts and sewing. She washed clothes in the sink, because they had no washer or dryer. When a friend asked why she put up with Wes' refusal to give her money for the laundromat, among other deprivations, Chris said, "Well, that's just life." She "thought all men were that way . . . just figured they were all abusive."

Several factors prevented Chris from leaving. She had no money of her own. When she called the police they said they couldn't do anything for her unless they actually saw Wes hit her. The concept "Until death do us part" was entrenched in her thinking, even though she wasn't formally affiliated with a church.

Wes was foreman in a cabinet-making shop. He had went from a regular laborer to foreman and then to purchasing agent. He was night watchman too, because we lived on the job. Since he was buying it and watching it he started stealing it. Every two or three days he was having these violent outbreaks and he was drinking constantly and eating speed and doing cocaine three and four times a day, just anything he could get inside himself.

When I found out he was playing around I couldn't hardly believe it because the only place we got along was in the bedroom. I was always fulfilled and I never denied him. Why would he need extra too? I found out he had been seeing this woman and I thought, "Well, it's time to go." I wouldn't have had the means to do it without the aid of my folks getting the police to take me to the Salvation Army women's home. I spent the night there and my folks were there in the morning and we packed what we could get in the truck.

After I left Wes, I spent a month with my mother getting on my feet. Then I moved thirty miles from home and got on the welfare system. I didn't know I was pregnant until after I'd left. I got a job in a nursing home and worked until I was about seven months along, but I was still on welfare because I wasn't working full-time. I know that people need welfare and I need it, but to me it's degrading.

Chris was able to get into a rehabilitation program to study radiology. Although in high school she had taken the easiest courses, she is enthusiastic now about all her college classes. She achieved excellent grades until the most recent semester when she overloaded by adding algebra and chemistry to other classes. It has sometimes been difficult to care for two young children and attend to her college work, and after shouting impatiently at the children once when they interrupted her studies, she arranged to do most of her studying at school or after the children were in bed. During her second pregnancy a welfare worker tried to persuade her to give up her baby son for adoption, predicting she couldn't handle school, a difficult child, epilepsy and a new baby. "Well, I'm handling it darn well," she says now. And only once did she waver in her resolve to remain separated from Wes.

We had one trial "get-back-together" and Wes didn't hit me, but I gave him two weeks to find a steady job and to be able to pay all the bills at the first of the month. The first rolled around and I asked him if he had the money for the rent. "No." Did he have a job? "No." I said, "When you come back I want you to get your clothes and leave." He just sort of laughed it off and left. He came back and I had all his clothes packed in a box and I gave him a bar of soap and a toothbrush and a few things and I said, "Bye."

For about a year after the divorce Chris was afraid Wes would follow through on threats he had made to kidnap the children. Then she realized that "No way would he have time to stay home and care for them." He had always made the threats in anger and had made no attempt to follow through.

She told him she was not afraid of him any more. He was shocked, and after that their relationship took on a different tone. Every couple of weeks he still goes to her for advice about the trouble he's in, and she's not sure why she listens. "I can't live with him," she says, "but I still care about him. I don't think a person can just stop loving somebody. I don't think it's something you can just turn off, especially when I grew up with him for a couple of years."

But Chris is not looking for the day that Wes straightens out. Nor is she interested in marriage. She has turned down two offers, but vows she will never get into a similar situation again. Her career comes first at this point. Along with two children it will keep her more than busy enough. She has had a tubal ligation to insure that she will not have to take her attention from the two children she has and loves. That decision was made difficult by five doctors who turned her down, believing that she was too young at twenty-two to know her own mind.

Chris hasn't had a grand mal seizure in a year, though she has had some petit mal seizures. They embarrass her, but her steady determination has seen her through difficult events, such as a seizure that caused her to wet her pants in a store. "I tied my sweater around my pants and finished shopping," she says matter-of-factly. "I figured that's the only way I can handle it, just face up to it and keep going about my business."

I became active with the Epilepsy League and even got my mother active. The time I gave my talk up there and she introduced me, it made me feel great. I think a lot of people who have crossed what I've crossed would have given up. I had a hard time with people when I first started going to school. I had went and got my GED and people at welfare told me I couldn't do it. I went to the WIN program to try to get help with babysitting and they told me I couldn't do it. All these people who are supposed to be telling me that, "You can do it, go do it!" were telling me "You can't do that." Well, I'm doing it, and I'll finish.

One day I was thinking, "Gosh, I'm not good for nothing," and then I thought "Well, just what have you done today?" I started writing it down and pretty soon I had a half of a page of stuff I'd done. I did the laundry and the dishes and mopped the floor, I sewed and went to school all day and pretty soon you add it all up and—"Oh, gosh, you've accomplished things, you do things. You're doing it. you're making it."

Now I can do anything I want, go where I want, buy what I want or call my folks long distance, without being told that I'm stupid or that I'm doing something wrong. A lot of people have told me lately that I have a pretty optimistic attitude. There must be something about me that's not too bad.

CHAPTER 12

Pauline

My father's dead and if my mother and I speak once a year, we're doing good. My stepfather beat me a lot and because of that I got married at sixteen. My husband wasn't physically abusive to me, but he was seventeen years older than I, and I had to ask permission for a lot of things. And I was raring to go. After ten years, I went through a very bitter divorce. I wasn't in love with my husband, but it was a big loss, and it was hard to pick up the pieces. I had been separated about a year when I met Matthew. He came from a background of social workers and so forth and at the time he was working for a local newspaper, which I thought seemed promising.

He was five years younger than me, and the opposite of my former husband. He was exciting and sex was good at first, one of the main attractions. He was what I considered at the time intellectual. I had gone with him about four months, when he informed me he had this little thing hanging over his head. He had dealt some dope, and he had to go to court. He said it was his first offense and he was sure they would drop the case. They socked him three years.

We had talked about getting married before he went to prison, so when he got out, we got married right away. At first everything was peaceful and happy and fun. About a month after we were married he didn't get home until four in the morning and I asked him, "Where have you been?" He beat me till I passed out, all over my face, my breasts. He bit me and squirted shaving cream all over my face and I came to, swallowing it and gagging on it.

The neighbors called the police a few times, but they didn't take the situation seriously, which Pauline attributes to the fact that Matthew is black and she is white. One officer told her, "It's your own fault you're married to a nigger in the first place." Matthew put her "through windows" and she was badly cut. He had many ways of frightening and demeaning her. Once he tried to pull a plastic garbage sack over her head. More than once he threatened to push her off tall buildings. He also humiliated her by telling her that other men thought she was a prostitute, and occasionally they did make that assumption and offered Matthew money for her sexual services. He told her if she left him she would meet worse men; she would be out there by herself with no money and nowhere to go. She began to believe him. "Slowly," she says, "everything edged away from me."

Health problems plagued her and exacerbated her dependency. She had an operation for uterine cancer and had no one to stay with during her recuperation. She was just beginning to recover when he raped her repeatedly. She got peritonitis, which necessitated a return to the hospital, and again she had "nowhere to go but back to Matthew." She had dropped from a hundred and thirty-five pounds to one fifteen and was "literally starving to death," because she was too sick to get up and Matthew refused to bring her food.

The worst was the last beating. The difference this time was that he really tried to kill me. Then I knew I hated him and that wiped out any other feelings. I took all my clothes and went to my girlfriend's place. A couple of days after the last beating the cops came and arrested him for dealing dope. He told them the reason he got busted was that I was a bad influence on him, so part of his parole was that he would never be able to go near me again. When I found that out, I was overjoyed.

When I left, I had no money, no job, no place to go. I had kept losing jobs because he would come in and rip me off so I would have to quit. In the end my health messed me up, but because of my illness I was able to get a welfare check and I went to stay with my aunt in California. It took me about nine months to get myself together to where I could get a decent job working for the state.

I can see how it happens, not only to myself, but to other women. He had this charming boyish innocent personality that hooks you. There is the extreme attention that most women aren't used to, and then when he's got you, slowly the reversal until you're like a slave. The worst of it was that I got conned into thinking he was a sickie and that I could help him. You get wrapped up in believing that it's your role to be supportive of his insanity. I always considered myself a strong minded person, but I was wrong. I will never have the arrogance to think that it couldn't happen again. I think part of my downfall was my arrogance. "I'm so strong, it can't be happening." It's amazing how quickly you can lose your sense of identity. You tend to think you're nuts.

At the worst times, it was money and no place to go that made me go back to him. But when I was separated I missed the excitement, the way he always had something planned that was fun—dancing, concerts, plays, lectures, parties. Nobody believed that he did what he did, that nice guy. "It can't be. You're lucky to have someone like him." He was conservatively dressed, he spoke intelligently. I thought he would take care of my need for excitement. I thought I had been deprived of it and that I couldn't generate it on my own without getting into trouble.

After I left while I was staying with my aunt I had an exercise class, I went to yoga and we had an all-women chess club, which was fun. I've always liked to dabble in oils, so I bought a small case and was doing that. And then I started accepting dates, which I never did before. I got a job as a typist and then I graduated to secretary, and met some people working there. You get invited to a lot of barbecues, swimming parties, fishing trips and horseback riding. It's good. It was such a radical change from the street and the night life. It definitely helped me get back together.

So then I came back to Phoenix and got offered a job as office manager for a real estate company. Later I got into hotel management. I'm currently managing a highrise that has short-term apartments, fully furnished. It's kind of a new thing in the Southwest, so I'm putting together a new manual and procedure book. It's a lot of technical stuff and a good friend who's an attorney is advising me. But I also do the interior decorating for the apartments, working with a designer.

Now I enjoy courteous treatment from men, not having to duck, not feeling that I'm going to be raped—that I could say yes or no, having my own life. I can pay my bills and buy my food and have something left over. That is a good feeling. I got my confidence back to where I could get a really decent job and put a lot of it behind me. My new husband's working at a night club so we get a lot of free passes for the shows there and I'm still doing art work. We go to plays, on helicopter rides, we're planning a trip to the Grand Canyon. It's exciting, but not dangerous excitement.

CHAPTER 13

May

May grew up in the Chinatown section of a large West Coast city, the daughter of first-generation immigrants who had been "matched" in China, at the ages of seventeen and fourteen. After the birth of the first child, May's father immigrated to the United states; thirteen years later he had saved enough money from restaurant and laundry work to send for his wife and teenaged son. May and her older sister were born in the United States.

May's mother learned very little English, but in Chinatown she could find everything she needed without learning the new language. "I think," May says, "my parents get along really well, for people who were matched. My father is really fair." Both parents worked hard, and though they avoided discussions of emotions and interpersonal relations, they rarely argued. May was a quiet child. In first grade she was in a special class for bilingual and "slow" children, and she didn't learn English until she was six or seven years old. It was not until fourth grade that she began to use English in conversation with friends.

I can't really remember grade school, except in small bits and pieces. I did have friends and in junior high school I became more sociable and involved in a youth center. My older sister was referred there because she was truant and I followed her one day, because I thought she was out to join a gang and I wanted to protect her. I felt like a big sister to her. I learned to play guitar there and met a lot of people.

In high school I did well and had a lot of friends. My parents got a little stricter because I started dating when I was about thirteen. There were blacks and Hispanics in the school, but I always dated Chinese boys. I would say those boys were pretty dominant. Most of the time I just wanted to be with my friends and didn't really want to go out with the boys, but I felt pressured by them.

My first boyfriend, when I was thirteen, was very dominating. He studied kung fu and he always had this front, and he often liked to spar with me, even though I never knew anything about kung fu. So I had a lot of bruises, but I never thought that he was being abusive to me. At that time I thought, "This is stupid," but I took it. I went with him for eight months. When I broke up with him I was very, very strong about it. He kept telling his friends he wanted me back, but I knew he was just not a very nice person.

I remember not wanting sex and yelling at him. It wasn't just talking me into it. It was force, but I never thought of it as rape until I was about twenty-two. I never told anybody until I was in college and was seeing a psychologist.

In high school May was senior class president and had many friends among the students who were monitors and office aides and who helped the teachers. Her parents pressured her to succeed in school and the friends she regularly studied with urged each other to do well. May excelled in honors classes, and also worked in a peer tutoring program. Her parents were determined that she become a doctor, so after high school graduation she enrolled in a pre-med program at an out-of-state university, in spite of doubts about whether she wanted a medical career.

She was fearful of the new university environment where she knew no one, but she wanted to leave home and she knew the school had a good reputation. There were only about twenty Chinese students in her freshman class. Away from Chinatown for the first time in her life, she felt lonely and ignored, as if she were different from everyone else. It soon became clear to her that she wanted to major in psychology, not medicine, but she was afraid to tell her parents. For the first time since her early years in school she faced failure, flunking all of her courses. She was given a "serious warning."

I met Ross in a psychology class and we started dating in the middle of the first semester. He didn't have too many friends either. A lot of people didn't like him that much because they thought he was arrogant, but I didn't think so, not until later on. He was pretty nice at the beginning.

What I didn't like about him was that he always expected me to behave a certain way. He wanted me to wear skinny heels, instead of wedge heels and I said, "I don't think I can walk in them." He wanted me to wear a skirt, and I didn't own one. I thought they were confining because I have to walk a certain way if I wear a dress. He would get upset if I took large steps, because ladies took small steps. I did buy the heels and the skirt, but I never wore them.

He was five-six and I'm five-three and he wanted someone much more petite, shorter and skinny. I was a little overweight. He wanted me to be shorter! I would say "I cannot be shorter!" After a while I thought he was crazy. It was almost like he wanted my feet to be bound, psychologically. From the beginning there was a lot of arguing. I was quiet, but I tried to be assertive. He would criticize my friends, but I would say, "They seem fine to me." He was very dominating, but I wasn't going to give in.

Ross tried to be nice and was always around and I liked that, but he called me names and didn't treat me that well. He was passing just about everything with A's, and he would say I was stupid because I wasn't doing so well in school. I had never failed anything before, except when I was six years old and couldn't speak English yet. In my freshman year I failed four courses. I saw a therapist a few times and the main point that came out of it was that I needed to make my own decisions. I decided I was not going to be a doctor, and after that I just picked myself right up. I got C's, but I passed. In my junior year I got A's. I took psychology, anthropology and sociology. It took me a year to tell my parents I wasn't going to be a doctor.

I don't remember the first time Ross hit me. It seems like if I don't want to remember something, I don't. I remember a time he chased me in his dorm. A couple of times he slapped me or punched me, but I don't know why these things happened. I guess I don't remember them because they were so irrational. Every time it happened I was kind of shocked and very, very angry. I would yell at him and a couple of times I would just leave, even though we were in my dorm room, and I'd just walk around campus.

He usually slapped me in the face, and I also had bruises on my arm. Once he split my lip. That was the worst and he apologized. He said, "I didn't know I hit you so hard." I said, "You're not supposed to hit me at all." He said he would never do it again. Now I know they always say that.

I knew I wasn't going to end up marrying him. During the first two years I thought I was in love with him and after that I felt sorry for him. Even though he hit me, I felt sorry for him! It doesn't make sense. He wanted to control me. I think it was my dependency on Ross that kept me with him. I didn't have that many friends and he was the first person I met at college. It just seemed like there was nowhere else to go. I had a lot of acquaintances, but not that many friends. At times I tried to make myself part of different groups, but a lot of students were also Christian and were part of Bible study groups. I didn't want to study religion and I felt like I couldn't share anything with them.

During the summer between my junior and senior year he was away and I worked with infants and toddlers in a hospital, and really enjoyed it. Senior year was a really good year. I was taking a lot of independent courses and I had my own apartment, and mentally and emotionally I was breaking away. We were still seeing each other, but that year I volunteered at a suicide prevention center off campus and that took a lot of time. It was a good experience. I became a lot more active and had more friends and I worked. I think once I started doing other things that were satisfying, I didn't care about him as much.

The battering didn't happen that often—every three weeks or so. There were periods when it didn't happen for several months and the severity stayed about the same. I didn't think much about it; it was not an issue. I just knew the relationship wasn't good, because we didn't get along that well. He expected certain things of me that I could not deliver and that I did not even want to.

In senior year I was applying to graduate school, and I knew I was going to leave and he was going to stay for three years. I applied to schools in San Francisco and Seattle.

By the time she was a senior May didn't care for Ross so much, but she wasn't quite ready to give him up either. They had been together a long time, and even on the few occasions when they had decided to break up, they had never remained apart for more than a couple of days. She also felt sorry for him because he wasn't emotionally stable.

After graduation May went home, started a new job, enrolled in graduate school and went out with another man once or twice. She decided she didn't want to continue the relationship with Ross and when she told him so on the telephone he immediately went to see her and tried to talk her out of her decision. However, she was adamant, and soon after she told him she was no longer in love with him he stopped calling her. She became absorbed in the hard work of graduate school, which included a psychology internship that was especially important to her.

After my college graduation I was a volunteer here at the Crisis Center for Asian Women, but I never even connected the issue of battered women with my own experiences until during one of the training sessions where the volunteers try to identify with battered women. Some of the questions were, "Have you ever been victimized? What do you have in common with battered women, if anything?" And I was thinking, "Hmmm, I think I have something in common with them." I thought, "I've been battered before." I got sad, very sad, and was feeling that for about a month.

Being a quiet person, not speaking up for myself, had kind of held me back from leaving. Even though I always tried to say what I wanted to say, a lot of times I was told I couldn't. I know a lot of Asian females are that way. Even though I was born here, I was raised very Chinese, growing up in Chinatown with parents who were pretty traditional. In the Chinese society the men are mostly dominant and a lot of Asian girls are told to be quiet.

I don't think battering is worse here in Chinatown, but women are more isolated here. People say that among Asians there are more close-knit communities, close families, but I don't agree. I think mainstream society sees that because they see a lot of Chinese people together in large groups. They have large families, but I don't think they share anything. Emotions are pretty much pushed back. Where I work, some of the Chinese families don't stay together any more or they don't talk any more. It's rare, but a few are even divorced. Women who are divorced might be rejected by men, but not so much by women.

I'm not so sure the women who call us at the Crisis Center want to leave, and I think it has a lot to do with their culture. First of all we find out if the person really wants to leave. They might not have anywhere to go, they might have been brought here because of the husband. Sometimes they don't even have their permanent residence status. For undocumented women, it's the hardest thing. They can't go to the police or they will be deported. They can go back to their home country, but they may not have people to stay with. The extended family may not treat the woman nicely, unless she told them what was done to her, and even then they might not. "You're an American, you're supposed to be happy."

Some women are emotionally abused, being told they have to work in the husband's laundry or restaurant, not being paid, not having any friends or any family. Or the husband might lock up all the women's papers. That makes it really hard.

I think Asian women should educate their own culture. Traditionally, Chinese families are not supposed to divorce. It's a shame to divorce and the wife's family might not take her back, but she has to know that she has to survive also. Living in an abusive relationship, no matter what culture you're from, is almost like living in a war zone. We try to help the women realize that they are strong people. They're strong enough to call us, they're strong enough to do something. They might just want to talk, but they often ask us, "How do I get a divorce?"

They go back and forth a whole lot, change their minds. We always call them back because we know the battering can get worse. Sometimes we house them for a few days and then they will go into a shelter. For the most part they don't leave their homes, but we work out with them what resources they have. We try to have a plan in case they do want to leave, or in case something happens. They always have a packed bag and all the papers they need. The volunteers at the Center have either been battered, their mothers have been battered or they are just very sensitive to the issue.

During our first press conference at the Center there were a lot of reporters, and one of them said, "I don't think this is going to work, because there is no problem like that in Chinatown." And we said, "There is." We had another press conference six months later and showed them our statistics.

In retrospect May sees her relationship with Ross as "a big waste of time." She wishes she could "go back to college and start all over again, make friends, do different things, become more involved in things." Yet she believes the relationship helped her make decisions about her life and made her a stronger person. She is active in her community and is developing many skills. She feels good about the way she lives.

Now I'm going to go to social work school. I enjoy volunteering here at the Center. I'm on the board of directors and I train volunteers for the hotline. I'm also the community education outreach coordinator. For Domestic Violence Awareness Week, we had a series of articles in the Chinese newspapers on the issue of battering, so I worked that out, had it translated and called the newpapers.

I'm a youth counselor and I do a lot of crisis intervention, but also counseling on day-to-day issues. I'm always, always, tired at the end of the day, even though I only work an eight hour day. I work the graveyard shift sometimes, and sometimes they call me when I'm not at work, if something drastic happens.

I like to go to the zoo a lot and take walks. My current relationship is really good. Actually my boyfriend was battered by an ex-girlfriend. I said, "No way! Men don't get battered," but he told me about all the bruises, cuts and scratches that he's had from his ex-girlfriend. I was always thinking, "There's never going to be anyone I could be satisfied with." He is a bit sexist and I point it out whenever I see it, but I think he's pretty fair as a person. He's pretty unusual for an Asian man. We talked about getting married, but I'm going to hold off for a while. I'll probably go to social work school next September and that will be for two years. I don't want to get married until after that. I'll probably work in family counseling, probably battered women in the Chinese community. It will be hard, because a lot of Chinese families don't want to talk about their problems.

CHAPTER 14

Grace

There was no actual violence in Grace's home when she was growing up, but she always felt the threat of it from her father. He insisted that tasks be done perfectly and if everything was not in precisely the right place, he would become "terribly upset and nervous." He was a member of the Ku Klux Klan in the 1930s and was an "uptight, very Christian, very proper man."

Grace was an independent adolescent, which put her at odds with the conservative minister of her church, especially over his racist attitudes toward a Japanese boy in the church's youth group. She was the pianist for the group and took a devilish pleasure in choosing songs and readings that spoke about brotherhood, which "drove the minister up the wall." Today she still laughs at the memory of the minister as he tried to stop the young people from square dancing in the basement—"Sin! Sin running rampant!"—and is amused at herself, recalling how righteous she was about her own causes.

Although she always had "grit and determination," she was unsure of herself in relation to friends. By the age of twelve she was physically well-developed and was made the center of attention by soldiers stationed at a nearby army reserve. Grace believes her father was attracted to her, and that his determination not to act on it increased his tension. For weeks at a time he wouldn't speak to her, "walking around the house an angry bundle of tension."

At sixteen Grace and her boyfriend were "two WASP kids who didn't have any other friends and just got in too deep."

She became pregnant, which was an "awful, awful thing to do in those days," and had an abortion. Grace believes her pregnancy was an attempt to get her father to reject her, because she was uncomfortable about his attention to her.

At nineteen Grace acquired a serious case of polio. She was hospitalized for a year and in the first month her weight dropped from a hundred and thirty to eighty pounds. She couldn't eat and was tube fed for eight months. It took a long time to develop the strength to walk, but with physical therapy she made enough progress to attend university classes. She enjoyed her studies, but it was a strain on her weakened system just to get from her living quarters to classes. Nevertheless, school provided a structure to keep her morale up.

I met Del at a Unitarian college group in 1950. He was a medical student, kind, warm and able to see past my physical imperfections. He was interested in me as a person. He dug out my medical record and said, "My God! You haven't got any reason to be alive! And you're out there bouncing around." We started going out in the fall, and by Thanksgiving we were wanting to get married. His father's classic remark was, "Well, you will spend more time taking care of her than in a medical practice."

Grace and Del were married the following March. During Del's last year of medical school Grace became pregnant with her first child and "blossomed," as she did with all five of the pregnancies that followed. All she ever wanted to be was to be a housewife and mother; yet she physically abused her children beginning when the oldest, Marta, was five months old. She lost control when she "felt closed in, backed into a corner." Marta got the brunt of Grace's anger for the way she had been raised, by "cold parents" who made her feel she was in the way. She believes her psychoanalyst's interpretation may be right, that she wanted all those children in order to have someone lower in the pecking order and also someone to play with, since she had been lonely as an only child.

She liked keeping house for her husband and the children,

and she and Del got along well, off and on, but violence was present from nearly the beginning. Grace remembers explaining to her mother, after a dish-throwing fight with Del, that it was better to "get some of this crap out of your system than to sit on it for thirty years."

In the late 1950's Grace and Del lived in a small town where he was in private practice as a gynecologist. They were very much looked up to by the community. It was during this time that Del dragged Grace down the stairs and banged her head against the kitchen wall. The violence usually started with a shouting match, but Grace was never sure when the "unpredictable volcano" would explode. Although she sometimes tried to retaliate, Grace usually just tried to stay out of his way. At a hundred pounds, and with weakened lungs, she knew she was no match for her two-hundred-and-ten-pound husband, who exercised regularly and had especially strong arms. She avoided many subjects of conversation that would arouse his anger, and she changed the way she reacted to his rage. She began to refuse to fight back, going for a ride, a walk, or to a neighbor's instead. Instead of yelling back at him, she let off steam by throwing canned food at the basement wall. "We had a lot of dented cans of soup in those days," she recalls. These changes reduced the violence, but Grace was still subjected to humiliation and sexual assaults.

> He would give sort of a sexual come-on, I would rise to it, then he'd say something that he knew would trigger a complete turn-off for me, and then demand his rights as a husband. If I wasn't turned on, I was a cold bitch. Then he would rape me. I came very close to leaving him.
>
> Four or five years into our marriage Del began to get strange. Bernie's circumcision had been perfectly normal, but Del went on and on and on about wanting to do Danny's himself, so "He'll have a good cock." He sent Marta away to school. She lived with a woman he knew and only came home weekends. I had been sick most of the winter with a serious chest cold, and I was pregnant with my fourth child. I think I objected to

Marta going away, but I was pretty battered by that time and thought that I was wrong, so I sort of swallowed my own resentment.

Del's comment about Marta was always, "What a sexy little girl," from the time she was tiny. And I was the prude for thinking that was inappropriate. He put it that there was a sexual tension between me and her in competition for him. When she got a little older he would make suggestive remarks to her, and make sort of passes at her. She had hip huggers on one day with a big brass buckle, and he began playing with the buckle, and she would say "leave me alone." It would go on until she would reject him, and then he would go into a towering rage and would go storming around the house.

A couple of times I got Marta out of the house to a girlfriend's and I would go out and hide. That left Bernie in charge of the little kids, which put him under a lot of pressure. To this day, he has a lot of problems dealing with his own anger because he doesn't want to explode like his father.

In 1962 Del went into analysis, but the beatings continued. He claimed it was normal for people in analysis to beat up whoever was around because they take out their hostilities on others. Del wore a thirty-eight gun when he went into tough parts of town, and I had a twenty-five caliber. Insanity. I knew nothing about how to use it. One day when it got too bad for me, I hid in the closet with the thirty-eight in my hand. Del is standing outside telling me what he's done to me is my fault and I've got this gun and I'm ready to go Kew! But then I said, "Hey, wait a minute. This is screwy. I'm not the one who did these things. He is the culprit." And I put the gun back in its hiding place in the closet and I began to do a turn around.

Grace had wanted to leave because of the battering and the damage to the children, yet she felt that her health and her lack of college and marketable skills would make it impossible for her to support all of the children. She didn't believe she'd get enough support from Del, even though by that time he was a highly paid specialist. She thought of leaving the three youngest children with him but felt certain it would do them irreparable harm, so there seemed no way out. By that time she was convinced that all the problems were hers. When she inquired about options from an attorney in the summer of 1962, she was persuaded that she was not likely to get enough support from Del for herself and the children.

Grace had sought psychiatric help several times, but it had not been helpful. Eventually she found a psychiatrist who pointed out that she was making Marta too much of an adult, due to her own illness and distress. Marta had been placed in the role of sounding board and emergency babysitter for her mother. On the psychiatrist's advice, Grace began to spend a day a week away from the house, which reduced her stress level and made it easier to take the pressure off Marta. Nevertheless, Grace's polio continued to exacerbate her problems. The back of her throat, her tongue, her right eye, parts of her lungs and other parts of her body are still paralyzed; one doctor she saw was surprised that she was still alive.

Beginning in the spring of 1965 Grace had a long affair with another man, and probably would never have had the nerve to get her divorce were it not for him. However, she feels that she didn't leave Del for Colin. It was more that he was a steady support person and "they put each other's feet on the ground." She gave him needed emotional support in his artistic work, and she learned that she wasn't "this shriveled up, frigid discard in the corner," that she could respond to a man in a healthy way.

By the summer of 1966 Grace had "had it up to here" and was concerned about her children, who said they didn't want to come home from summer camp because the house was such a battleground. She was especially concerned about the girls. She realized that to save her children she would have to leave Del. Her therapy and the relationship with a loving man helped her develop the courage to file for the divorce and to follow through with it. Grace's life has improved, but she doesn't regret her relationship with Del, who played a crucial role in her life when she needed someone, desperately.

He kept me alive. The only thing I would do differently is somehow or other be able to gain more sense of myself earlier, for both my own satisfaction and my kids. It's all a growing thing, you have to go through certain things before you can leave it, and I gave it as much time as I could afford to give. I'm a very different person now, much more relaxed and accepting.

CHAPTER 15

Dee

I grew up in a small university town and we had excellent schools and teachers. I just read like crazy and spent a lot of time in the library. But I also had a lot of friends and liked to run around and do wild things.

My father worked as a farmer, and then a machinist. He was was quiet and tried to make peace in the family, but he never had any parental control over me. My mother worked a few years as a proofreader. She was emotionally abusive to me when I was a child and that continued later when I became emotionally ill. I was frightened of her while the fur was flying, and I didn't know there was such a thing as two people living together without screaming at each other. She dominated me, and the peculiar thing is I respected her. She's a very, very intelligent woman and well read, so on anything other than a personal basis, conversation with her can be stimulating. Most of the time it was a real good relationship.

My mother and father were fighting tooth and nail and I had to get out of the house. I wanted to quit having my mother running my life and to get out in the world, and I was bored with school, so I quit in eleventh grade, moved to Tucson and worked in a law office. I rented a little one room apartment and managed to support myself on two hundred a month, if you can believe that. Most of my friends were older than me and were living in Tucson, so I wasn't lonely.

Before I met Pete I felt pretty good about myself. I

was assertive and pretty strong. I met him at a bar, where I was out drinking with a bunch of friends. He came along and danced with me, then took me out and two weeks later we were talking about getting married and two months later we were married. He adored me, just treated me like a china doll. He knew his own mind, was confident of his own worth and not easily shaken. He seemed emotionally stable. I was sixteen and he was twenty-six. I've always been more comfortable with older men.

I was something of a radical at that time and my parents were violently anti-Mexican, so dating Pete was a defiant thing to do. But after they met him they thought he was great. My mother just adored him. He's charming as hell, big, tall, handsome, ingratiating—a beautifully charming man. You would never in a million years think he was capable of being violent. Like with my mother, when the fur wasn't flying, things were pretty good. When he was mean and hateful to me I would be terrified and terribly hurt, because I adored him. The worst part of it is you love this person and you almost feel sorry for him, that he's doing this. You feel like, "It's my fault. If I didn't behave this way, maybe things would be different."

Pete worked at a hardware store and had been a security guard before that. Later I found out he had been fired for beating up on a woman he stopped for shoplifting. He had also been court martialed in the marines for beating up another marine. He didn't seem able to control himself in any sort of a stress situation. But there were no clues before marriage.

We were only married two months before I discovered I was pregnant, and six or seven months later I was up in the middle of the night having pains and very uncomfortable. I was crying and he wanted to sleep and didn't want to be bothered with my noise. He got up and wanted to know what was the matter and I told him my back was hurting me and I was having pains and I was scared and I wanted him to keep me company. Well, didn't I have better things to do? He had to work the next day. He threw me down on the floor, sat on my stomach and slapped my face until I just passed out. I didn't know people did that to each other. I was just appalled. I don't think I talked to anybody about it.

During the next few months Dee went to work with purple finger prints on both arms where Pete had grabbed her. After that he beat her about once a month. "He's a very impatient person," Dee says, "and wants things his way. It seems like whenever anybody crosses him, just with the slightest thing, he reacts violently." Pete was in Vietnam and told Dee a story about having been a guard on the perimeter of a camp. He heard footsteps and fired into the dark. In the morning he found he had killed a woman and two children. Later, Dee says, "he had nightmares and would get up and walk in his sleep and shove all the furniture up against the door."

Pete bragged about special courses he had taken in the marines, which taught him to land nearly fatal blows without leaving any marks on the body. After the first few times he hit Dee, he left no signs of his violence on her. Whenever she reminded him of his violence toward her he would say, "Show me your bruises," and there were none to be seen. It felt like he was saying, "You're really crazy, lady" and she began to wonder, "Am I crazy? Is he right? Who am I? What is my worth? If I didn't behave this way, maybe things would be different." She saw a psychiatrist and often talked with her mother about how to save her marriage, but she is convinced her mother didn't believe Pete was beating her. When she sought shelter from friends their attitude was, "How can you say that about such a wonderful man? You've been going to a psychiatrist, are you sure you're not imagining it?"

During the last three or four years of the marriage there was no sexual intercourse, but "just fellatio on demand," and occasional painful rapes. "You fight for a little bit, and then you just let it happen, because there's nothing you can do about it." When she accused Pete of rape he said, "I'm not raping you. You're my wife."

Pete abused the children, too. One of them has a deformed leg because Pete refused to take him to the doctor to treat his broken knee cap. "My daughter was sick and wasn't allowed a doctor, until she burst her appendix. He also let the dogs die out of neglect. He has never been sick and thinks it's imaginary. The one time he broke his own leg he wouldn't see a doctor for that either." Dee often stopped the overt violence against the children, but she couldn't always protect them, and she didn't see how she could take care of them if she left either.

> I was only making two hundred a month and the babysitter alone was costing us forty dollars or something like that. There was no way I could have supported myself and the kids, or I didn't see how I could have anyway. I was afraid of him, afraid if I mentioned divorce he'd just flat out kill me. I don't think there is any way I could have gone to my parents and said, "Take me in, I'm gonna divorce this man," because it just wasn't that kind of relationship with my parents. What it would have been is, "We told you so. You're on your own."

Pete told Dee she was selfish, self-centered, a snob and lazy, and before long she began to believe it. When she wasn't working outside the home, he was virtually her "only communication with humanity" other than the children. The worst of the emotional abuse was not a single incident, but the continual fear of doing something he didn't like or neglecting to do something he wanted. During the last two years Dee was terrified simply by his presence. "He always had murder in his eye when he came after me," she remembers. "He told me many times, 'I didn't hurt you. If I'd have hit you full force, you'd be dead.'" Dee used to think of killing him, but knew she couldn't actually do it. She hoped that he'd be killed on a job.

Dee left and returned countless times, but until the end she was never able to stay away from her children, nor could she find a way to take them with her. She tried many ways to stop the violence. After she called the police Pete hid at his boss' house and the prosecutor was unable to serve him with a subpoena. After four days in hiding, he turned himself in and Dee took that as a sign of willingness to change. She bailed him out. After that, with one exception, he never seemed to hit her as hard again, and Dee felt that "he was trying hard not to do any more damage than he was doing."

During the later years of her marriage, Dee was mentally ill, often hospitalized, and even less able to cope than earlier. "I cried most of the time," she recalls. "It was a very bad depression, and I was suicidal a lot, very nervous and took a lot of medicine. He hassled me about all the medicine, and I felt guilty about every pill I took, which increased the nervousness, which increased the need for the medication, which increased the nervousness. It was just a vicious circle." Dee is sure the unwillingness of most people to believe what had happened to her was what pushed her sanity "over the brink." However, during one hospital stay she heard many patients' stories about not being believed, which helped her realize she was not alone, and when she left the hospital, she was able, finally, to trust her own experience. She decided that would have to be enough, and that it wasn't necessary for other people to believe it. That new perspective was important, but she regrets that no shelter was available to help her through the next phase.

Each of the countless times Dee left the family, the children encouraged her, saying things like, "Mom, you've gotta get out of here, he's going to kill you." Once she was away three months and went to Tucson to work. She wanted to go home every weekend to see the children, but Pete wouldn't let her visit unless she was willing to stay. She couldn't support the children on her four-hundred-dollar-a-month salary, and she missed the children so much that she finally gave up and went home.

> I just couldn't face life without my kids, and he had sworn that if we ever got a divorce, he'd tell the judge I was crazy, anything he wanted to hear, just so long as I wouldn't get my kids. I knew he'd do it and he did exactly that. There was no way I could have taken the kids.
> The final time I left, I had gone to Tucson to visit my father and was astounded by the difference between my "prison" and the fear I lived with, and his home, where no one was angry or yelled at anyone else, and I realized

that my father cared. But I also realized I'd lost everything that was worth having, and on my way home I called to tell my father I couldn't take it any more and had to kill myself. He said he'd come and get me, but I said there was nothing he could do. I just wanted to die in peace.

So I got back in my car and I took all these pills—Valium, Meloril, I don't know what all—and I drove off the highway and took a bunch more pills and I just lay down on the seat. I lay down on the seat to die, and the next thing I knew my father was there opening the door, and there was a cold rush of air on my face. He put me in his car and took me to the hospital. Later, he said, "You know this just can't go on. Come home with me." And so I did. I went home with him and tried to start a new life.

I wasn't with him very long because I went to work in Tucson, again. Pete and I filed for divorce separately, but he got to the courthouse first, and I was served with the papers at work, which shattered me. Soon after that I was in the hospital again, and the diagnosis was manic-depression. This time I stayed three months, determined to get well. When I left I felt like I was free. It was probably like walking onto another planet or something. It was a total relief. Yet at the same time I felt like I was going to cry all the time and I did cry about the kids. This went on with decreasing frequency for a couple of years. But at work I forced myself to put them out of my mind.

I had to convince myself that he was the monster because when I got away I kept remembering the good times, so a couple of times I called him and I pretended to be begging him to let me go back, and he would be cruel on the phone to me, and then I'd hang up and I'd say to myself, "Right. That's the reason you left." I knew he wouldn't want me back, and I knew I couldn't go back, but I had to sort of hit myself one more time so I'd know: "You're not going to change, this really is the way it is, it's really over."

When I went up there for the final hearing on the divorce, I went over to his house so we could have a conference about splitting up things, and that was very amiable. When all that was settled, he said, "You're going to have a long line of men in Tucson waiting to see you and I'm gonna be standing in line there." It just broke my heart. He got down on his knees and he was crying and he said, "Don't do this. We can work it out." And then it was me that had to say, "We can't work it out. I know it can't be worked out. I've got to go." I think that was one of the hardest things I ever had to do, but I saw that I was losing my mind. I knew I would kill myself if I stayed with him, I knew I would.

Dee did attempt to gain custody of her children, but Pete used her history of mental illness against her, alleging that her petition was a lie from start to finish and that she was a totally unfit mother. Dee was defenseless because she hadn't been able to find a lawyer to take her case—they all told her there was no way to defend her mental record. The judge ruled that she was an unfit mother and could visit the children only in her husband's home at his discretion. She asked what she could do to make her home fit. "Get a husband," said the judge.

The kids have been so used to seeing their father react violently to every frustration that I think they feel that is normal. For instance, the two youngest ones, even though they're able to understand intellectually that it's wrong, their initial reaction to any kind of frustration is to hit or to react violently. I think when you grow up in an atmosphere like that, you probably figure that's the way people act, and you just do it.

Because of my background I feel that I'm going to be crippled for the rest of my life. I still have nightmares virtually every night in which I'm always getting into trouble and I'm dependent on somebody else to help me out.

After I left, it was traumatic for all the children at first, but in the long run it's going to turn out to be best, because now that I'm married to Tex and we have another child we have a living example that people can be happy and decent to each other. I used to try to instill in the kids how the real world should be, and it probably didn't make much sense in that atmosphere, but now they have a place to come and see the contrast.

My fifteen-year-old, Stan, ran away from his dad to me, but then went back. He's interested in the same things his dad is. His dad has horses and he fishes and he wouldn't have any of that with us. When Stan was here for three or four weeks he said, "Boy, it sure is boring around here." I'm worried about my daughter, because she's nervous and jumpy like I was when I was living with Pete, but he doesn't seem to pick on her as much as the boys. All I can do is hope that the contrast of the two environments is going to have some lasting effect on them. That's what I'm counting on.

I see the kids once every other month. I used to be on the phone with them every week and just be at the mercy of Pete and his moods. Sometimes when I'd call he'd scream and holler at them afterwards, so I gave up calling for a while and then they started calling me collect, behind his back. That worked out okay. I wait for it to be his idea for the kids to come because if it's my idea it never works out. The only one of the kids that I don't have anything to do with is Brian, who is twenty, and that's because I think he has decided that he has to take sides. I can't see anything wrong with that as long as it's not hurting him, and I just figure ten or fifteen years from now he's going to come around and say, "What really happened?" and then we can deal with it.

I can remember years and years of saying to myself, "I love this man. How can I help him?" I would never go back to him, because I'm so happy here, but I still love him. I don't think a person, once they really love somebody, ever stops loving them.

A man is important in my life, so after I left, I said, "Go where the men are." I went to Parents Without Partners and found there's a bunch of good people there. I think some people don't go there because they have a "I don't want to be part of a "losers' group" mentality. Well, other "losers" are more sympathetic and you find people in those groups who understand you. I went to the theater just because I like theater, but it turned out that's where I found Tex, the man I married.

My husband is a music teacher, a very good pianist, and a ceramicist and he sculpts. He's just sort of a Renaissance man and a delightful person. He says the medicine that has worked strongest for me is his unconditional acceptance of me. Even when I have been crazy he remains calm. We just enjoy each other enormously. We talk to each other, we have friends over and he plays the piano, while I play the guitar and we all sing. We belong to a very small church and we're active in its music program. Tex has been a member of the church council and I have been elected recording secretary. Our life centers around the church, educational programs on the television and good literature. Even the baby has a stack of books. I can't say that we do anything that would excite anybody else but we sure have a hell of a good time.

I had written before, but just poetry for friends, and now I've discovered that I can write my story. I've absolutely forced myself to write when I get depressed, because there are parts of the book that can only be written when I'm depressed or it couldn't be right. That's not the easy way to do it, but it works. My plan is to publish the book and on the strength of that to become a professional writer. It's stupid, I know, but if I can have the confidence that comes with somebody publishing my book, I can say, "Okay, now you're a writer. Now you can do all those things you've dreamed about doing."

After I left I found out who I was and I kind of liked me. I found out that I could do all the things he was telling me I couldn't do, that I wasn't stupid. I found out I was an okay person, and that was delightful because that was the first time I had felt okay since I was a kid. Life is marvelous now. I enjoy everything because I don't have this cloud hanging over me. It's just like living in a new world. The sunset, my garden, everything is different because I don't have somebody picking on me all the time. Just the freedom is great.

CHAPTER 16

Hillary

My father worked as a civilian for the army. He came from a really poor background and ended up with a Ph.D. in chemistry. He pulled himself up and that affected my background, because I grew up with a lot of issues around money and background and not fitting into the social class we were a part of. I grew up in upstate New York, in a middle-class, white, Protestant town. My parents were Jehovah's Witnesses. My mother was working in the home and she was sick a lot. Once in a while she would get a job and then would have to give it up because of her health and having three kids and trying to balance everything.

As a child I was very good, very proper, an overachiever kind of child. When I took flute lessons I practiced three hours a day. I did really well in school, especially in English and all the subjects that girls are supposed to be good at. I think my family was pretty rigid in terms of sex role socialization and expectations. When my mother was sick I cooked, even as a young child, and did a lot of housecleaning and all the ironing.

I remember sucking my thumb as a little girl and having my grandfather tell me that he would cure me of that and having him put his penis in my mouth. I remember him coming into my bedroom at nap time and touching my breasts and genitals and jerking off. I know that the sexual abuse had started at least by the time I was four and I think that affected how I felt about myself. I also remember my father coming into the bathroom when I was taking a bath and jerking off, but not touching me.

In high school Hillary was active in church activities, popular and successful. She had a boyfriend who was a "nice fellow, approved of by everyone." Hillary wore his ring with yarn wound around it, and they were a "cute couple." She did all the right things and was concerned about approval, yet she felt fat and ugly and believed she was a "bad person." She went away to college and felt that she didn't fit in. However, she made friends with a small group who were "outcasts, politically and socially" and soon she was smoking marijuana and taking hallucinogens. She had two abortions within a short time, one of which was the result of a pregnancy from a rape.

Hillary worked two or three jobs at a time, took "more credits than anybody else" and got all A's. Yet she continued to get "stoned every day, all day." She began to date mostly black men she met at a bar where pimps, prostitutes and other street people gathered. During several summer vacations she went to Europe and gained self-confidence. She lived happily with a Greek man in Athens, much to her parents' distress, since they wanted her to be involved with someone of her own background. When her mother had an operation Hillary returned to the United States to care for her. After her mother recovered, Hillary resumed her studies.

She graduated with a double major in English and psychology and enough credits for another degree in music. She then worked in a bank during the day, and in an art gallery at night. The gallery was close to the skid row area where prostitutes and strippers gathered. When Russell came into the gallery and asked her to dinner, she accepted.

I was going out with a lot of men and looking for someone to pay attention to me, and mostly what I was getting was one-night stands. When I met Russell he paid me a lot of attention and I was thrilled. He told me he was a pimp and that whole thing was kind of appealing to me. It was different, I guess. I thought it might be glamorous and interesting. It has a kind of mystique to it. So we saw each other for about two weeks and he never asked me to be a hooker. He told me he was on methadone and I went, "Well, yeah, he's a junkie, but he's working on it, it'll be okay." He wasn't flashy at all. He was interesting, charming, intelligent and fun to talk to. I liked the way he thought.

A prostitute who worked for Russell discovered his relationship with Hillary and caused a scene at the gallery, so Hillary lost her job. Russell fired the woman and told Hillary he didn't know what he would do for money or a place to stay, so she offered to let him stay with her. Hillary earned only about a hundred dollars a week at the bank, and she offered to try working for Russell so she could support them both.

A guy pulled his car over and I was scared, but I got in his car with him and we went back to my place and I turned the trick. He wanted a blow-job and I had never done that before. He came in my mouth and I almost threw up on him. I should have. That freaked me out a lot. Also, it took about two minutes and then I had thirty dollars and it was over and it was really easy. I went right out and did it again and again, and in three or four hours I had made over a hundred dollars. That was more than I had made in a week. I thought, "This is great. This is easy."

Before I got into prostitution I was depressed all the time. I had pretty low self-esteem and I was thinking that if I had sex with someone they would love me, but I was feeling worse about myself after doing it. Now, at least subconsciously, everything became so much more clear. I wasn't giving out sex randomly, hoping to get something back from it. I was saying, "Here. You can have this, and this is what you have to give me, this is where you have to go, this is what you have to do, this is how long you get. And if you don't do these things, Goodbye." I had never been tough in my life, but I liked it a lot. It felt really good to me to be streetwise and tough and take care of myself. So I was really taking control in the immediate situation. In the bigger picture

I wasn't at all.

The jobs were playing into low self-esteem for me too, 'cause I had these expectations put on me. "Go get through college and get a great job." But I didn't really have any direction on how to do that. I needed either to go on to school or else have some really good skills on how to do a job search. I was still planning to go back to graduate school but I wanted a break and I wanted to work for awhile. Generally, I felt like a failure in a lot of areas. I think I was frantic a lot; I was a pretty fast-paced, compulsive person, but I really wasn't doing anything that was interesting to me, so I felt a lot like I was spinning my wheels.

I got arrested a couple of weeks after I started being a hooker and, looking back, Russell loved it. It was another hold on me and it was also a clincher for giving up my job. He reinforced me giving up my status in society —how much status does a woman have anyway?—saying, "You're outside of society, you have a record, you can't ask people out there for anything. Don't ask them." I bought into that.

I was ready to give up my job at the bank. I was tired. I'm sure on a subconscious level, I couldn't live those two lives at the same time, being really submissive and polite and proper and nice in my job and going out on the street and having to be tough at night. When I quit my job I still had the idea that if I wanted to get out of this I could. It was probably a month later that he was physically violent for the first time, and that's when it came to me, I was trapped.

I remember in the beginning liking my sexual relationship with Russell, but now I feel like our whole relationship was a rape relationship. I usually didn't want to have sex with him or to do what he wanted me to do for as long as he wanted me to do it, but if I didn't, I would get beat up. That started after a couple of months.

My grandmother had sent me some money and I was going to take that twenty dollars and spend it on myself. He wanted me to give it to him and I refused. He hit me and started yelling at me, right in my face, about how I had to understand that it doesn't matter where that money comes from, he has control of it. I wasn't used to being yelled at and I don't like it, so I pushed him away from me. He started beating me up, hitting me in the face a lot and he threw me against the wall and would jump on top of me. It went on for a couple of hours and I had a bloody nose and lots of bruises on my face and a black eye. I felt really helpless, like there was no one there I could ask for help. I had a stubbornness about asking my parents for help and I was afraid they would find out what I was doing.

Hillary was beaten about once a month, until toward the end, when the violence escalated to once or twice a week. In addition, both "tricks" and police periodically assaulted her. A plain clothes police officer took her to the station without booking her, looked up her record and then raped her in an alley at gunpoint. Before long she began to work out of a bar, which was a little less dangerous. She enjoyed the company of the other women who worked there; they exchanged personal confidences and she found she could also rely on them for information about dangerous men. Twice, Hillary had sexual relationships with women, but she didn't think of herself as a lesbian until a few years after she had left Russell. One of the women she had a friendly relationship with was killed by a customer, and Hillary, against the code of the streets, identified the murderer and testified at his trial.

Hillary liked Russell's intelligence. "He knew a lot about history and read a lot and, and he liked to talk and make up stories." There were good times when they listened to music at a "players" bar and when Russell showed her off to other pimps at after-hours parties. She like that. "I was being attractive, a kind of prize, a middle-class, educated, white woman and I made a lot of money, so I got a lot of attention." Now Hillary sees that the attention was a result of the racist attitudes that are as pervasive in street life as in the rest of society.

As the relationship with Russell continued for over three years, Hillary began to have fantasies about someone or something killing him, but she notes that she played a passive role even in her fantasies. From time to time she planned to kill herself, but there was always "just a little glimmer of hope" that kept her from it. Hillary left once, early in the relationship, to work for another pimp, but she was afraid of what Russell would do to her and went back the next day. The second time she left, she intended to stay away. "I felt," she says, "like if I didn't leave him, one of us was going to die and I was really worn down and I knew I wasn't taking care of myself in my work, which is pretty important. Deciding whether or not to go with a trick is pretty much a life or death situation, so it's important to be on top of one's survival skills. I wasn't being careful."

One of Hillary's regular customers, a kind of "sugar daddy," bought her a plane ticket to New York and after resting with her parents for a few weeks, she went back to the city where she had been working and got another job in a bank. Russell found her and began to harass her. He threatened to tell people she was a prostitute and even to kill members of her family, so she went back to him out of fear. Additional motives were that she "had to have a man" and she was still in love with him, although she notes the feeling of love was "more when I was away from him than when I was with him."

Three days after she returned to him, he beat her up. Later, after she had become pregnant, he kicked her in the abdomen and broke her ribs, which resulted in a miscarriage. Her gynecologist was supportive and didn't judge her and she felt heartened to know that at least one door was open where she wouldn't be blamed. She told Russell to leave and he agreed. Then he asked to come back just to get his clothing. She agreed, and he beat her with a leather belt and kicked her with his boots. Thinking he was going to kill her, she tried to jump out of a sixth story window, but he restrained her.

She needed money to get away again, and appealed to a "loan shark," but was turned down because she had already left once and gone back. But a bartender friend asked a couple of his women friends to take her in. They gave her good care, and when they saw her bruises, insisted she go to the hospital. She had broken ribs, a broken collar bone and a crack in a bone in her leg. They persuaded her to press charges aginst Russell for battering, which made her uneasy because it was against the code of the street, but she didn't see any alternative. During the painful period of the trial she was comforted by her brother's presence.

Russell was given a year's suspended sentence for assault, and although he didn't batter her after that, he continued to harass her. Hillary chose another pimp, Chip, who was good to her. Chip tried to talk Russell into leaving her alone, and when that didn't work, he beat him up, which did work. Hillary began working on her own, out of her home. During this period she abused alcohol and drugs, habits she had resisted until near the end of her relationship with Russell. She fell in love with a white man she met at the bar, who bought her clothes, was romantic, and took her "fancy" places. After a while, he wanted to be a pimp and asked Hillary to give him money. It was hard to risk losing him by saying no. But she did turn him down and he left her.

> I had this really good friend who shared my apartment for awhile. She lived out of town and about four days a week she would come down and use my apartment to work out of, and we would sit and talk for hours. We were both trying to get out of prostitution. She wanted to go to nursing school and I wanted to get a job, so we sort of pulled each other out. I don't think I could have done it without her support, without her doing it with me. After that, women used me in a similar way. I had done it, so they connected with me real strongly and identified with me. "If you can do it, I can do it."

Hillary found a job in a law office and during the next two years she did little other than work. Her roommate persuaded her that she could rise above her doubts about her competency and apply to graduate school. It was hard for Hillary to believe, but she was accepted for both law school and a program in creative writing. She moved across the country and enrolled in the creative writing program. After she moved, she told her former roommate about her past work, feeling certain that she had somehow figured it out. "I was sure that she knew. I was sure everyone knew. But she was blown away by it."

I was in a big identity crisis for a couple of years and it came to a head when I moved here. At first, I felt really out of place and I had a lot of fear someone would find out about my past, and if they did I'd lose everything. I felt like if people who were becoming my new friends knew about my past they wouldn't be my friends. I did a lot of affirmations about it. I would just say, "Well, logically how would they know? Look how you are dressed." I also overcompensated with how I looked and how I acted. I became extremely polite and passive, a lot like I was as a child, and I wore very conservative clothing and gained a lot of weight. If the conversation got off work, to personal issues, I would just turn it back to work. Yet I wanted to talk about my life, all the time.

Now, it's hard for me to be vulnerable with someone and I just have this fear that if I let go a little bit, I'm going to lose it all, and the person's going to take me over. I don't totally trust my judgment. A little over a year ago I was in a relationship with a woman and after about two months I recognized that she was emotionally abusive and that my self-esteem was being affected. I felt powerless a lot and I told her, "This is emotionally abusive. I can't be in this relationship any more." I'm trying to remind myself that I did that, because I need to know that I can set limits.

I wish I had known about shelters when I was trying to get away in 1976, although I don't know if I would have felt safe using a shelter facility as a hooker. Shelter programs need to start looking at that issue because there are so few options for women who are prostitutes. Feeling outside the mainstream makes battering even more isolating.

It was working on prostitution in therapy that led me to my incest experiences, because I had those totally blocked from memory. I see a pretty strong connection there. The feelings that come up for me around incest are similar to some of the feelings that I have around

prostitution—powerless experiences. It's kind of a para-
dox to talk about power issues around prostitution.
There is that sense of "I'm taking my power back in a
particular situation, by being in control." But at the
same time I was being physically, sexually, emotionally
battered, really brutally, in my primary relationship and
in a few other relationships too. I don't want to say every
single bit of it was abusive, but there was abuse every
day during that time in my life. And I was in a position
in society where I was really an outcast. I was just as
powerless as I was as an incest victim. In leaving Russell, once I felt like I had some control and like he wasn't
going to pop out of every corner, I felt really light and
really free.

I feel strongly that a woman's life is her own. Her
choices are her choices. In making a choice it is really
important to have information and support. I see prostitution as a set-up for women, in that prostitutes are the
epitome of the madonna/whore split. "Some girls are
good girls and others are bad girls." Essentially we're all
property of men. Prostitution is a viable occupation for
some women, one of the few ways that women can make
a lot of money, and I don't want that to be taken away
from women. At the same time, I think it's a part of a
system that's abusive and oppressive of women. If I was
still in that lifestyle I would want to work on having a
support system of other women and to work on legal issues. It's difficult to be in a relationship with a man in
this society because of the power imbalance. I think
prostitution is a more dramatic playout of the same issues. It is important that it be talked about in the battered women's movement and the women's movement
in general.

Part of how I worked that through is through my writing. I have a manuscript that I'm getting ready to send
out, that's about my life as a hooker. In graduate school I
gradually started writing about it and bringing it to
workshops. I got a job and went to school part-time for
three years to get my degree, and I got up in front of
seventy people and gave my thesis-reading of my

poems, which are mostly about prostitution. But I didn't claim them as my own life. About a year later I gave a women-only reading in my home and claimed the poems as my own.

I got involved in facilitating support groups for battered women and incest survivors, volunteering at the shelter and doing abortion counseling. Then I did peer counseling at the women's center. When the position as center program coordinator opened I wanted it, even though it's a real low-paying job. Mostly the work is with incest survivors. I'm wanting to move toward education, because I'm really good at public education and I like it a lot.

I've been through all of this, and I'm going to use it as well, and as constructively, as I can. I'm going to talk about being an incest survivor. I'm going to talk about being a prostitute and talk about being a formerly battered woman and talk about having been raped, talk about the fact that I'm a lesbian and I'm going to talk about it out loud. This interview is part of that. One of the biggest ways that I've been hurt is by silence. And I'm not going to be silenced any more.

CHAPTER 17

Lisa

Lisa, a Tlingit Indian woman living in Alaska, was fifteen years old when she met Fred. She was unhappy with her parents, because they drank too much and didn't give her what she needed. Her father fished for a living and her mother worked at a cannery. Although her father was an alcoholic and violent toward her mother, he never hit the children. Lisa was the youngest of eight, and was close to her brothers and sisters, yet she often felt insecure and alone. Her friends took advantage of her inability to say no by coercing her into buying things for them.

I was working at a concession stand at a theater and Fred kept following me all the time. I wasn't interested in him, but he was pushy and I started going out with him. I went with him almost a year before I married him. He was funny and he was considerate of my feelings and listened to me. He was five years older than me. He was white, which was a shock for my parents. He threw temper tantrums once in a while when we were going out, but he never hit me until after we were married.

I was pregnant when we got married. He was in the service and got transferred to Alabama, where his family lived. I left Alaska on a Saturday and the next Saturday the baby was born in Alabama. Things started to go downhill. I was from a small town and a big family that I was very close to. They always took care of me and it was a culture shock to go to Alabama, 'cause there was so much prejudice there. My mother-in-law and I did not get along so hot. When I first met Fred's family we had this big dinner together and they were so loud. I felt so alienated from everyone else. It was like I was on display for all the aunts and uncles. "Are you really Indian?" Twenty questions at the table.

I enjoyed the baby and I really thought Fred loved me. I put so much into the marriage and I really thought we were devoted to each other, but when the baby was six months old the violence started. He was too young to be married and have a baby. I am a very outspoken woman, always have been, but after that first time he saw I was scared and a light bulb went on in his head: "Oh, I've learned something. I've got something to threaten her with." After that he just had to threaten me and I would be quiet right away. He would put his hand over my nose and mouth and make me hold my breath till I fainted. Or he would get me on the ground and kick me in the head and stomach and the back. I'd just roll up in a ball. It got to be almost once every two weeks before I finally left. He gave me a black eye one time, which he said was because I moved. If I hadn't of moved he would have hit me in the "right place," where it wouldn't show. Usually he would keep it away from my face.

He liked to spend money on the dog races. I started working at a restaurant and he started to take away my tip money and hitting me around because I wasn't bringing any money into the house. He hit the baby too. He got beat up when he was growing up and he thought it was okay. I'd never been beat up by my parents and I said, "No. You don't need to hit a child." Sometimes he would be getting ready to hit me and I'd think, "please don't cry" and my daughter would look at me and she wouldn't cry. She would hold back.

Sometimes I think it would have been nice to be violent back. I hit him a couple of times, but I was only five-three and he was five-seven and I'd think, "God, what did you do that for? Here it comes. You know it's going to be worse, now." One time I was waiting for my family to send me money to send me home, because he got all my money. He had took a swing at me and the knife was there and I backed off and went at him with the knife and he just barely moved in time. It was stupid to have gone after him.

The first time I left I was gone one month. He kept calling me and saying he loved me and he could talk real good. He was very convincing and I was real young. I thought I had no future, that if I did get on welfare I would never get off. I stayed with my parents when I left and then I went back to Alabama. My mother was upset, but when you're young and you're in love, you don't listen. You think you know everything.

The violence and emotional abuse continued and Lisa was afraid to go out of the house. In the oppressive summer heat of Alabama her tank top and shorts exposed her bruises, and Fred threatened to make things worse for her if anyone saw her black and blue marks. He also persuaded her that no one else would love her, that she didn't know how to be a woman, that she was too young. She was devastated by the verbal abuse and the second time she left for home, it was for good.

Fred followed Lisa and tried to persuade her to come back. He didn't dare hit her because she was on her own territory and had the protection of her large, devoted family. He did harass her though, pursuing her for nearly a year. He also spread stories about her to her teenaged friends, who all believed she was a "whore." She was hurt that they would turn on her, but she told herself, "I'll survive, I won't let this get me down."

After I left, my daughter wouldn't let anybody touch her for a long time. I didn't push her when she wasn't ready for it. Now she's not afraid any more. She's very outspoken. I feel very inferior still. I want to be pleasing to everybody else. But I saw a psychologist three or four times and that helped.

Any man that rubbed me wrong once, he was gone. I just thought, "I'm not going to get hurt any more." Then I realized they did not deserve the treatment I gave them. I started to work at a nightclub as a cocktail waitress and I met Clark, another service man. He's Caucasian too. He was after me for about two months before I broke down and said, "Okay you can walk me home." Then he started to come around more and more. I said, "I'm not ready for this." But two weeks later he was telling me he loved me and then it was moving-in time, and putting our money together.

Clark said, "How could a man hit you like that? I would never do that. I will take care of you." But then alarms went off. I could feel something was wrong after I moved in with him. He liked to turn the car lights out and speed when he wanted me to agree to something, even if it was just something like where we were going to eat. The first time he hit me I was getting close to knowing who he was going out with and started questioning him. He twisted my arms black and blue.

After a while when I was beat up, I didn't even feel it. I felt the initial impact but you close yourself up, you're just not there mentally. He would try to make love after he beat me up. He raped me, but I didn't call it rape then. After he beat me he bought me things all the time.

I was in love for the first time with Clark. I believed miracles could happen. I would go back to him because he threatened to beat up anybody I went out with and none of them was as big as him. He was about six feet tall and played hockey. He looked like a football player. I didn't want anyone else hurt around our relationship. I couldn't relate to anyone, couldn't explain how I could be locked into one little corner of my mind and not remember anything. It was like going crazy. I had to get out, otherwise I probably would have gone right over the deep end. He moved out and we started making new lives, but he was at every one of the softball games I played in, just watching, making me nervous. Then he started calling me at work and bringing me flowers.

Lisa stayed in a shelter and grew stronger. She saw others who were much worse off than she, more like she was in her first marriage, "just gone." She began to cry less and express her anger more. Talking with the other women made her realize that others cared about her and that she was able to help them too. She returned to Clark, but she began to set some limits. He continued to slap her once in a while, but the beatings stopped. Lisa knew her rights and was angry. She was determined that things would be different.

I said to the women in the shelter, "None of us are strong enough to leave, but we've got to start." After I went back to Clark, I took my own advice. I was scared, but I jumped up and put my face in his and I spoke out for myself. It was like I was just taking off from my chair into space and there was nothing holding me. I used to work out in gymnastics and get high off that—just being in the air—and it felt like that. I felt like grabbing my body. It was shaking. I'd say to myself "Geez! This is nice. I'm not as low as anyone thinks of me or as I think of myself." When he did slap me I would go right back to the old feelings again, but I would still say something. I found out I usually didn't get hit when I stood up to Clark. A real new experience! Ding! Round one! I felt ecstatic. I felt lightheaded.

He got out of the service and wanted me to go to Chicago with him. I wouldn't go. I had a whole year to get ready mentally, to work up to it. I started planning things with friends without him. I thought my daughter, Melanie, deserved ten times better. I want a good life for her. I was always with Fred and Clark and people who wanted me to not be myself. After I left I found out who Lisa was. It's not like being reborn, but it's sure close. I'm through with the Freds and the Clarks for the rest of my life.

I'd like to see a psychologist about the violence I have in me. I'm not through yet. I have to grow. I get angry and throw things. It was always supressed before, but after I left Fred it started. I have a lot stored up and I don't want to ruin it now. I keep waiting for the mirror to break because this is too good.

I've been married a year and it's a fairy tale. My husband is too good. He's in the service too and he's Caucasian. I was in a bar and he tried to talk to me, and I told him, "Just don't bother me." He would not budge. I told him I have no respect for servicemen and he just kept giving me positives. I slipped out and he ran after me.

I knew him three days and he left on patrol. I get this eight page letter in the mail. "If we got married we could . . . " I thought he was joking. He took leave for two weeks and flew down to see me and after that we saw each other maybe three or four times until we got married five months later. Then he took off for five months. This has got to be cuckoo, but he has really been good to me. He really loves me.

I really feel lucky. I got my GED and trained for clerk typist II. I was paid to go to school and now I make sixteen thousand dollars a year working for the state. I'm going to go for Administrator I. I'm moving up and that feels good. I'll go as far as I can in my career. My biggest fantasy is helping the Tlingit people with their culture. I'd like to go to college and study Tlingit culture and teach my people to be proud of what they are. In the past two years I'm finding out who I am and I'm on the way up now.

CHAPTER 18

Gwen

My father and mother were separated most of the time. My father was an alcoholic and one time I watched him beat my mother very badly. I've seen my mother's arm broken and my dad rip her dress off of her and strike her. He'd be gone for months at a time and come home drunk and she was afraid not to let him in.

Gwen's mother earned twenty-five cents an hour doing other people's housework, and Gwen had to walk almost two miles to public school, usually with no breakfast and no money for lunch. She loved to read, write and draw and early in life she learned that she would have to get the things that were important to her through her own initiative. When she was twelve a man who taught drawing classes gave her free lessons. When he became physically too familiar with her, she told him she wouldn't come back unless he stopped, and he complied.

Gwen was afraid she would have to drop out of school because of the family's poverty and because the public high school was too far away to walk to. A Catholic school was closer to her home and one day she just walked in. She was befriended by a nun who admired her drawings. She met the priest in charge of the school and when he saw her work he invited her to teach art to the younger children in exchange for her uniforms, books and a little extra money. "That's how I got to high school," she recalls.

Jonathan and Gwen were "properly introduced" when she was still in high school. He was talented in music and an ex-

cellent dancer, "just a perfect gentleman, very considerate."
He also had a reputation for practical jokes that "weren't
jokes at all"—that were sometimes even dangerous—but at
the time she could see no flaws in him.

I never did see any signs of temper and that was a
very nice period. I was eighteen and had known Jonathan a year and a half when we eloped. We were married a year and a half when the first child came. He was
colicky and often cried and cried before I finally got him
to sleep. Jonathan marched through the house playing
tunes on the baby's toy and was acting more juvenile all
the time. I finally just locked the front and back doors,
but he came in through the window and grabbed me and
turned me over his knee and pounded my rear good. I
struggled to my feet and slapped him, but he was a big
six-foot-three and I'm five two, so it didn't have much
effect.

I'd seen my mother beaten and I didn't think men
should be spanking their wives. I was the one being responsible for the baby and I wasn't going to be punished
for something I knew was right. I'd just had a little baby
and my mother had just passed away, and I didn't have
any other relatives, but I just wasn't going to live that
way. So I talked to the attorney and he told Jonathan
there would be legal action if he continued to act like a
lumberjack. He told me he was sorry and that seemed to
work well for a number of years. He didn't lay hands on
me for a long time.

Then he started doing silly things. He'd get me up on
the garage roof and then playfully set the ladder away.
One time he got me on the floor and sat on me and said
he was going to lick my eyeballs, and he'd get his tongue
clear in there. He'd peek in the windows and he scared
my daughter many times. He would hide in a closet and
scare me with a horrible face. These games started when
our daughter was about ten and our son about twelve.

He threw me up in the air one time and I bumped my
head and had a headache for three days. I called a

gym and arranged to take self-defense classes. The lady I was going with called and mentioned to him that we were going and he wanted to know what was the idea. I said, "I wanted to show show you how it feels. I was going to flip you right on your back." He said he was sorry and he quit it, except he couldn't resist a little window peeking.

I was very optimistic, so happy to have a home. I irrigated the yard and did all the mowing because I'd been raised during the Depression years when you were just really lucky to have a home. I worked as hard as I could to live up to that impossible ideal we see in every women's magazine. The beautifully set table and all that. We used to love to dance when we were going together, but after we were married he never would take me. We didn't have many good times. We were working really hard to establish our business and our togetherness was just around the children, the house and the business.

I married during the time when you were your husband's possession. All of the gifts that you had really belonged to him and it did not matter if you worked all day, there was still women's work to be done at night. I believed in God and I was Jonathan's wife. It was as simple as that.

I gave private art classes and I was very stingy with my money. I put it away and bought my supplies wholesale. Until the very last with Jonathan, he really did not keep me down. There was a little free something in me that he did not own. The painting really did something for me.

My family never knew I was taking college classes. I took the classes after lunch and before they got home for dinner and I still had real nice meals. If I let the least thing go I knew Jonathan would get on me about it. I had to ask for anything I wanted. If I wanted a bra I would have to ask for the money, and he would give it to me two or three weeks later and tell me not to spend much. I really resented that, because I earned a sizable check every week when I was the main salesman at the store, but I never saw the check because it went right into the bank.

Gwen was involved in artistic and community activities and in the mid-fifties organized a Nevada art exhibit. She wanted to include dance and theater and decided she would invite an anthropologist to discuss the various arts in different cultures and times, so she simply called Margaret Mead, who accepted the invitation. Shortly after that she entered a state-wide art competition. For years she had kept her painting secret from Jonathan, and she assumed he would never find out she had sneaked some of her paintings to the gallery. She won the first prize in contemporary painting and was stunned to see her picture in the local paper. Her great pleasure was only slightly diminished by Jonathan's anger over it. Gwen also did the publicity for the state art association and wrote feature articles for the local newspaper. It was satisfying to deposit paychecks for her work in her own account.

Shortly after the children graduated from high school Jonathan was hospitalized for manic-depression, which was the first time Gwen realized there were serious problems. For the next two years Jonathan often sulked, refusing to speak or to join the family at the table. Gwen would bring him a tray and try not to make waves, but she was increasingly reluctant to live that way. Her son was at home caring for Jonathan and she decided to spend the summer studying with a colorist at an art colony near Sante Fe.

Jonathan agreed that she could go and for the first time in her life Gwen was off on an adventure of her own. She found an inexpensive room to share with another woman. She arranged to do the publicity for the annual music festival and got a part time job in an art gallery. She attended classes, worked in a studio, made friends and realized she didn't need her house and garden back in Nevada. "I was my own person," she recalls. "I decided I was never going home. I knew it would be a struggle, but if I was ever going to get out, well, I had better go."

During her second week away she received an emergency call from home. Her son, Matt, had crashed during his first airplane solo. Gwen went home. When she arrived she found that Matt was dazed and in shock, but basically all right. However, Jonathan was complaining of painful headaches, couldn't move his arm, and needed care. She had a feeling she would never leave again.

The emotional abuse and physical violence from Jonathan became worse. On one occasion Jonathan pushed the refrigerator door into her, dragged her across the floor and slapped her. She tried to call for help, but he tore the telephone off the wall. She got away and went to a hospital where she was told she was hysterical and kept for six days. When she came home, Jonathan apologized, but he continued his displays of temper and forbade Gwen to pursue the public relations work she was doing. About two months later he stopped speaking to her. Then he broke her hand, and she went to the police, but was told they could do nothing. She sought advice from Jonathan's lawyer who advised her to run away, but by then she felt there was no place she could go. Jonathan's psychiatrist told her there wasn't a thing that could be done about him. Gwen was "going downhill," losing weight and feeling helpless.

One night, without apparent cause or warning, Jonathan jumped up, opened a drawer, pulled out a gun, put a bullet in it and stuck it in his mouth. Gwen tried to force his arm down and kept hanging on to it, crying and talking to him "like he was out on a ledge." Finally she gave up and went next door for help, trying to ignore his shouted threats, "If you go out, I'll be dead when you come back." He was still alive when she returned with the minister who lived next door. He talked to Jonathan all night, and the next day the doctor came and gave Jonathan something to put him to sleep. The day after that Gwen took him to the hospital mental ward, hoping they would keep him until he was over his acutely suicidal phase. The psychiatrist just gave him a prescription and let him go. Gwen was afraid of the violence that Jonathan might inflict on himself or her and had counted on the psychatrist to create a safety zone by keeping him in the hospital. She felt he had betrayed her, and she was running out of people to turn to for help.

When Gwen asked Jonathan to sleep in a separate bedroom he took her head between his hands and squeezed it. "I could just feel my eyes popping out," she recalls, "and I screamed, 'You're murdering me. You're murdering me' and he let up." For a month her face was covered with bruises and she stayed in the house. When her friend, Nancy, came to see her and expressed her outrage at Jonathan for treating Gwen so badly, Jonathan "shot out of his chair and grabbed Nancy by the throat and then dragged her by the hair over to the door." Gwen intervened, telling him he'd gone too far, and to her surprise he let go. When Nancy said she planned to file assault charges, Gwen was relieved to know someone else would be validating the fact that Jonathan was dangerous. But a few days later Nancy's husband talked her out of it, fearing it would make them more vulnerable to Jonathan's violence. Gwen was devastated.

Gwen's lung collapsed and she had to be hospitalized. Jonathan visited her daily and brought her gifts. During one visit he said, "I could kill you right now with a pillow and nobody would know the difference." Gwen quietly asked him to hand her the Bible and for reasons she doesn't understand he suddenly stopped threatening her. A sympathetic nurse agreed to keep him out of Gwen's room, but no one had a plan for what to do when she was released from the hospital. She was still so weak she would need a walker at home.

One time he reached out and patted me and said, "Thank you for understanding about my illness." What could I do? It's my nature to be forgiving, and he was so sweet when he said those things. Besides, I couldn't get any help from anybody.

After he broke my hand it just seemed like time didn't mean anything. It was just going like water, because I wasn't able to express myself, to concentrate on anything. It was just the bottom for me. Always before that, I felt like there was some place where he couldn't get at me, some place he couldn't reach, that he never really did completely own me, even if I had to maneuver around him. That time was gone. There's a song about being so full of sorrow and pain that you forget to eat your bread, and when you begin to eat, the tears are mingled with your food and it tastes like ashes. I think that describes it.

One night he went out and didn't come back until almost four in the morning, and when I started saying I was worried about him, he tore into me verbally, much worse than he ever had before. His eyes were different. They were dilated clear out to the edge. I turned around with my walker to go to the bedroom and he grabbed it and threw it. I went crawling to get it and he threw a chair at me, calling me names like he never had before and getting more and more worked up. "Shut your mouth!" I said, and he did. No one was more surprised than I. A friend came over and said to Jonathan, "Aren't you going to take care of Gwen?" and he said, "I think not." That's the last thing anybody ever heard him say.

Later I got up and said to Jonathan, "Please don't give me any trouble, but I'm going to call someone. We can't keep going on this way." As I turned in my walker, one of the legs got caught in the shag carpet, the walker tipped over and I fell to the floor. I checked to make sure I was okay and started to get up. Just as I reached for the walker, I heard this awful noise. When I turned to look at Jonathan, he looked just the same, and just then a little trickle of blood started. I could hear a woman screaming and screaming—it was me. I started crawling, dragging my walker into the kitchen. I couldn't seem to get up. I reached the phone, called the operator, who calmed me and told me to go to the front door, that someone was already there. I found a policeman there. I was put in bed and the bedroom door shut.

The children were called and arrived, both drunk. They made the funeral arrangements, but also went to the police station and suggested that it may not have been suicide, that perhaps Gwen had killed her husband. There was a thorough investigation and Gwen was exonerated. "I just thanked God," she said, "that killing Jonathan never did occur to me as a way out. But can you imagine how I felt when I was accused?" The children were more of a trial than a comfort. Her daughter made a habit of getting drunk and calling in the middle of the night to scream "You killed my father and I'm going to kill you." She is manic-depressive and blamed Gwen for giving birth to her and for passing Jonathan's illness on to her. Gwen hasn't seen either of her children since the funeral.

Gwen had enough money to open an antique shop and gallery with two partners and they all did very well. Nevertheless, the years with Jonathan had taken their toll and her health continued to be troublesome. She tried to work through her problems by keeping busy, but after Jonathan took his life, Gwen went through periods when she was haunted by the thought that suicide is "the preventable death," and she wondered what she could have done. "Then my thoughts would be like a tape going over and over some of those incidents. How could I have made them different? As I began to mend, I couldn't really put blame on myself that much. If there was any way I could blame myself, it was for being so stupid, for just staying in there in an impossible situation. I just feel like I have to do something intelligent and halfway important to make up for the time I've wasted being stupid." Gwen continues to ruminate over what was the right thing to do and arrives at contradictory conclusions, sometimes taking comfort that she did all she could for Jonathan, and at times feeling resentment for devoting so much of her life to him.

I'd always been very devout and whenever I gave my word or when I took my vows, I felt that I had to abide by them. I had to do what I felt was right within me, and that probably kept me with him, especially after I came home and found that Jonathan couldn't move his arm and needed care. If he had taken his life while we were separated, it probably would have bothered me even more than it did. This way I tried to be a friend to him, I did go that extra mile with him and if there's a God, he knows that I was really in there doing all that I could do under those circumstances.

My minister advised me to pray for Jonathan. At the time I didn't realize why God didn't intervene, but I

later realized I had free will and had gotten enough messages to leave. I don't believe it was my duty to stay with
a psychotic who had no conscience.

CHAPTER 19

Janine

As a kid I was very active, I had a lot of friends and I was basically very happy when I wasn't at home. Although I did have a lot of parent pressures, I could go with my friends and just tune that out. I did volunteer work at a hospital, took piano lessons and was in a music group. My parents, especially my mother, wanted me to be the best. I think she felt she let herself down by marrying my dad so young, having so many children. She had five children and she wanted me to take a step beyond her. I was afraid to fall on my face, and that I'd never hear the end of it. I wanted either to go into music or writing or teach at a high school. I know I would have tried if things had been different.

Janine's father worked for a bank and her mother was a part time secretary. Her father was manipulative and cruel; he frequently assaulted her younger brother and sometimes broke promises to the children as a way of punishing his wife. He hit Janine just once, when she was sixteen, and she hit him back. By the time she was a teenager her father was regularly beating her mother, and Janine was the one who would pick her up and take her to her room after her father stormed out of the house.

When Janine graduated from high school she took a job in a photography store and continued to live in the cold atmosphere of her parents' home. They refused to speak to each other for long periods, during which "ice would form" when the family sat together for meals. Other aspects of Janine's life were equally joyless. She discovered that the gifts her boy-friend had given her were stolen and that he was living with another woman, while dating her. When that relationship ended she had no interest in meeting someone new, and she was feeling generally dispirited at the time she met Raul.

When I first met Raul I was working with his sister and he would come into the store to talk to her. I couldn't stand him at first. I thought he was a pain in the butt, and he was always hanging around. He was always calling, acting very pushy and I didn't want anything to do with him for a long time. I didn't want anything to do with anybody. It was around six weeks until I finally dated him. I finally gave in, I think, because I thought it would get him to stop pestering me. I was mean to him in the beginning, too. We were dating pretty steady and I'd sometimes date somebody else and he'd just have a fit.

I was just a kid, just eighteen, and nobody had ever been as in love with me as Raul was. It was very com-plimentary. I knew him a year and two months and I guess I finally realized, "This guy is really crazy about me. This is my ticket out." By that time I did like him and he wanted to marry me and he'd take me away from home.

I was only married a month before he hit me. His family had stayed in my house while we went away and it was a mess when we got home. We got into an argu-ment about it and I got punched around. I had a black eye and he felt terrible. He wanted me to go home, and we called my parents and my mother was very upset and said, "No, you can't come home. You stay there and you work things out." I think he realized he wasn't really ready to get married and I had very ambivalent feelings. I didn't want him to hurt me, but I didn't want to leave after only one month. So I stayed and things were fine for a couple of months, and then it happened again. It happened about once a month and he began to be emo-tionally abusive and I began to believe it was my fault.

He didn't want a baby, but I thought a baby would

level things off. I had a miscarriage and then was pregnant right away again. He didn't want me to tell anyone about the pregnancy and was very stand-offish. He had his school and friends and I was alone and neglected a lot. I took it out on myself and gained fifty pounds. When I was seven months pregnant I took one of the worst beatings. I think he was trying to hurt the baby because he knew it would have totally destroyed me. He punished me severely and I had bruised and maybe cracked ribs. They couldn't x-ray me.

My M.D. was very strict about check-ups and twice I had canceled. I didn't know how to explain the bruises, and on top of that my husband would go in and sit there and listen to what I told the doctor. And God help me if I told the doctor he punched me in the ribs. I told the doctor I tripped and I'd say, "I just touch something and I bruise" and I'd laugh. I'm sure he knew and he'd say to Raul, "You take care of her and the baby."

There were other injuries. My dentist filed down my teeth so much there's almost nothing left. I had cracked teeth and I'd laugh and say I'm getting my iron from eatin' nails. I had broken fingers, and they're all twisted and gnarled. One of them was stiff for almost a year. I wish I'd had medical attention, but at the time I was afraid he'd say, "You ran off to the doctor and told him the whole story, "and then I'd get it worse.

He was very, very, very, very possessive and jealous. If somebody would call me and he found out, he would go harass the person, try to start a fight with him. I thought it was complimentary. I didn't realize he had a problem. I have to attribute a lot of it to my age.

Raul's sister had told Janine that he had severely battered a girlfriend, and Janine was shocked but she said to herself, "I'll be so nice to him he'll never hurt me." She tried being quiet and meek, but he would explode anyway, and when she held in her anger, eventually it would come out. She broke his things, and then lied about what had happened to them. After a while she joined Raul in blaming herself for the battering. Janine took a part-time job, but Raul harassed her there too, until she was forced to quit. Then she started school, but Raul made her nervous when he drove by the school to see who she was with. She didn't have the will to continue.

When the baby arrived she consumed so much of Janine's attention that Raul felt left out. He began to spend long hours at work and Janine rarely saw him. Her mother often visited her and the baby or took them out, and Raul didn't like that at all. He became more violent. When Janine told her mother about it, she warned her daughter that if she left Raul she wouldn't be able to support the baby and herself. She also suggested that, since she herself had taken it for twenty-five years, her daughter could too. "Wait," she advised, "until you can buy a house. Set yourself up a little bit." Janine was at a loss to know what to do.

I was emotionally trapped. I was convinced that I was a loser, that my parents had had a bad marriage, I had a bad marriage, that this was the way it was. I had heard that from my husband and my mother. "This is the way it is. You stick it out." I was so lost. I knew I couldn't function, support myself and my baby. I wasn't strong. I had to hang onto him. He was the provider, he did everything for me, and for three years he convinced me I couldn't do it myself.

And yet at times he cherished me. Oddly enough the good times were after he beat me. He'd bring me a box of candy or flowers. He was making good money and he did let me buy what I wanted, clothes, and a lot of things for the baby that were luxuries. And he couldn't do enough for me in front of other people. I thought, "How could anybody like this do anything to me?" After a while my love for him was just a dependence on him. I know, when I look back, that I never really loved him. I always knew deep down it wasn't a permanent situation, even before I got married.

He'd say he couldn't stand me, he didn't want anything to do with me, except to have sex. And that was a big emotional thing to me, because he was so hateful and nasty to me. I hated it! I hated the sight of him, I hated his smell, I hated his hands on me, I hated every-thing about him. He'd drive up the driveway and I'd cringe. If I didn't more or less put out for him, I paid for it, but that was my duty, too. I was married to him, I was his wife. The worst thing he did was to call me a whore and say I was nothing to him, that I'd never be anything to anybody else, because after a while he said it so much that I believed him. Definitely a few times I was raped. I wouldn't have said that then, because I didn't think anybody would believe me. On TV they say, "Well, that's your husband, you have to let him."

I was always afraid. I went to a shelter and they said to press charges, but I was afraid if he went to jail he'd come out and kill me. That's all there was to it. I thought if I left him he would always come looking for me. I knew I'd never be through with this man. Still today I'm not through with him. I'll never be through with him.

I often thought of killing him. It started as a fantasy and got down more to a plan. I think I was almost to that point where I really could have. I used to think of it at night. I was going to put a knife under my pillow and when he was sound asleep I would slit his throat. It became a part of me, and yet it upset me because I've al-ways been a very passive, easy-going person, totally un-aggressive. It upset me that he got me to that point. I didn't want to go to jail and lose my baby. That was really the only thing that kept me from doing it.

He worked out of town and just came home week-ends, and I was alone with the baby, so I could think. I started to use my brain again. I lifted the cobwebs off and started to realize a lot of things just because I was alone, and I wasn't afraid. I started to stand up and get a little strength. He'd come home on weekends and I'd cringe, but I had the whole week, and if I could hold on for the weekend he'd be gone. Plus I had a very, very good friend who was very strong and some of her strength rubbed off on me. A lot of the strength that I had inside started coming out.

When the baby was a year old we got into an argu-ment about whether to visit his parents. He said, "You'd better be ready to go." I said, "Those people are mean to me and the baby and I'm not going." He just totally blew up. He beat me very badly. He kicked me, shoved me, slugged me and pulled my hair, and my daughter was screaming and screaming and screaming. What made me leave him was that that little baby got in between us and was pushing him off. That did it. I was so shocked, that did it right there, 'cause I said, "That's no way to raise a daughter. I can take this myself, physically and emotionally. I can probably take it for twenty more years, but I can't do this to her."

We went to the women's shelter and stayed there quite a while. There was one little girl there, I'll never forget her. She was nineteen and she had two children. She said, "You know what's going to happen? Your husband's going to call you or you'll call him and he's going to say he'll never do it again and he wants you back. But he'll always beat you again." She'd been through it so many times in five years with her husband that it made me realize it was true. It would start up again, no matter what he promised, no matter what he did.

I was scared and confused. I felt I'd had my insides ripped out and thrown on the ground, and I was relieved at the same time. There were so many things coming down on me all at once, but the main thing was I had taken the steps. I could pick up and walk again. After three years of marriage I knew the further in I'd get, the less I'd be able to do, and the more I'd believe him and the more dependent I'd be. I knew if I could take those first steps I could do anything. I could go through with it.

When Janine came home from the shelter she found that Raul had moved all of his things out of the house, but soon he began to call or show up on Janine's doorstep three or four times a week, pleading that he missed her and the baby. But Janine was relieved to have him gone and bought a gun to protect herself. Raul had a good job and Janine took seven hundred dollars out of their account when she left. When she had spent it, she was frightened, but she was learning to do without many things. Her grandmother offered her a house and paid the utilities, and she received food stamps and an AFDC allotment of 186 dollars a month. She persuaded Raul to pay for her daughter's swimming lessons and occasionally he gave her a hundred dollars or so. Her mother (who had divorced her abusive husband) bought Janine and her daughter clothing.

After she left the shelter Janine found she was often depressed, sometimes barely able to get up in the morning. She began to see a counselor and after a few months the depression lifted, except for occasional short spells.

One of the things that helped was getting totally involved with my daughter. She gave me lot of strength, because I had somebody else to look after, and I had to do it. When Raul and I were still together she'd catch a cold every time you turned around. She had ear infections, she was fussy, she wouldn't sleep good, something was always wrong. Once he left she gained weight, she grew, she just really changed. She's happy. She shines. She picks up things very fast. A big weight was lifted off of her and she was allowed to grow. That's the big thing that made me not want to go back to him. I didn't think I had the right to take her peace of mind away. I knew what it was like growing up with my parents, it was an ugly thing, and I didn't want to put her through that.

Hispanic husbands are very strong, very macho, and that is a bad characteristic. We're very family oriented and not until very recently did Hispanic women leave their husbands and get divorces. Even my mother faced this. You get alienated from your friends and family for doing this, and I've lost both Hispanic and Anglo friends, but I found out awful fast who my friends are. The ones that have proved to be my friends understand that I was drowning and I had to get out.

I'm going to community college in the fall. I was going to go away to college, but right now I really need my mother, my sisters, my brother. I need them to lean on. So I'm going to stay here and take a two year degree and after that I'd like to go to Albuquerque and finish a four year degree. I'm going to study public administration. I applied for a grant to go to school and got not only that but work-study. I'll be working two or three hours a day, so that makes me look up because I not only get the money but I'll be improving myself. I can do anything now.

CHAPTER 20

Joan

Joan grew up in a small rural town. Her father was a church and community leader, a strict disciplinarian who had been a World War II marine. He was a big man who controlled by his voice, a voice Joan remembers as always harsh. People from the community would look to him for advice and he would use the Bible to counsel them, but he never had a good relationship with his children. Joan, the oldest of four, was close to her siblings, but her mother was a cold and undemonstrative person. Joan didn't have many friends, though she was close to one girl in high school and had one boyfriend before she married Randy.

Joan began dating Randy shortly after high school. She was troubled that she had no goals and "just felt nowhere." Although Randy had no serious plans for the future either, he was a hard worker, independent, mature and seemed unafraid of anything. He had his own car, a job, was poised and polite. He treated her well and his ability to take charge of things gave her a feeling of security. She also liked his good looks and build.

After a year of dating they were married. Joan tried hard to be a good wife and then a good mother to their two boys, who were born not quite a year apart. She was a "homebody," mostly content to sew, read, watch television and care for the children. She and Randy only went out together to visit their parents or to attend the annual Christmas party Randy's employer gave.

She had expected that she and Randy would share responsibilities "fifty-fifty," but Randy didn't recognize any obligation to help with the children or housework. He made that attitude clear in their first year of marriage when Joan asked him to carry out the garbage and he responsed by dumping it on her and all over the living room couch. Joan cried and decided they should separate for a time, but he was contrite and affectionate and she changed her mind.

Randy often told Joan she would "lose her teeth" if she didn't comply with his demands and threatened her with a raised fist. He slapped her on several occasions, but each time she convinced herself it wouldn't happen again. She tried to put these events out of her mind, but often she was anxious, bewildered, "walking on eggs," and intimidated unless Randy was out of the house at work or engrossed in working on his car. But her fear of "that certain look in his eye" became a more salient part of her life. She tried to adapt by always serving dinner on time and never confronting Randy with anything unpleasant.

From the time Randy dumped the garbage, Joan frequently thought of leaving him, but she took her marriage vows too seriously to act on the idea. She was also afraid of being on her own and couldn't find answers to the chronic questions of "Where would I go? How would I get income to put groceries on the table for these kids?" She was too wary of supporting herself and the children even during a period when she had a fairly good job in a lumber mill. As a "putty-patcher," she earned "the best money a woman could make at that time," and felt proud when she was selected from twenty women to work on some new machinery. During that same time Randy was fired from his job at a department store and bought into a fast food restaurant franchise. But he went bankrupt and decided to look for work in a city a few hundred miles away.

While Randy was gone Joan thought about how nice it would be if he never came back. When he did come home to visit he was frequently violent. He eventually found work and Joan felt obliged to join him. She was unhappy in the strange new surroundings and missed her home and job. Randy threw her over a porch railing, breaking her arm and injuring her leg. Again she thought of leaving, but there were too many reasons holding her back. A doctor had said he wouldn't

give the marriage six months and Joan wanted to prove him
wrong; she wasn't ready to give up the dream that the relationship would get better; no one in her family, including two
aunts who had married alcoholics, had ever been divorced;
she believed Randy when he said she would never make it
out in the world without him.

Not yet ready to leave, but reluctant to stay, Joan sought
help from a counselor, Peter. The therapy with Peter developed into a complex relationship, which alternately helped
and hindered the process of leaving Randy and establishing
herself as an independent person. In the first stage, which
lasted about a year, Peter's support and caring enabled Joan
to gain self-confidence and to develop the belief that "a human being doesn't have to live that way." She decided to
leave Randy. He agreed to a divorce and to move out of
the house. Joan saw a lawyer and explained to Randy that
he would be served with a restraining order, but she made
the mistake of listening to his pleas not to have the order
served.

He says, "Don't have them serve a restraining order.
I couldn't stand that. I'll do anything you want to, but
don't have them do that." So I agree, because I feel that
it's hard for him to leave his home and his kids and me,
and he's cooperating. He did leave to stay with friends
and he was to talk to the attorney I'd picked out. Then
the next week we were to discuss finances.

During that next week my seventeen-year-old son
came home and took my two-year-old son, John, for a
ride. My other son was gone too. I was alone in the
house and Randy came to the door. I let him come in,
just to talk about finances. He said "I have seen an attorney and since you haven't served that restraining order on me I have just as much right to be here as you
have and I am not leaving. If you want to leave this marriage, you get out and I will have a restraining order
served on you. The kids are with me, they read those
divorce papers and they don't believe a word of them.
They have agreed to stay with me, so you either agree to

stay in the marriage, or get out and I'll get the house, I'll get the cars, I'll have everything."

At first I said "No way," and kept screaming at him to get out of there. Then he said "All I have to do is make a phone call and they'll come and serve the restraining order on you and you'll have to get out." I was totally devastated by that. Here I was alone, he'd taken my kids, and I fully believed there was somebody who was going to come and make me leave. It was quite a shock to have my children taken away, and I could not withstand that. I felt helpless, trapped, stripped, hopeless. I caved in and agreed to stay. He took me in his arms. And I hated him. I just hated him. Taking my children away completely erased all and any feeling that I'd ever had for him. It was just gone.

Randy had gone to see Peter that day and agreed to start counseling, but it was too late to make any difference to me. And then he convinced Peter that he was the one wronged. I stopped seeing Peter, and he called and he says, "You can't leave now, we're not through with therapy." He talked to me for a whole hour. Here was this man giving me a very warm response, appealing to me not to leave, so I came back.

Peter was very tall, very good-looking, very dark eyes, quiet. He was a hard person to get to. I thought, "There's a person there some place and I want to know that person." So I proceeded to get to him. I sympathized with him when he had a cold. I shared with him that I was genuinely concerned about him. I was mothering him and I knew it. That touched him and he began to open up a little bit. His voice softened and he discussed himself personally.

I knew he had left a relationship. Of course the fact that he was single appealed to me and I developed a very strong attachment to him. I discussed it with him and he handled it very well at first. He was very strong in telling me this was a therapy relationship and there was no romance, so I was satisfied with that. But then these romantic inclinations toward him would continue to develop and as time went on, he softened, his expression grew warmer and it was a very deep relationship. It was obvious the romantic feelings were returned, though he would never say anything.

He would see that things were getting out of hand and would try to draw back and say, "This is a therapy relationship." I would get very angry and upset, and threaten to leave and that would threaten him and then he would soften again and I would soften. When things weren't going my way in therapy, that was the way I manipulated and gained control. I wanted very much to have him respond to me openly, and I wanted to have an open relationship.

I did feel that I was sexually attractive to him and I learned that I was desirable and needed and that I had a power over someone. I'd say, "I'm sick of this and I'm getting out." And I knew what his reaction would be. He would appeal to me to stay. That's how I kept in touch with his feelings. It made him uncomfortable, I'm sure, and he didn't like to be in that position. He'd try to get back that power he gave me and I wouldn't release it.

He was manipulating me, too, by directing the conversation to more suggestive sexual subjects. I had a dream that we were having intercourse and he wanted me to elaborate on that. He was very intent and he was turning on. He undressed me with his eyes a lot and I was needy. Here was someone I confided in, whom I could trust, and I just couldn't believe that someone could be that interested in me. It was very flattering, and that was the happiest time of my life, that relationship. We both looked forward to my coming. He increased my coming from once a week to twice a week, which intensified all this and we both fed on it.

I think my relationship with Peter had a positive effect in the sense that it developed my self-confidence. It was detrimental to the degree that he would deny his feelings one week, and the next week turn on again. I couldn't handle it any more. I was getting depressed, I couldn't stand it, but I was hooked into him and I couldn't leave.

He was very controlling, and disapproved of my reading any books that might help me. He felt that he alone had the only answer to my problems. I was very much afraid of his disapproval. But I had gone to a women's group without telling him, even though I knew he would disapprove.

It was the women's group that helped me evaluate things. I was just amazed at the stories of these women and the similarities to mine. They were talking about me and my life, the hiding from everybody, the men hiding the violence from everybody. Someone brought up the fact that her husband always was trying to know who called, what was said. It was exactly how Randy behaved, and suddenly it dawned on me I don't have any friends, that Randy discouraged it by criticizing people that I wanted to bring home. I had thought it was all something that I was doing. Peter didn't understand what I was talking about, the feelings, but I could relate to the women, because they had gone through it. I got support and took down a lot of telephone numbers and whenever Randy wasn't there I called. That helped a lot.

Peter wanted to see Randy in therapy and once he started seeing him he changed his mind about what he thought I should do. Before he saw Randy he thought I should get out of the relationship. Afterwards, Peter would say he didn't think it was a good idea to get a divorce and he was very cold to me. He deserted me emotionally. He couldn't see me for four or five days, he was nowhere to be found. I was very bitter toward Peter after he threw me to the wolves, so to speak, but there is a part of me, too, that remembers him as the only person that I felt genuinely loved me.

For a period when he was seeing Peter, Randy went to church with Joan, spent time with the children and even brought her flowers. But the last thread of her caring had been broken when he tried to take the children away from her. Joan was only waiting for another slip so she could feel justified in leaving.

Randy sensed that she wanted to leave, and he took all

their money out of the savings account. Joan told him that was the last straw, and he went into the bedroom after her, saying "You're not leaving." She wasn't sure what he was going to do, but she felt menaced and backed away. He calmed down. The next day when he went to work she gathered her things together, took her son, John, contacted an attorney and stayed with friends for a couple of days. This time she got a restraining order.

Once she had separated, Joan realized she expected people to take care of her, yet it seemed demeaning to ask for help. When she first had car trouble, she recalls, "I cried, broke to pieces. I got so upset because I wanted to handle this myself, on my own, and I didn't know what to do." It was hard to ask for a ride home or for someone to pick John up. The first time a request was turned down she was devastated. She felt as if the whole world had turned against her and she wanted to just give up. But she learned to cope with occasional rejection and also dealt with some of her car's idiosyncracies herself. "One time in desperation I took off my shoe and hammered on it with my heel and it started!" Women at work suggested a good car mechanic and friends at church helped Joan learn how to do her income tax.

In retrospect, Joan realizes she had hardened herself against any intense emotions and she regrets not being more sensitive to her children. Now she's becoming more attuned to her feelings and realizes that being emotionally expressive needn't keep her from being a strong person. Her self-worth no longer depends on Randy's responses to her, and she has had no trouble staying away from him.

I expect people to know that I'm a valued human being, that I'm sought after, that I can contribute something of value. It's a great source of satisfaction to me if somebody calls me—especially somebody from the women's group—that has a particular question and I can answer it, help her along on her journey toward getting free.

I vacillate between wanting to be a part of someone's life, to share things, to have a companion and at the same time wanting to expand myself, to know myself better. At work they have acquired a word processing system and that has rejuvenated me. They'll need a supervisor and hopefully I'll obtain that position. I think I'd like to get involved in the stock market. I want to improve this house, and I'd like to go to school. I'd like to learn how to sail. As soon as things kind of even out here in terms of getting this divorce over, getting through this wild fling and wonderful time I'm having, maybe I'll get down to business.

I feel like a load has been lifted off my shoulders. I'm able to make decisions by myself without having that second person looking over my shoulder supervising, constantly telling me when to get up, when to go to bed, how to wear my hair, whether or not to color my hair, what route to take as we are driving through town. I don't have to put up with that any more. I feel very much at peace.

CHAPTER 21

Sue

My dad was an industrial contractor and my mom was a high school math teacher. My mom and I fought a lot and she'd make me feel guilty. Once in a while it was a hairbrush across the face or a slap. Once my dad tried to hit me and he missed me and hit the refrigerator, knocked it over and put a hole in the wall. I think it surprised him, because he didn't know he was hitting so hard. He would take me into my room and slap me around and I'd run away. At school if I had a male teacher and the classroom door was closed, I'd start shaking uncontrollably. I was just a nervous wreck, couldn't pass a test, and started getting ulcers. I just assumed I was a bad kid.

Three days before she turned eighteen Sue's parents asked if she wanted to go live with her grandparents in Idaho, and without a moment's hesitation she agreed. Two years later, after a year at a university, she headed toward the West Coast and settled down in Portland. She earned an associate degree in engineering and soon was making twenty thousand dollars a year at an aircraft company, but she was lonely. Then she met Ned, who lived in the same building. He worked as a mechanic and at times he helped Sue out by working on her car. Everyone who met Ned thought he was the "sweetest, most gentle man" and he was strikingly handsome. Soon they were dating and for six months they got along well. He was five years younger than Sue.

The honeymoon was over when Ned began to do things

that made Sue feel crazy and undermined her career plans and her confidence. She took night school classes to upgrade her skills and Ned tried to sabotage her ambitions in various ways, such as borrowing her car and not returning it in time for her to get to class, or keeping her up late with exhausting questions. She believes he also wanted to get her fired from her job.

Ned told Sue he would like a birthday party, but the day before the event he announced that he was not going to attend. Sue was left with the embarrassing task of telling his friends the party had been called off. On another occasion he gave her a ring and the next day spent time with another woman. Since he and Sue lived in the same building, it was humiliating and when Sue let him know how she felt about that, he moved the woman into his apartment for two weeks. He took things from Sue's apartment and when she discovered them in his apartment he denied they were hers. His friends believed him and thought she was "crazy." Sue became consumed with the relationship and her mind became progressively "cluttered with confusion and feelings of desperation." "I wanted to trust him," she says, "but the more I would tell him about myself, the more he would use it against me. He knew how to tap into me and hurt me."

About six months after we met, Ned slapped me, but then swore up and down he would never do it again. The next time, he kicked me and chased me with a hammer. I went to a shelter for a few weeks and then moved in with a friend. But then I found out Ned had tried to kill himself and I went to visit him in the hospital. He was crying and saying, "I'm sorry. Things will be better. Don't treat me like an animal." I said, "Look what you've done to me. My friends think I'm crazy, I'm a nervous wreck all the time, I can't concentrate, I'm miserable. I tried everything I could to make you happy. What do you want from me?" He said he would go to counseling, so I made an appointment for him. I didn't want to be there but I was afraid not to be there for him. I was afraid he would kill himself, because to me he seemed like a real mixed up person.

I was having my own problems and I felt like a basket case, so I started to go to counseling because I thought, "Gosh, I must be crazy." I said, "I can't stand this guilt," and the counselor said, "Well you can't be responsible for other people's lives." I said, "That's easy for you to say. What if he kills himself?" He didn't have any answers for me and I decided to go on seeing Ned, but I kept my own apartment.

I was resentful and felt angry and humiliated, almost as if I were prostituting, because I didn't want affection from him and was lying about still wanting to be with him. He missed four counseling appointments and I began to realize he was in no danger of killing himself. Then I saw him with his arm around another woman. "This is the guy who is going to kill himself over me!" I realized he wasn't honest with me and was just manipulating me and using my sense of guilt against me, and I was really angry. I should have walked away, but instead I pulled him aside and told him how angry I was. He tried to break my glasses, and he knew that when I went to class I couldn't see the chalk board without them. I was enraged and I looked around for a way to get back at him.

He had several pairs of sunglasses on a table and I just cleared them all off in a blind rage. I looked like a raving maniac. I just jumped up and down and broke every one I could, just stomped on them in a fury. He hit me and I grabbed a pair of scissors, but I couldn't bring myself to use them against him, and he beat me up again. He was six-feet-two and weighed one sixty-five. I was five-feet-four and weighed a hundred and seven. His friends were there and watched him beat me, and didn't do a damn thing. They saw me pick up the scissors too, and I might have stabbed him, but they just stood there.

I left then for the final time. The relationship had lasted ten months. I moved, changed jobs and didn't even keep in touch with my friends. I wanted it to be the way it was in the beginning before I met him. When you realize there's no way it's going to go back, something snaps inside of you. You don't care any more. I left it all behind.

At first Sue wanted to go out with someone and to be held, "to feed her crushed ego." She has learned to recognize men with traits similar to Ned's whenever they give her the message, "Poor me, nobody gives me a break," but she's dissatisfied that she doesn't always pick up the clues immediately that a man "wants to be mommied." She still has trouble differentiating between the situations in which she's not patient and understanding enough about the inevitable rough times in relationships and those in which the interaction is one way, with Sue doing all the work. She tends to keep an emotional distance from men and is relieved that she doesn't need a man to tell her she's all right. She says she's now happiest when she's not involved with a man.

Sue feels that one mistake she made when she was trying to "rehabilitate" herself was taking on goals that were too big. "Something that really helped me is to have little goals. I'll get the checks mailed today. I'll iron a dress." Dressing well helped her feel better and that helped her be more friendly to people. Jogging and good nutrition were important to her. She also joined a church. Her stay in the shelter had given her a perspective that stayed with her.

The shelter was really good for me. I was so embarrassed. You feel like you're the only woman it has happened to, but then you realize all these women are in the same boat and they know exactly how you feel, especially during the few days' period after you've gotten hit and you're in shock. You start to do something like the dishes and in the middle of it you forget what you're going to do with the pan. It's a strange experience, like being high (though I don't get high). You've really got to concentrate to get normal stuff done.

After I left it took a long time to rebuild myself. It was excruciating coming to grips with what's real and what's not real. I was really confused. I did things to build my self-image, but I still have a problem with it. The happier periods get gradually longer than the slumps and it's worth it, but it seems forever at first. I was depressed and all I wanted to do was stay in bed.

I thought I must be a real pain in the ass to be around. You set up to go shopping with the girls and you realize you break into these crying spells every half hour, so you think, "They don't want my company," and you decide not to go. But my friends were supportive. "We understand. We've all been there. Let us give you some affection and support." It reinforces your confidence to have people around.

Sometimes I'd get really angry. I had so much anger in me I didn't know what to do with it and I'd fantasize about getting doberman pinschers that would kill him. But I'm not like that. I'm the most mild-mannered person. I'm very accepting. And sometimes I think I would have done it all the same. It's a learning process.

I was twenty-three and Ned was eighteen. I had more schooling and a nice job. I think I intimidated him. When you're nice to people who don't think very much of themselves, they're just sure you're out to get 'em. So then he had to intimidate me. And I didn't want to be a real person, a grownup. But now I've started taking responsibility for my own feelings. I've decided to take care of myself emotionally as well as financially.

I can't say when the transition was. I think my self-image is getting better all the time. I think that's the basis of everything. I have a lot more freedom, because I own my own feelings and I'm not consumed by these flashing thoughts like "I wonder what he's doing right now. Why can't he love me?" I feel a lot more freedom not having a boyfriend, a lot better.

Work is much better. I just zip through so much work, whereas before it was hard to get any work done at all. I don't walk around afraid like I used to either. And I'm a lot less lonely. I used to feel lonely at night by myself, but it doesn't bother me now. I've got a lot of friends and I've got myself. Before, I didn't feel like I had that. And I got myself a teddy bear! I think an adult should have a teddy bear.

My interests are simple. Playing with the cat, sewing, doing little projects, reading a good book. I love comedy shows. I do believe there is a God up there and that he wants us to love people and love ourselves. I live alone now and it's a very secure feeling knowing I've got control over my environment.

CHAPTER 22

Maddie

Maddie's mother married twice, and Maddie had a close relationship with her four stepsisters and her brother. They all lived together with Maddie's parents for a few years, but when Maddie was three her mother died. That was her earliest memory and her sorrow was compounded by the removal of her stepsisters to their natural father's home. Later, through the help of her aunts, visits were arranged among the children and she re-established important relationships with them.

Maddie was molested at the age of three by a neighbor. Her father was furious and threatened to kill the man, but Maddie was aware that he had molested her sisters and some of her school friends. By the time she was six her father had married her eighteen-year-old babysitter, and soon she had a baby brother. When she was nine, her stepmother divorced her father and left her child, so Maddie, who already was devoted to him, became "almost his mother." During that period, her father worked day and night, seven days a week.

My father would beat us so bad, sometimes we couldn't go to school for three days. I would run away and he would chase me down the street and drag me back, or I would willingly go back, because I loved my father. Most of all I just hated leaving my baby brother.

One night my father caught my older brother and me outside playing instead of being home, and he beat us so hard with brooms and sticks that he raised welts. Then he was out on the steps crying, and he'd come back in and cry real loud and say, "I'm so sorry." He had a drinking problem, but I didn't realize it. He was always having car accidents and the car would be torn up, and then he would come in late at night, crying. He was always crying and I hated it. I hated it.

Maddie tried hard to succeed at school, but there were too many problems at home and she didn't do well. Her art work was chosen for the covers of programs for school events and she was in a musical group as the lead singer and choreographer. Just before her graduation from junior high school she participated in a talent show.

I came out in an outfit my cousin had lent me—a long dress and long gloves—and this guy was waiting and took my fur, and I handed him my gloves and my cousins were all there, and everybody stood up and clapped, and there were pictures taken, and I really *performed*!

But those moments of feeling appreciated were of minor significance compared to other aspects of her life. "My father was killing me mentally," Maddie says. She was so unhappy at home she wouldn't even eat there. She recalls feeling both lonely and angry. She developed physically at an early age and by the time she was eight she had started dating a high school boy, who thought she was older. She was thirteen when she met fifteen-year-old Rick.

Rick had eyes that just lit up! You could spot his eyes across the park! And he had these pretty white teeth. When he smiled those teeth would just glow. He thought a lot of himself and he cared a whole lot about me. He was very sweet and he walked like he thought he was cool. When he saw me he did a double take and that was *it*. He saw my eyes and I saw his eyes, and it was just Maddie and Rick all the way.

Maddie's father didn't share her enthusiasm and tried to make her stop seeing Rick, but she wouldn't give him up, so at sixteen she left home to live with a sister. All her sisters

had married at sixteen, and they supported her decision to
stay away from home.

> We tried to get pregnant. We were going to get mar-
> ried and I wanted to be a June bride, but we didn't care
> which came first. We had no training, no one to talk to. I
> was sixteen when I got pregnant and married. That's
> what everybody did. You are in love, you live together,
> you make love, you have a baby, you get married.

The first violent incident occurred before Maddie and Rick
were married, but when Maddie was already pregnant. Jealous of another man's attentions to Maddie, Rick hit her several times. She took off his engagement ring and threw it at
him, but when he apologized, "explaining" that he only hit
her because he loved her, she forgave him.

Rick didn't hit Maddie again until after they were married,
but for the next ten years he kept Maddie on an emotional
roller coaster. He was alternately cruel and then sweet and
loving. Three or four times a year he kicked and beat her and
she called the police, who usually made him leave for a little
while. Once, shortly after she had given birth by caesarean
section, he knocked her to the floor and left her.

About "seventy-five percent of the time" the relationship
was exciting and fun. After a beating Rick would "call and call
and call," would say he was sorry, would insist that he loved
Maddie and would tell her how much he wanted to be with
her and the children. Maddie would listen to her children call
for their father, would think about her "motherly commitment and wifely commitment" and would take Rick back. After a separation the two lovers would spend several days together skipping work and ignoring other relationships.

> We'd usually go somewhere and spend days totally by
> ourselves. No work, no anything. Just romance. Sex was
> important. We'd play games with it. We'd turn out all
> the lights and play hide and seek, and when I'd see him
> coming at me, I would get so excited I would scream and
> laugh and we would fall over and laugh and laugh. We
> had a lot of fun. We would go to the parks and take pic-

tures all day and run and play and the kids would laugh and play with us, and we were like kids. We were *all* kids. Everybody thought we would never leave each other.

But the fun and games, the good sex and the romance were diminished by Rick's unwillingness to hold a job and were punctuated by his physical assaults, drug abuse and involvement with other women. Periodically the couple separated, but then Maddie would become convinced that Rick was going to change. At one point they had been separated for a year and a half when he persuaded her that he had pulled himself together and had a job. His claim seemed to be backed up by the fact that he was driving a Cadillac, so Maddie began to see him again. She was working at a new job and doing well. Yet she was impressed when Rick dropped by and gave her large sums of money. "We never had a phone most of the time or a car or anything and he was dropping off hundred dollar bills." One night when Rick didn't pick up Maddie as planned, she called him. When a woman answered, Maddie questioned her, and the woman admitted she had been Rick's girlfriend for about two years. She told Maddie that the Cadillac Rick was driving, the diamond ring on his finger, and the money he gave Maddie all came from her. Maddie was furious and the reconciliation was off once more. Again she went through a bad time, but she loved her husband and eventually they were reunited.

Maddie says now that she must have infuriated Rick. "I had such a dirty mouth," she says, "it would get me beat up. One time, when he tore up the Monte Carlo we had owned just thirty days and that I had paid for, I found a lady's shoes in it. I was so mad I provoked him to fight, but as I got a little older I learned to keep my mouth shut."

Rick said he wanted to travel, so he joined the service, but partying and getting high were more important to him than the risk of being AWOL, so he soon became an ex-serviceman. Then he joined the merchant marine, and Maddie decided to go back to school while he went out to sea. But Rick didn't use his sea papers. He was spending his unemployment checks on drugs, so Maddie packed up and went to another city where she stayed with her father until she could get herself established. She got a job the second day after she completed the move. After a brief period of unhappiness in the new city, where it always seemed cold and rainy, she began to appreciate its beauty and to get over her loneliness. She made plans to open a daycare center so she could make a better living and felt pleased with the new life she was making for herself and the children.

And then Rick reappeared. She gave up the daycare plan, they rented an apartment and celebrated their anniversary together.

> He took us out to dinner, me and the kids, and we all had steak and lobster, and the kids had Shirley Temples and we had our Margaritas and it was so nice. The next day, because I had had such a wonderful anniversary, I came home on my lunch break to tell him, "I love you, and I thank you"—and he had a lady there!

Maddie left, but didn't stop seeing Rick. Soon he beat her again; she hit her head and bled profusely. Her daughter became upset and pleaded with her father to let Maddie alone, jumping on his back in a vain attempt to stop him and then running out of the house. Maddie was worried about the effects of the violence on the children and describes it as a terrible time. "But it wasn't enough. I let him back in a couple of weeks later, and the same thing happened." That time Rick made her move all her things into her car, and she and the children were forced to live in it for three days.

Through a girlfriend, Maddie had met another man who called her every night for three months, trying to persuade her to go out with him, but because of the children she wouldn't. "Real square," she says of herself. Nevertheless, the attentiveness of this new man had an impact. She was trying once more to make up with Rick, but once more she had become angry at him, and for the first time she said to him, "I don't give a damn what you say. I don't care what you think of me." She says she had the strength to say that because she knew there was another man who appreciated her.

Rick managed to get into the house one more time. He

locked Maddie in the bedroom and tried to strangle her, but fortunately her brother was there and tore the door down to free her. Rick threw him across the room. After Rick left, he called her all night, and all the following week, alternately telling her he'd kill her and that he still loved her and needed her. But that was finally the end.

I was stretching, waking up from this long sleep, but I didn't know what it was. I was in a daze. I could almost say I was born again. I didn't know what kind of thinker I wanted to be, I didn't even know what kind of mother I was going to be, wha' 'nd of *woman*. I had never thought about what kind of house I liked, I had never thought about how I wanted my children to be. I never thought about anything but Rick coming back and the fighting and trying to make this marriage work. That was it. When I was with him, all I thought about was him and the kids. Anytime things were really getting good or I was thinking about doing something, we would end up fighting and all my attention went to that. But when we were separated, I was in tip-top shape. I would even buy myself clothes when he wasn't around. "I'm *me*, now." I felt *up*!

It's hard developing myself, making myself stop procrastinating. It's hard when you're a single woman and you don't have a man or anybody. I don't have anyone I can count on. When I was in the hospital for a few nights, my kids were by themselves from after school to bedtime. I had to ask for help from a friend, and I'd never learned to ask for help. I keep bumping my head on a lot of hard things.

I get mad at myself, because I like to have company. That's been the biggest thing for me. I miss having somebody to share and communicate with. Sometimes I want to talk to somebody and tell them what's on my mind. I want to share my life with someone, and that's been a big problem for me.

I *miss* a man. I *want* a man. But I'm not really looking for one. Being a young, black, single woman is tough, because first of all the majority of black men available are not at the level of awareness that I have been blessed to be at. What I mean by that is not only recognizing what you want in life, but having the courage to sacrifice to get what you want. Being young and single attracts a lot of men of all ages and they want to promise me the world. I know better. Lots of times on a Friday night I want to go out, but if I went out it would be to find somebody, and no telling what you bring back home.

Maddie did live with a man for a brief period and he was kind to her, but he became involved in drugs and she left him. Now, when she is tempted to go out and find a man, she plays a game with the children or calls a friend. She thinks positively and gives herself pep talks.

"Listen. When the time comes, you'll be okay. In the meantime, take care of your hair, take care of your skin, take care of *you*." I have confidence in myself that, "Maddie, you've always been able to attract a man. It's not that you're spending this time by yourself because you have no one. It's because you're being selectful at this point in your life, and that's the positive part." I fell in love when I was a child, so I never knew anything else. I want to *choose* who I'm involved with this time.

I didn't realize how very seriously affected the kids were until now, until I left the second man. I had been involved with him, and then lived with him, beginning soon after I left Rick. I didn't move into my own house until about five months ago. It's been absolutely amazing to see my kids comfortable. We have a home now. I also see that the year we were going through the divorce and all that, they probably missed all the basics of language to the point they have learning disabilities. Little Rick has a temper and he will fight and he will cry. (A little bit of both of us.) He said, when I finally left Rick, "Mommy, you don't ever have to cry again." And my daughter had drawn a picture of me with tears. I can see now that my kids suffered a lot.

If I had it to do over again, I probably would have still got married and had kids, but I would have thought about how I want to be, how I want to raise my kids. I would have left him though. I probably shouldn't have given Rick more than three or four years of my life. But that's all right. I'm still young.

I've decided to try new ways. I've never had anybody teach me how to take care of myself, never. So, I might be considered, the last few years, a child, learning to take care of herself. I'm dealing with *me*, and that's hard. I'm developing myself, I enjoy people who get out there and take care of their bodies. God gave you a body and if your body's not in shape, that holds you back from a lot of things.

I skated with the kids this summer and I loved it. My mind was *so* clear. I just skated around the lake and I didn't know I could skate so good! So I bought myself skates because that's the kind of life I want to live. And for Christmas I bought the kids and me bikes, too.

I went to an aerobics dance class, and man, I would come home and I would put the radio on and I would dance every night before I would go to bed, and my mind was clear! I realized I'm a person who needs a little physical activity, but all my life all I did was sit and mope and cry and think. Now, I need physical activity in order for me to write. I write poems. I write short stories. And I draw.

I can do things. I'm very capable of doing whatever I set out to do. I surprise myself. I have surprised myself with my ability as a woman to attract men. I never looked at myself as being attractive, or I always thought it was a sexual thing. But I learned about me, my ability to take care of myself, my ability to take care of situations, my awareness.

I've worked in a hospital for three years, in the personnel department. When I started, my paycheck was about three hundred a month, after taxes. My rent was three-eighty. Childcare for two was three hundred and forty! Welfare took up the difference. Now, I'm taking home about four hundred every two weeks, and I have a small business of cleaning offices on the side.

I want to go into the service. I have this deep desire

to see the world and I hate the idea that I have to save for it. I'm thinking about my future. I want to own my home and I don't want to just exist. And I don't want my kids to be all of my life. There may be some negative things about being in the service, and everybody's going to tell me about it, I know that. But I'm talking about the opportunity for education and to travel with my children and maybe when I get out, the opportunity to buy a house. A friend's kids came back talking German. That's impressive to me, a little black girl talking German. I get excited about boot camp, lifting things and running, building my body. I'm scared, but I don't have a man or anything holding me back now. I want to go for it. I want to break out of the norm.

CHAPTER 23

Jane

My father was a lawyer, and my mother was a house-wife and raiser of children. Girl Scouts, church choirs, standard middle-class, small town New England upbringing. There was no abusiveness. None. To be impolite was about the major sin.

We were all pretty normal kids in my family. I'm the middle child of three. I'm more aggressive probably than many women who wind up in this position. That's part of why it was so shocking. But I've always been very independent and fairly intimidating in my own right. As a kid, my house was the center for neighborhood activity and kids came to see what I was planning to do today. I was a leader, but I also spent a fair number of hours in solitary pursuits at the beach or the woods.

I was twenty and pregnant when I married the first time. I had known the man for three years of college and my parents, his parents, everyone thought it was a great idea we should get married. I really didn't think it was a hot idea, but I thought well, all right, I'll try it. We were married five years and had two kids. He's a very nice man, but I'm not very good at being married, staying home and taking care of babies and the house at all. It just was so confining and so unstimulating.

When I left my first husband I went back to my parents' house and finished my last year of college, and I was single, then, for two years. Gerald and I started seeing each other almost as soon as I got back to town. I had the two little kids and I was in school full time, so I was really busy and didn't have any intention of getting married.

Around Christmas time he started pressuring me to get married and I said, "I don't want to talk about it anymore. I can't really think about it until May." Next thing I knew, May was when we were getting married. I really should have had more control over that part, but I had the kids and, coming from the kind of background I did, women—especially women with little kids—were supposed to be married.

I got my degree and we were married. It's hard to say whether I was really in love. Probably not. He was nice, he was fun to be with, he seemed to respond to the same things I responded to. We knew a lot of people in the town in common, so it was a social convenience. He was madly in love with me, which is very unhealthy. I really do take a percentage of the blame for the situation developing, because I should have known he was not equipped to deal with me. It was not a fair thing to do.

Gerald is an only child, his father had been through thirty jobs in his adult life and both his parents have been hospitalized at one point or another for mental disorders. However, I didn't even meet them until maybe four months before we got married. Looking back it's very easy to see the clues that I should have seen. His father was physically and emotionally abusive and his mother was a cowering, self-sacrificing crazy lady. Crazy! As a child, Gerald always had to be in control of the household. He was the sane one, and from the time he was really young he took care of his parents.

Jane believes she fit Gerald's picture of a socially desirable wife from a prominent family, and they were "well matched aesthetically," but there were significant differences, too. Gerald was a silent drinker, politically conservative and at six-foot-three, an imposing figure "used to being accorded respect for his size alone." Jane, an athletic five-seven, was a liberal activist in women's and civil rights causes and "aggressively articulate." She believes it was inevitable that Gerald would be intimidated by her and feel out of control.

Even before the marriage it was apparent that Gerald was "insanely jealous," but since Jane wasn't interested in other men she thought that wouldn't be a problem. His jealousy became so extreme, however, that by the end of the relationship "every size, age, gender and person in town" was suspect to him. Nevertheless, he bought Jane sexy clothes, insisting she wear them to parties. She felt uncomfortable, but wore them to placate him.

When Gerald disliked something Jane said, the veins in his neck would stand out and he would grip the arms of the chair "as if controlling himself by great effort from leaping across the room to rip my head off." Soon after the wedding Jane wondered what she had gotten herself into, but she didn't think of leaving. In her social background there was hardly room for one divorce, and certainly not for two. She told herself, "You did it, you're stuck with it."

Jane worked part-time teaching adult education and tutoring, but mostly she was at home with the children. Gerald, who owned a jewelry store nearby, called "fifty-seven times a day," came home for lunch and sometimes arrived unannounced in mid-afternoon. About six months into the marriage, he had come home at noon and Jane made a political comment as she walked toward the kitchen with the lunch dishes. Without warning Gerald picked up the teak dining room table and threw it against the wall next to her. "It worked," she says. "I shut right up." That was the first time she knew that violence was going to be a problem. "My skin literally crawled. They talk about the hair standing up on your body. It's literally true."

Jane felt she must be doing something wrong, because if she were a good wife and a good person she wouldn't be making Gerald angry. She even began to think she must be flirting with other men without realizing it. She hadn't confided in anyone about Gerald's threatening behavior or her fear of him, so there was no external check on her judgment of the situation. Only once was the violence witnessed by friends. She and Gerald were in their kitchen with another couple when, suddenly, without any explanation, Gerald punched Jane in the face. No one said anything. Jane's mouth began to swell and she said she was going to bed. For reasons Jane never understood, the woman guest urged her not to, and Jane acquiesced. The two couples continued polite conversation for half an hour, and then the guests went home, nothing having been said about the violence.

The most frightening times for Jane were waking up in the middle of the night to feel Gerald's hands around her throat. "It was as if he was doing this in his sleep, but he wasn't." He would be "glassy-eyed and out of control." Jane would talk to him until he was calm, and gradually he would ease up on her throat. As the relationship deteriorated, Jane lay awake in terror more often, and during the last six months the choking occured as often as once a week.

Gerald often prowled around the room and stared at Jane "with an about-to-go-over-the-edge look." The teenaged babysitter was the only person other than Jane who saw him behave that way and she was outspoken in her reaction. "Does he always do that? That's weird! I don't know how you can live with that!" "You mean it's true?" Jane asked. It was a relief to know it wasn't just her imagination.

One Saturday Jane was especially unnerved by Gerald's obsessive surveillance. She told him he had to leave her alone, and he agreed. He then went outside, climbed onto a ladder and started washing the windows outside of the room she was in. "That was his idea of leaving me alone, staring at me through a window instead of staring at me in the same room."

Although Jane was not actually beaten until just before she left, she felt hopeless and terrified. "It was the hands around the throat, it was talking to me in the kitchen while playing with a butcher knife, it was punching the wall." A great deal of Jane's thought and energy went into trying not to make Gerald angry, being charming, entertaining his friends, not saying anything that would upset him, being careful not to interact with any men, contradictory as those requirements were.

One night Jane had a particularly hard time getting Gerald to take his hands from her throat and was frightened enough to say she was leaving. He said he was sorry, he loved her, and that if he ever laid a hand on her again he would leave.

Jane gave in, because, she says, "I was still expecting him to be a sane and rational human being." But this time she moved downstairs to sleep on the couch.

For a year Jane entreated Gerald to go to a therapist, and finally, after she threatened to leave him, he agreed. Jane listed numerous problems to the therapist who turned to Gerald for his interpretation of the difficulties. "There's no problem," he said. "If Jane would just relax, everything would be fine." The counselor said to Gerald, "If you insist on playing ostrich I can't help you; but Jane, I think you could use a little help." It was a relief for her to have an objective person say, "He's denying it."

We had been married two years and he decided that I was having an affair with someone. He came home from the bar and I was asleep on the couch and he just flat out came at me with his fists flying, cursing and just calling me every name in the book and beating on me. I'd never had anyone attack me that way. And I was already lying down, so when he came at me I was not in any position to defend myself. I was totally trapped against the back of the couch. He punched me in the stomach, knocked the wind out of me, and then I was curled up in a ball trying not to get killed, I guess. I don't know how long it lasted, but I thought I was dead. I was unconscious by the time he stopped hitting me. I came to as he was walking up the stairs to do something about my daughter, who I could hear standing at the top of the stairs screaming.

A half hour later he came back down and paced back and forth across the room staring at me, and I thought, "If he comes at me again, I'm going to kill him with the fire poker, because if I don't he's going to kill me." But he took his suitcase and drove off.

In the morning I found that I was really hurt and couldn't walk. Still, I couldn't call the doctor. This was the man who had known my family all our lives. He was a social friend. Obviously it's some problem that I've had a hand in, and I have to deal with it. It would never have occurred to me to call the police. Never. Fairly typical middle-class story. You just don't admit to that kind of problem in your house.

Monday morning the phone rang and Gerald said, "Hi! How you doing?" This was typical behavior after a scene or a threat or choking. Very casual, as if nothing had happened. He said he went to a shrink who told him to move back in. I called the shrink and said, "Did he tell you what he did last night?" He said, "Yes." "Did you tell him to move back in?" And he said, "Well, now calm down. Gerald told me a little about your problem and I think you should come talk to me, because I've had some success in dealing with women with your problem." I hung up and packed and within a half hour I was out. I never went back.

Leaving and getting a divorce were not guarantees that Jane was finished with Gerald. He continued to harass her on the telephone and through the children. But Jane had underestimated people's willingness to help. With the support of her lawyer she told Gerald in no uncertain terms that if he continued to talk to the children in destructive ways, she would not let him see the children at all. With her therapist's backing she learned to hang up on him when he called. Jane moved into a group house, and one of her new housemates made his dog available to her for protection, twenty-four hours a day. Her women friends accompanied her when she retrieved her personal belongings from her house and refused to be intimidated by Gerald standing at the door making obscene remarks. Two male friends taught Jane self-defense exercises, which "felt great." She began doing twenty-five push-ups a day and feeling strong.

Jane's mother was a great support, but her father failed her in significant ways. Jane was hurt when Gerald gained her father's ear after she had left, and this was compounded by her father's denial of the violence months after he had been told about it. Jane respected and loved her father but these were not the first disappointments from him. About six months before she left Gerald, she had told her father Gerald was making her believe she was "crazy," but her father insisted she could handle it. Jane says "the propaganda is that Daddy is strong and will save you, but there's a point at which you go to women because Daddy's unable to handle the emotional turmoil."

After several years of separation Jane is able to be civil to Gerald on the occasions when she encounters him. She sees no signs of psychosis in him, and believes that she "drove him to it." "I know it's there in him, but the kind of person I am triggers the release of that. I don't think he would beat the woman he lives with, because he doesn't beat for pleasure, but reacts with violence when things are out of his control. She says 'Yessir' to him, but I was out of his control."

Jane found no more difficulties socially after her second divorce than the first, but this time she moved to an urban environment and made a new circle of friends, many of whom are single. Jane was "twitchy and nervous" for the first year, and only slowly able to add needed weight to her one hundred and fifteen pounds. She did begin to date, but looked for men who demonstrated non-violent attitudes and even chose those who were close to her own height. The first man she became involved with was a verbally abusive alcoholic, but she was able to end the relationship quickly. She is very assertive now in setting her own limits. She guards against men who are "like little boys," emphatically stating that she already has two children to mother. She is ambivalent about whether she would do things differently, given another chance.

I wish I had been strong enough to break out of it when I knew it was coming. It was impossible to have any light outside of that terror, and that's a really sick thing. On the other hand, I would not change any of it because it was a growing time, eventually. I wish I'd been able to see it as a learning experience, a trial by fire, rather than as being mired in that terror. It was horrible, but I don't see how I could have gotten to the point I'm at without that.

There is no comparison between my life now and then. I feel very much that I have chosen to be where I am. I feel independent of restrictions, either by other people or by society. My needs are not met in marriage and now I am taking care of my own needs and it feels terrific. I feel blessed to have really close friends around me. I have a steady job typing manuscripts and at fifteen thousand a year I'm financially secure. But I'm about to quit the steady job and get back to writing full time. I feel as if twice I sold out for a financial security that the rest of my family thought I should have, and I don't need that.

I have great control over my sexual life. I'm in a relationship now that's emotionally reasonably satisfying. He lives out of the city and we see each other on weekends and the rest of the time he doesn't ask and it's none of his business. I am not afraid. If I'm in a group and I start to feel hostility, even if it's not specifically connected with me, I leave. I go some place where I'll feel better.

At thirty-five I feel the relaxing of the restrictions. I'm a grownup, so no one can tell me what to do any more. My future as far as I can see is totally unlimited. I am free now in a way that I have not been in my entire life and it feels wonderful.

CHAPTER 24

Lucia

Lucia began life in South America, the child of a housewife and a kitchenware salesperson. Her mother was "bright and talented." She had been a teacher before marriage and had rebelled against the social norms of her wealthy family by marrying a poor man. He was an alcoholic who periodically refused to give her household funds, but he wouldn't allow her to work outside the home. She managed the budget by selling her arts and crafts and from periodic subsidies from her mother.

I remember seeing my mother with bruises twice, but three years ago when I confronted my father about them, he denied having hit her. My mother was good at covering up for him and taught my two sisters and me to love and respect him. My mother was always ill and when anything went wrong I felt responsible. I was a nervous child, I had a tic and had problems concentrating at school. When I was ten years old my mother decided it would be good for me to go to the United States and learn English, so I was sent to Texas to live with my two aunts and my grandmother. I missed my mother and sisters, so after a year and a half I was planning to go back. That was to be in June, but in May my mother died of an aneurysm. Instead of me going back, my sisters came to the U.S.

Lucia had a difficult time during her first year at the North American school and was helped through to adjust to the new

country by two Latina girls. During the second year she
learned to speak English and did exceptionally well in school,
even in English composition. By her third year she was in the
most advanced classes and in the sixth grade was chosen vale-
dictorian. School had become her refuge. The rigidity of her
grandmother and aunts became especially oppressive as
Lucia reached her teens and became interested in boys.

My grandmother needed to be in control of everything. She and my aunts were afraid of the bad influ-
ences of the city. They knew about drugs and all that, so
I was not allowed to go out, except very rarely, and I
could only date if my male cousin came along. My
grandmother listened in on my telephone calls. She and
my aunts got involved with the Charismatic Catholic
movement, and I went along with it because I was allowed to mix with other teenagers at church events.

A priest came on to me, though and I began to change
my ideas about the church. About the same time I read
Karl Marx's ideas and began to be political. I had to
clean my cousin's room and iron his shirts, while he was
free to do as he liked. I was argumentative with my
aunts and grandmother and rebelled against the rigid
sex roles, but I felt I wasn't a bad person. I was outspoken, but I was such a goody-goody, there was no reason for my aunts not to trust me. I felt I had to prove
myself to them.

When I was a junior in high school I met Juan, who
was twenty-seven. In my senior year I began to cut
some of my classes to see him. After a fight with my
aunts about something else I threatened to leave with
Juan and after that I was forbidden to see him. I felt so
hopeless about my family that I made a suicide attempt
with an overdose of pills, but I threw them up. My aunts
didn't acknowledge what I had done. I hadn't wanted to
get married, but I couldn't think of another way to get
away from home. Juan didn't want to marry yet either.
He was also from South America and he had a North
American sponsor, but hadn't yet received the "green

card," which would enable him to live permanently in the U.S.

Lucia thought Juan was a "wonderful man." They had much in common, including a desire to eventually do liberation work in South America. By the time she was nineteen he had his "green card" and they were married. He readily agreed that they would share all the household tasks equally and was supportive of Lucia's plan to continue college. In addition to her studies, Lucia had a part-time job in a crisis intervention program.

The first year he was a very nice, understanding, sensitive, caring, human—genuinely good. He helped people out, lent them money, tutored kids and helped them in school. We had fun together, took trips and he was a good companion. In between the beatings, when they were only every two or three months, he was making up for the beatings, and it was crazy-making. After he visited his family in South America and saw the privilege his brothers' wives gave them, he started making the housework all my responsibility and blaming me. He started saying it was school that was taking my time away from home.

I started seeing it as a problem of drugs and thought, "How could I be working in crisis intervention and not be able to help him?" It felt like it was my responsibility to get him away from it. He changed little by little. First it was a push and a slap and a lot of screaming and the next time was three months later and then one month later, and the second year it happened frequently. The last six months it was maybe twice a week and the abuse became much more severe.

It usually exploded when he knew I was studying for finals. I was terrified of him. I used to hide in the bathroom and once he broke the door down. My only recourse was to take a knife, but he took it away. I knew that the next time I was going to be able to stab him and that became very, very scary. I actually did make several attempts. I did fight back, but he was much bigger than I, so usually I would just try to get away. I didn't know about orders of protection. I read about battered women in my classes, but I didn't want to see myself as "a battered woman."

Lucia thought there was no way out, because if she told her aunts they would say, "You wanted to get away from the house and now you see what happens." She felt that she had no one to talk to. However, she did leave twice, one time spending the weekend with a friend. Juan promised to see a therapist, and after she went back to him, he said he had seen a psychologist friend who told him there was nothing wrong with him. The second time she left, she did go to her aunts' and stayed a week. To her surprise they were supportive, but she didn't want to tell them very much. She went back to Juan because she wasn't feeling totally welcome at her aunts' and she still felt responsible for helping Juan with his drug and drinking problems. In addition, she was very frightened that Juan would have her deported.

When Lucia had come back to the United States, after going home to her mother's funeral, her sisters had obtained student visas, but she was not able to get hers renewed. One of her aunts hoped that if she adopted the girls she would be able to sponsor them to get "green cards", but by the time the adoption proceedings were completed Lucia was sixteen, and too old to be allowed that kind of sponsorship. Once they were married, Juan had applied to be her sponsor, but it was taking a long time to get the papers approved. She wasn't questioned, but she did think it necessary to lie about her country of origin on her college admissions application and "there was always the fear and the threat of being deported," she says. "I got by, but that's very rare. Most undocumented people don't speak English and don't know the American way. They don't know how to survive."

He would always use it against me, that he would withdraw the papers, wouldn't be my sponsor anymore, that he was going to have me deported, was going to tell them I had been working illegally. He used it as one more tool to intimidate me into not doing anything about the abuse. It was a big part of why I went back to him. I didn't want to, but if I could just kind of take it until I got my "green card," maybe I could get away from him.

He scared me in the way he exaggerated the risks involved. Now that I know immigration law, I know I would not have been deported, or not as quickly as I thought, because I had been living in the U.S. so many years and have been a good citizen. I didn't know what I would do if I went back to South America, how I would survive.

Everything Lucia had confided in Juan was used by him against her. He said that she was such a troublemaker that nobody cared about her, that no one would want her because of her "big mouth." She became much more quiet and submissive, withdrawing into herself. She gave up her friends, her school activities and the political action she had begun to be involved in. One of the more painful beatings occured when she was recovering from having two wisdom teeth removed. She reacted by taking an overdose of codeine and other medicine, along with alcohol, and was taken to the hopital where her stomach was pumped.

At first I was very depressed. After the suicide attempt it was very scary to see myself almost dead. But I decided I wasn't going to kill myself because of this man. I thought "He's not worth it." That was it. I wasn't going to take it any more. And I started feeling hatred. I actually started thinking that I was capable of killing him, and that was very disturbing because I didn't want to be a murderer.

I knew I had to leave, but how was I going to explain to my family that I had, by their standards, failed in my marriage? I still cared about him, so how was I going to leave him without hurting him? What would I do with myself, where would I live? I didn't want to live with my aunts. They have this Victorian idea that once you're married, it's the end of your life. I was afraid they would see me as a divorced woman and they would have to guard me or I would be this promiscuous woman. I would have to regress. Even with Juan I had some level of freedom I didn't have with them. He would go away for a month or so to training and they were vacations for me.

I had been working at the crisis center and I resigned and started to look for other kinds of work. There was an ad for a counselor to do education with teenagers about battering. I don't know what made me send the application in but I did. I was offered the job, but I said I would feel like a hypocrite, and then I told the woman I was being battered and she was wonderful. She told me about orders of protection and about shelters. I was at such a point that it was enough for me just knowing that there was somebody there. She gave me support and told me I was not the only one. I needed to hear that it wasn't my fault, that there were a lot of other women going through the same thing and that there was a way out. It opened my eyes. I met her in June and I left in September.

I didn't go to a shelter, but I got an order of protection a week later. I hadn't served him with the papers yet, because I was terrified about how to do it. We went to this party and he got drunk and he started beating me in the street. I called out for help, but no one would help. He punched me in the stomach and in the face, and he kicked me with his cowboy boots, he banged my head against the cement and he tried to choke me. It was very bad, the worst beating I had ever gotten. I took advantage of one second when he let go and I took my shoes off and ran and hailed a cab and asked him to take me to the police. I had to wait and wait at the police station and I made the police come with me to the house, and I showed them the protection order. Juan resisted arrest and called them names and that really made the cops angry and they arrested him immediately. That was the final beating.

He was arrested and told not to come around the apartment, but of course he did. I went to a friend's and then to my grandmother's. Then I moved in with a friend. And that was that. The same woman who had interviewed me told me about a job at another shelter. She told them about me and six months later they hired me. The fact that I was a formerly battered woman was respected. All of a sudden it was a good thing, not bad. And I could put my experience to use.

Several things contributed to Lucia's decision to leave and her ability to stay away. Her fear of her own anger was one motive. In addition, the last beating was terrifying, and by calling the police she felt she had pretty well burned her bridges. "When I finally called the police," she says, "it meant that I was ready to leave. I had never called them, because he is a Latino man and I knew he was going to be treated very badly by the police. And I knew it would make it bad for him because he was politically active and I had felt responsible for protecting his image."

When she reached the point at which she knew she had to leave, Lucia had more hope of surviving than previously—she had learned about protection orders, she had finally obtained her "green card" a few months earlier, and she had graduated from college. She recalls college as "the only sane thing" in her life. "No matter how bad the beatings were," she says, "and no matter how hard he tried to make me fail, I kept going. It made me maintain my self-respect and feel like there was something good about me. I don't know how I managed it, but I never got a failing grade in any of my courses. While I was in school I was able to think about other things, to meet other people. I really felt like he was taking pieces of me apart, but in college I was doing something for myself that he couldn't take away from me."

Once I left him it was amazing how clearly I could see things. I had taken a couple of courses in women's studies, but I had never used the term "feminist" for myself. I think that all along I really was a feminist, but I never saw myself as that, because feminism has such negative connotations, especially for Latina women. White middle class feminism wasn't going to do it for me. Women's liberation didn't mean having the same job as a man. It meant more being treated with respect.

The first year at the shelter was tremendous. I was so hungry for knowledge, I worked from nine in the morning until nine at night. Everything I did felt so important and I was getting so much out of it, learning so much, experiencing so many wonderful things. It was then I really started seeing as myself as a feminist. The second year at the shelter I started looking at racism and how battering is different for Latina and other women of color, and started pushing for racism work within the project.

A lot of people would perceive my story as typical: "Her mother was a battered woman, so she's a battered woman." Well, yes, and no. I saw it happening to my mother, and I struggled against the current, but I wasn't strong enough and it took me over. It wasn't learning the behavior so much as understanding the role expectations. Women are supposed to be a certain way and men are supposed to be a different way. My family wasn't all that different from a lot of others, but it was the two cultures clashing that left me feeling unclear about who I really was. In the U. S. a woman is more able to go out and do things on her own, or at least there's a feeling that women are able to be more independent. This is all different from Latin cultures.

My aunts, in some ways, lead feminist lives. They relied on themselves, did things for themselves, with no men in their lives and they are very strong women in some ways. I had strong role models. It was very confusing because they were telling me men were the ones that had the last word, were smarter than women, yet they were showing me it was possible to do things on your own.

Something good came out of the ugliness. The abuse made me a better person. I've learned to appreciate myself and to be more sensitive to others, especially women. It made me stronger. I know that I have to rely on myself. And now I know too that it's okay to rely on others.

What would I say to undocumented women who are battered? Don't give up. You might not think you're worth very much, if you're at risk of being thrown out, you don't speak English and you're perceived as a criminal. But you are worth very much. Try to be strong. If you can't be strong alone, identify with someone else who is. You can find a safe and secret place to be. You can find help and learn the truth about your rights.

Life is very busy. I like doing the things I'm doing. My relationship with my family has improved because I can set limits with them now. They have learned to respect me. My sisters are very important in my life.

I felt like I had put myself on a shelf and locked myself in, dedicated my whole life to Juan. When I left it felt as if I had found the key, opened that shelf and gotten myself out, dusted myself off, and started a new life.

CHAPTER 25

Margaret

I had one sister. She passed away when she was three, so I was really raised as an only child. I can't ever remember living with my father. I had a stepfather. I don't recall seeing any violence in my childhood. My mother passed away when I was fourteen. One day she was home and the next day she had to have an operation and she came back home and they rushed her to the hospital again. Everything was kind of hazy. No one ever bothered to tell me exactly what it was she died from.

My father was a single man, he lived in a hotel room, drove a cab, and there was no place for a fourteen-year old child. I lived with a girlfriend, a little here, a little there, it was very disjointed. My father paid for my room and board, you might say, but never what I needed. He never bought clothes for me or anything like that. Then he went away and I was more or less on my own. I was a good student when I was little, but in high school it seemed like I just couldn't get anything through my head. I dropped out in my first year, basically because of not having proper clothing, and maybe not having anybody to take an interest. I sold shoes, worked in a restaurant, in the shipyard, in a laundromat, did pressing, anything I could learn on the job.

Margaret was married to Ken just before her eighteenth birthday. He was an alcoholic and began to batter her almost immediately. He gave her black eyes, bruises and threatened her with a gun and an axe. She managed a laundry, often working a twelve-hour day, seven days a week. Ken drank at the local bar while she worked and when he came home he often accused her of having a man in the back room of the laundry. She's not sure why she finally left, but after twenty years she had had enough. Their five children were mostly teenagers at the time of the separation.

Margaret had lost the laundromat job before she left Ken and he was often unemployed, so she had to support her children even when they lived with him, which the boys sometimes did. She couldn't qualify for public assistance because she and Ken had been buying a house, which was seen as a financial resource. She sold her furniture, her dishwasher and everything she could get her hands on and received a little bit of help from her stepfather. She was lucky that she had a friend who told her when Ken was working and when he got paid, so she occasionally could get a little money from him. Through the state employment office she was able to take a course in wiring, which qualified her for work at an aircraft plant. She made a good living at it for about two years and then her next-door neighbor introduced her to Roy.

He had a very good personality and he really was easy to get along with. I loved him. We liked the same things. We liked to go camping and fishing. He was an outdoorsy type person. We were just always going and doing something. He loved the grandchildren, was always good to them. He had a pretty hard life. He was about seventeen years old and he wrote a check for a pair of cowboy boots that wasn't any good. They put him in prison for about a year. He was involved in something else and they put him in for five years for that. I didn't know this for a long time.

He had a lot of complaints. He was a baby sometimes. He liked a lot of being waited on. When he was drinking he'd say, "Margaret, fix me a drink. Margaret, open me a beer." I always took his coffee into him in the morning in bed. Weekends I'd take him his paper. He'd stay right in the bedroom and read the paper, but if I took off he'd be on that telephone until he ran me down.

When he was drinking his temper came out. The first

time he hit me was in '66. I sit and think that this didn't start until later, but it really started right away. I guess you really don't see it as that. You hide it, you lie about it. You have a black eye or something, gee, you fell down or ran into a door or something. He could be very nice. I'd come home and find a present on the table, things like that. He'd say he was sorry, but he didn't want to get into it. He didn't want to hear any more about it. Period. When you're hurt you want to talk about it and find out why. I just didn't figure I deserved it.

If I could run, I ran. Sometimes I went to my daughter's, sometimes to friends, and he would get on the telephone and be calling all over. If I went to their house, then they knew something was up. Or if they came and there was a big fight going on, naturally they knew, but lots of times I didn't even tell the children. You're not too proud of something like that.

He broke my nose a couple of times. I'd been in an accident where I'd had my ribs broke. They were just about healed up and he knocked me down and broke both of them again. Another time, in our friend's camper, he got mad and he hit me and knocked me into the wall and broke a big chunk out of the camper and gashed my head. I just pushed it together, you know. There were a lot of times I should have gone to the doctor, but didn't. That's like washing your dirty linen. I know now it's better if you go and you talk. I think it's great to have the shelters.

The kids would maybe use the tools and not put them back and he could just get furious with them. When Sally was about sixteen he went after her and knocked her down about three or four times. She's real stubborn and she'd get right back up. She didn't figure he had any right. Once he called up the kids and told them it was open hunting season on my son, Steve, and all his friends. I don't know what in the heck that was about.

I called the police once. He was threatening me with a gun and was gonna shoot me and I ran in the bedroom and I called the police and I stayed in there. He was hollering at me that if they did come up, he was gonna shoot the officer. When the officer came Roy put the gun behind the door and then he answered it. I was still worried and I told the officer where the gun was, but he just looked at it, picked it up and told Roy to leave. That's all he did. Roy said, "That will be the last time you call the police," and I never called them again.

He beat me in front of a Chinese restaurant and some people who drove into the parking lot seen him knock me down and called the police. They took him to jail and called an ambulance and took me to the hospital. I had a head injury. Even though I didn't call the police I might just as well have. He was very uptight about it. I figured if I called the police after that, it was just going to be twice as bad. They don't do anything anyway.

Roy was an ex-convict and if he broke parole, or if I'd pressed charges and sent him to jail, they would probably have taken him back to prison. I didn't want to press charges because I was afraid of what would have happened when he got out of prison.

I didn't care about the drinking when we were fishing, but if he got violent on one of the trips then it kind of spoiled things. Sometimes he'd come home from his evening shift and he'd sit there 'til four o'clock in the morning and drink. I would see him and my next-door neighbor sit down with a fifth of whiskey and it's gone. I'd have maybe two or three drinks out of it. At the very last, he went in for an operation and he had something wrong with his back. He didn't work for two months and all he did was drink. He would be drunk in the morning.

After that operation he was terrible. He had me running, waiting on him. There was nothing that was right, it was constant. I couldn't sit down. I couldn't clean the house, I couldn't do anything. It was nervewracking 'cause he was worse than any child. He'd be up at the tavern every weekend. He'd go up there and he'd play poker and drink. Sometimes he'd be very happy, but you never knew what was going to upset him. I think he had eight D.W.I.'s.

I didn't drink as heavy as he did. I had a beer with

him when he came home or something. But I think my drinking would be classified in excess. I was reading an article and they say if you get drunk two times a year, that's in excess.

I thought about leaving and I called once about a divorce, but I thought I'd be lonely. I guess I was pretty dependent on him. He was a machinist and a very good worker. He could be out 'til two o'clock in the morning drinking and he'd be on the job. When I try to talk to somebody about Roy, I think it'd be pretty difficult for them to understand. He wasn't always bad.

The night that it happened he was just as nice as could be, all day. There was no argument, there was no fight, nothing I could pinpoint. It was evening, about dusk. Roy and his friend, Henry, sat around drinking and then Henry went home and said, "Why don't you guys come on over later?" And Roy sat around for a while and he wandered over there. When he didn't come back I went over, too. When I walked in the door he told Henry to tell me to go home.

Henry said no, he wasn't gonna do that because I had as much right to be there as he did and I was invited, too. And then Roy got up and he went into the restroom. Instead of coming back into the kitchen where we were sitting he walked out and got in my car, so I went out and asked him where he was gonna go. He said he was going home, and I said, "Move over, I'll drive," and I drove the car on home.

We got in the house and I think Roy went into the bedroom right away and got undressed. I went out and started to get something for dinner and I asked him if he wanted something to eat. He got a little upset about it and I told him he should eat something because he'd been drinking so heavy. The next thing I knew, he hit me in the head and chicken went flying all over the house and I ran into the bedroom and I was gonna go to bed. He came in after me and started hitting me again and grabbed me by the hair and pulled me across the bed.

He drug me, pulled me across the room, had me by the hair and the gun was on the floor. I don't know whether he'd had it underneath the bed or what, but it shouldn't have been there. We had a lot of guns in the house, pistols and black powder guns and rifles and shotguns. There was a lot of guns, but we didn't keep any of them loaded because I have nine grandchildren.

So I picked up the gun. I was trying to get his hand out of my hair and I had the gun in my right hand. I don't remember pulling the trigger, I really don't. I remember grabbing the gun, and that's just about it. It just seemed to . . . it just went off and that was it. But I consciously don't remember pulling that trigger and I didn't aim it. No way.

He fell partly on the bed. I got him up on the bed and then ran for the telephone. I called the operator to get an ambulance and I called my daughter. It was just mass confusion. My son-in-law was just down the road and he got there first. I was trying to hold Roy on the bed. He kept slipping off. I kept trying to stop the blood.

I guess the police came next. I'm hazy about that. One minute there was just my son-in-law and I, and then I remember somebody else coming, police, ambulance, I'm not sure just who did arrive. The next thing I knew it seemed like the whole house was full of people. All the kids, the next-door neighbor, the detective. I felt kind of numb. I didn't want to live. I knew he was dead, and yet I didn't know. It couldn't have happened, it just couldn't have happened.

I felt down about everything, just everything. I don't think that there's anything that could have been worse. Losing my mother, my father, basically it's the same thing, except I felt worse because I had caused the death. I had to have caused it. There was only two of us. It's something I did. I'm part of this, I did it.

I was in jail for about nine or ten days. It was terrible. At first my attorney told the kids he didn't want me out anyway. I was suicidal, so he figured I was better off in there. It bothers me still to talk about it. It was about a year before the trial came up. I had to pay a thousand dollars bail and no one had a thousand dollars. I still have a list of things that people sold and of the people who gave money for the bail.

I lost my house insurance. The day it came out in the paper they just canceled it, for no reason. I couldn't get a job. I put in for one of the grocery stores and talked to my attorney first and he said if they asked about felonies I had to tell them the truth. I watched them tear up the application. If you do tell them the truth, forget it. You're out. If you lie to them it's the same thing.

My daughter and I were together in a restaurant and she said hello to someone she knew and introduced me to him. The man came unglued. He was ranting and screaming in this public place, that I should be in jail. There were other episodes like that, that went on for about four years. I wouldn't go anyplace, except where people were expecting me.

I got a job as outreach worker in a children's hospital. My daughter got in a fight with her in-laws and her mother-in-law called them and said I was a child abuser. I was immediately fired. I went to my attorney, but he said because of my record of the felony and being accused of child abuse, I had to keep a low profile. Both son-in-laws called up my boss and tried to explain it, but she wouldn't listen.

A lot of people I thought were friends were not. But a lot of people did stick by me. The next-door neighbor, who was Roy's best friend, was very supportive through the whole thing. Roy's mother stuck by me and people knew how Roy had treated me. My son said he knew it would happen some day, but he always thought it would be me. People can be supportive, but you're by yourself, regardless. That's all you can say, you're by yourself. Where do you go? What do you do? There didn't seem to be any place to go.

Margaret finally found a job putting components in form boards, but several months later she developed nerve damage, which paralyzed her arm and she temporarily lost some speech. During that period she lived with a daughter. "My kids supported me all the way," she says. "Without them I couldn't have gotten through it."

For reasons that were never clear, the prosecuting attorney didn't talk to Margaret, so she didn't have an opportunity to tell her side of the story until she was on the witness stand. She feels strongly that if she had been given that chance, she would never have been charged with first-degree murder.

As it was, she never imagined she would be convicted. "Why, I figured," she says, "as soon as I tell my story everything is going to be fine." In spite of unrebutted evidence that on the night of his death Roy was assaulting Margaret and that he intended to seriously injure or kill her, she was convicted of second-degree murder and sentenced to twenty years in prison.

Margaret was given tranquilizers and slept for three days. Her attorney appealed immediately, and she didn't have to go back to prison during that process. Three years later the state supreme court overturned the conviction on the basis that the trial judge had given the jury an incorrect instruction. For over a year Margaret was kept in suspense about whether the prosecutor would choose to try the case again. Finally, the decision was made not to do so.

That was four years ago and for a couple of years I just felt down. I think I cried for two years until I finally come to the realization that if you don't do something for yourself there's nobody else's gonna do it for you.

Vocational rehab. paid for my books and tuition and I went to college. I was scared to start and I was so surprised to find out I can really learn, I can really do this. I can get A's. I always have been a real nervous person and I'd go in for a test and I'd be in a sheer panic. My stomach would get going and I'd be shaky and perspiring. I'd know the answer and I'd just completely forget it. I'd just sit there and tell myself, "Now, before you go in, do this deep breathing." There were about thirty students and after two years, only four of us got our certification as occupational therapists. I graduated with a 3.6

or 3.7. I'm very proud of my degree. I just wish I could have gone to school years ago.

Before I got my certification a friend introduced me to Erik and he asked me to go to a dance the next Saturday night. It was as simple as that. The day we met we hit it off and we've been together ever since. We lived together for a while and then got married. One of the main reasons I didn't go back to work is that he's a superintendent for a construction company and a lot of his work entails going out of town. He'd just have a fit if I wasn't with him, even if it's just a short distance. I don't like living in the motor home but he doesn't like to be alone either, so you go, whether you want to or not. We both make decisions, but if it's something he really wants, he'll ge it. He's got a heck of a temper, but the man is not physically abusive.

I tell Erik he's so nasty tempered he can't retire; I can't stand to have him in the house. He rants and raves. I holler back at him, mostly over the children. There's a lot of jealousy there. He thinks I'm too involved and dislikes it if I call them. My daughter and I get on the phone and talk for hours and he doesn't like that.

I know he wouldn't hit me, but if he did, I'd probably hit him back and then run. The one time he was drinking and got verbally abusive, I called his son and told him to come down and get him out of here and he did.

My husband just bought me a nice new sewing machine, so I do a lot of sewing. I keep up my certification and I told my husband I'd like to go back and take a review course to keep up to date. He doesn't really understand why I want to do this, but even though I am sixty years old, I might need it. Something might happen to him.

Do I wish I'd done something different? Doesn't everybody? Probably I would have divorced Ken the first time we broke up after I had my first child. That was a big mistake. But then I wouldn't have had my other four children. I used to think about hitting Ken with the frying pan, but I was always afraid of hurting somebody, and yet look what happened.

Naturally, I'd have probably left Roy, too. I don't know when I should have left, but I should have gotten out. The other day I was thinking and I got really angry at the things he did. I think that's the first time. I thought, "What's going on here? All of a sudden I'm getting angry." It was a strange feeling for me to be angry at him now, and saying, "Look what you did to me." I often wonder what I did with my anger before. I didn't kick the dog, but I probably felt like it. I guess I did a lot of house cleaning and banging around. I think I broke a lot of dishes.

Sometimes I think I have completely forgiven myself and sometimes I don't feel like I have. I think this has had a great effect on my children's lives. Their attitudes changed. It's made my daughters more aggressive toward the men in their lives. I feel responsible.

I don't think it's the way to go. It does too much to you, that you're just not going to ever get over it. Sure, if you have to do something, you have to, you're going to fight. But do I advocate it? No.

CHAPTER 26

Ruth

I'm the youngest of four children. I don't remember seeing abuse, yet my mother tried to commit suicide and I heard about things my father did, this horrible disciplinarian. They were separated by the time I was five or six, but they weren't divorced until I was eleven. It was on again off again, in the house, out of the house. "How are we going to get Dad out of the house?"

I was also aware that my father had raped my mother, thinking that if she were pregnant he wouldn't have to leave. I even used to think that I saw the rape, but I don't know if I made that up from hearing stories from my mother and her sister. I was supposed to choose between my mother and my father. He was not a great father by any means, yet he was the one that was fun, that played with us. I can remember neighbors asking about the divorce and making it obvious that my family was different because of the divorce. And we were different because we were Jewish.

I was very athletic and very shy. In school I didn't have friends. I always felt like the outsider. I was very involved in the temple and with the family I adopted, which was the family of the rabbi. The temple was a half to three-quarters of a mile away and the rest of the family was not into it, but I would walk to it every Saturday. That was sort of my salvation.

I spent all of my time in high school in the gym and around the gym teachers. My life was volleyball and swimming and for the first time I was getting all this at-

tention for being an athlete. I didn't date at all and I was
always aware I wanted to be with women. In college I
decided I didn't know if I was a lesbian, but I decided I
wanted to sleep with a woman. By that time my friend,
Bella, had come out to me, so one night I told her I was
frightened to be by myself and told her to come over.

I was maybe just eighteen and now we had slept together and now I was stuck with her for the rest of my
life, and all I had wanted to do was sleep with her. I
didn't even like her that much. I stayed with her maybe
seven or eight months, and then I cheated, I slept with
Alice, this other woman on the volleyball team. It was
the first time that here was someone I really wanted to
be with. Bella found out about it and I stopped seeing
her after about three months.

For reasons she can't explain, Ruth went back to Bella until, a few months later, she again slept with Alice and was
caught, which ended the relationship with Bella. But Ruth
found herself once again commited to a partnership, this time
with Alice, when all she had wanted was a quick sexual connection. Although she doesn't say that Alice battered her,
Ruth was afraid of her because she was "mean," and once
threw an iron at Ruth.

Ruth continued to live at home, but didn't tell her family
she was a lesbian. Although she found it exciting to be in an
"underground world," she didn't feel good about deceiving
her family. She wasn't happy with her college major in physical education. Teaching was not a stimulating idea; what she
really wanted was to keep playing. Then her mother upset
her by marrying an anti-Semitic man, getting a "nose job"
and moving to a new city where "there were no Jews anywhere."

Alice's best friend, Jean, was involved with Robin,
who was this wild woman, sleeping around all over the
place. I was twenty-two and she was eight years older,
worldly, she did drugs, she was black and she would
come on strong to me. I was in lust, there was no doubt
about it. We would be sitting around and I couldn't even

breathe from the sexual tension, yet Alice and Jean were not even aware of what was going on. When they were out of the room I would be literally running around a chair to get away from Robin, but there were times when we kissed for a split second and then I pulled away.

The problem was it was so exciting. I wanted to be there. I had a lot of black friends and I thought I was very open, but looking back now, I probably wasn't. I was scared to death because I couldn't imagine what her body was going to look like. I said that to her and she got up and proceeded to show me in a really crude way what it looked like. It was really scary. Now I had gone too far and she was standing up there and showing me. I was at Robin's apartment and she said, "You wouldn't be here if you weren't looking for it, and you might as well just admit it." She was right, but I felt so guilty.

Ruth was afraid of Robin as much as she was excited by her. "Robin was so crazy, just sexually, she was so crude, she couldn't walk down the street without something happening." Again, Ruth wanted the sex, but not a commitment, yet she felt that one went with the other. Finally she did sleep with Robin and told Alice that their relationship was over. Then she felt committed to Robin, committed to being "the good Jewish girl."

About six weeks later, Ruth wanted to take Robin home for Thanksgiving dinner, but her new stepfather, Clyde, said no, and Ruth said, "If she's not welcome here, I'm not welcome here," and she moved out of her family's home. Yet she didn't trust Robin and didn't think the relationship was going to be good. Although Ruth smoked marijuana she didn't drink and she always had the feeling she couldn't keep up with Robin, who was "always high" and seemed to have no limits. Robin worked for an underground newspaper and said she had been to college, but later Ruth discovered she hadn't finished high school. Ruth often did her written work for her.

I got my first job and was very nervous the night before I started. I was getting into bed, and she said,

"You're not sleeping in this bed." I said, "What do you expect me to do?" She told me to sleep in the chair, and I went to the chair. I just waited for her to go to sleep and I was going to go home and forget this whole thing. I got up to go to the door and she said, "If you touch the door, I'll break your arm." I got back into the chair and stayed. I didn't have any sense of her rage before that. That was the first time I knew I was afraid of her.

The abuse started very fast. I remember feeling very caged. She kicked and pushed and I just remember always being beaten. I was afraid to get out of the house. I was afraid to be in the house. But I always said to myself, "You're strong, she hasn't broken you. She'll never break you."

I was taking a shower and she pulled me out and I backed up and said, "Just don't touch me, just tell me what you want." And she said, "Get out of the house." It was the middle of winter, and she said, "Get out of the house now, without your clothes on." We lived on the top floor and I went up the ladder to the roof and just tried to hide behind the skylight. I went to sleep up there, and eventually she called me to come down and I came in and she was holding me and crying and saying, "Why can't you love me the way you love Alice?" I remember thinking, "She broke me." That was it. I knew she had.

There was still fear and terror, but it was sort of like she was beating a dead person. I was in such a state of grief over my own death in some ways. There was a part of me that was dead, and it almost just didn't matter. At that point I was almost completely isolated from friends and family.

Patrice, my best friend since I was a little kid, knew Robin hit me, and I would run away to Patrice's house after a battering. Robin would call and say, "Come back or I'm going to tell your job you're a lesbian" or "I'm going to tell your family." The job thing didn't matter much because I wasn't even functioning and eventually I was fired, but my family did. Or she would say, "Come back, I'm sorry." Whatever it was, I always went back. I don't think when I left I thought I was going to stay away, until that last night. I didn't realize up to that point that she was going to kill me, although she had come after me with broken bottles and weapons.

One time she said to me, "I don't want you to see Patrice any more." I knew that if I gave up Patrice I was dead. I said, "You've taken away everything. I will never give up Patrice." And the next thing I remember was being on the floor and she was on top of me and hitting me.

The worst of it was the feeling of insanity, the feeling that you can go too far and never come back again. Mostly it was from terror. Everything I did was going to get me abused. She was sleeping with this guy and she knew I hadn't been with any men, and she used to tell me she was going to bring him over and that I was going to sleep with him. I was terrified of that.

One night I said, "I'll stay with you, but I will not sleep with you." I was stupid enough to think I could get away with it. I tried to go to sleep and she started coming on and becoming more and more aggressive and I was saying I wasn't interested. She went to the bathroom and I thought, "This is my chance," and I got up to get dressed. I got my stockings on and my one boot and the next thing I knew I was hit from behind and she was punching me and punching me and she was telling me that she was going to have me and I remember hearing the crunch when she bit through my nose.

Then I thought, "It's just not going to happen this time, and I smashed her as hard as I could between the eyes with my fist. Unless I'm mistaken, I think I could have taken down a cow with that punch. She just smiled down at me, and I can remember thinking, "This is it," and she took me by the hair and was smashing my head against the wall. I remember watching the wall turn red and all I wanted was to remember the day I died on. I must have been screaming because somebody called the police and they were knocking on the door. She must have stopped long enough that I got on the floor and was crawling to the door.

She was still kicking me and biting me and I remember feeling like I was in a movie. I remember reaching up and getting the door open and seeing the police there and then she fell back against the wall and said, "I have a lease to this apartment, this woman is trespassing." My father was a police captain and she said, "Her father is a police captain and she's a lesbian and a Jew and she works for the Catholic Senior Center." The cop said, "This is great: a nigger lesbian and a Jew that works at the Catholic Senior Center. Did you ever think of going on The Gong Show?" The other cop was very good. I remember him picking me up and taking me to the bathroom and washing my face and trying to see how bad things were.

They took me outside and the cop said how he'd been married for so many years and, "I've never done this to my wife. Why are you a lesbian? You probably just need to be with a man." I remember looking up at him and saying, "Why don't you just go fuck yourself?" I had had it.

I slept for days, I just slept. I don't know how much later I went in to work and at that point Robin called and—are you ready for this?—she said she was going to the hospital for a hysterectomy and would I come? She had no family and they needed somebody to give blood. I remember saying, "I've given enough blood." And that was it.

I came out of there pretty racist. I saw black as drugs and sleeping with anybody, stupid, not educated. Before that I felt really open. I had never dealt with it in any kind of political way, but just on a gut level I had stood up to racist remarks and didn't want any part of anybody I thought was a racist. It took a very long time for me to see that a lot of it wasn't black/white, it was who Robin was.

Ruth began going out with Donna, her first feminist friend. She met feminists and other politically aware people and was exposed to an analysis of racism and sexism. She became involved with a committee against violence against women,

which helped her broaden and deepen her political awareness and it was to them that she came out as a battered lesbian. One of the women on the committee is black and Ruth
says, "Her softness and positive strength couldn't have been a
better role model."

Ruth and Donna worked together and they "sort of
courted," but never had sex. Ruth was enjoying her freedom
and never wanted to be in a relationship again. She was willing to be just friends indefinitely, even though she was attracted to Donna, but Donna finally decided she wanted
more than a nonsexual relationship, and persuaded Ruth to
go into therapy. Ruth's "flashbacks" of her experiences with
Robin made it difficult for her to develop a sexual relationship, but Donna was gentle and patient and after a long time
Ruth began to feel good about making love.

I was so fearful of confrontation. If anything gets hot
at all I still use humor to get out of it. Getting out meant
finding myself. Now through therapy and other supports
I can see the connections between why I got into that relationship and my early years with my family. I was
brought up to be a peacemaker, peace at any cost. If you
want me to cook, I'll cook, if you want me to clean, I'll
clean. I'll never hit, I'll remain the nice Jewish girl.

Telling people what was happening would have
meant coming out all over the place and at that time I
was still interested in teaching in the public schools.
Robin would say to me, "You'll never teach because of
the coming out stuff." There were no services for battered lesbians and there was no information about options. Who would even think of it? The other thing is not
being able to put a label on it, because it's a woman. For
instance, my definition of rape was penetration with a
penis.

I had always used the phrase "beaten up." I saw myself in a bad situation, not as a "battered woman." I
would have been horrified, scared to death. That means
I'm one of *them*, somebody out of my experience, and
that I'm weak and out of control. And straight. I went to
a conference for battered lesbians and even though I had

been working on this problem for a while, I had never seen another battered lesbian—and when I saw another battered lesbian it wasn't a good feeling. On some level it was great that we could recognize each other and support each other. But my God, *I didn't make this up.* This really was happening.

Now I teach computer science and I'm working on a book about lesbian battering. It has allowed me to get rid of a lot of my anger. I have great women in my life, I like who I am, I'm comfortable with who I am. I feel like I have control of my life.

CHAPTER 27

Terry

I grew up in Taiwan. My father was a seaman, but when I was in fifth grade he went to San Francisco and worked for a rich Chinese family as a housekeeper, and he came home only once or twice a year, so I don't really know him. He would stay with us one or two months. I know him as a father who sent a check every month. My father liked to hit people. Every time he come, I start shaking. I don't like to see him home. Too scary. My mother get upset when my father hit us, but she won't say anything. She know it won't do any good. She just cried.

Terry's father would banish her from the house when he was angry, even when it was snowing and she had no boots. When she was about ten years old she was caught with stolen money and her father punished her by waking her up in the middle of the night and hitting her; this went on for several nights. She felt she deserved to be punished, but not so severely, and she was in such despair over his treatment that each day when she looked at a kitchen knife she thought, "I'm going to kill myself tonight."

Terry worked hard in school, but she believed she wasn't smart and had trouble memorizing lessons. A teacher hit her hands so hard that she couldn't use her fingers for some time. Her reaction to the fear of more pain was to get up at four o'clock in the morning to study, and after that her school work improved.

In high school Terry became a model student and was rewarded by receiving a certificate of merit. There were strict rules at the all-girls school she attended, and anyone who dated or attended parties was subject to expulsion. After graduation at seventeen Terry wanted to go to a fashion design school, but her family had barely enough money to eke out a living. Her father had insisted that the family move to the United States, but Terry refused to go, and because her mother wouldn't leave without her, her father stopped sending them money. Her mother was forced to sell the family house and after two years their savings were depleted. Terry gave in and the family moved to the United States.

A few days before she left Taiwan a neighbor took Terry aside and showed her a picture of a woman she claimed was Terry's natural mother. She appealed for compassion, and asked Terry to give her a picture of herself for her "mother." She said "Your own mother is so sick, she's crying so much, because you're leaving the country." Terry could not believe it, and refused to give or take any pictures. She was puzzled and upset, but felt she couldn't ask her parents about it.

When the family moved to San Francisco, Terry could only find work in a sewing factory. For the first few weeks she and her mother—joined by her brothers after school—cut threads from newly made clothing for three cents a garment. Terry could earn eight dollars a day if she completed work on two hundred jackets or pairs of pants. She recalls those days with disgust. "I could smell the dead rats. It was an old building, and they would die and we could not find them. We would get there at seven in the morning and at the latest we would finish at eleven o'clock at night. If you sew you make more money, but no one shows you how to use the machine and the needle goes so fast. The joke is 'If one day the needle goes through your hand, you graduate.'" Nevertheless, Terry did learn to sew and began earning sixteen or seventeen dollars a day. Six months after arriving in the United States Terry started college, concentrating during the first year on the study of English.

I went to college in accounting and got a bachelor's degree. I didn't date at all. My father wouldn't let me, and when I was in college I just put my mind on school work. I just want to survive, that's all. The guys are afraid of me, I heard from people. One guy said, when he saw my schedule—class, work, study, work, study— "My god, Terry, you are a female soldier." I just want to be good, to survive. This was the first time I was around people who weren't Chinese. I was the minority. I don't feel they're friendly. Usually I sit in the first row in the middle, so I can concentrate.

During those five years it is difficult. I work and I study, I discipline myself, but my father loves to come home and yell. When I get upset I can't concentrate, nothing goes in my mind. When he's asleep his mouth is closed, it's quiet, so I get up in the middle of the night and study. We work hard at school and work and we have a right to peace. It comes in cycles. Every time I get my period I get very hyper, and when he yells at me I talk back to him. You're supposed to respect an elder, but I would yell back at him. I tell myself I get a job, get out of here.

When I was twenty-five my father still refused to let me date. My friends' friend asked me if I'd be interested in seeing a Broadway show. I told my parents, "I will be home late tonight." My parents said, "You're supposed to bring him over and let us see if he's a good guy. How do we know where he's going to take you after the show? He might take you to a hotel and rape you." We had big argument and my father start cursing me and saying, "You were born by a prostitute." He could name me anything, but not that. I said, "You're not my real father." I was so angry. Every time he curse me, I would start shaking. They won't tell me who I am, and I can't ask them. I always want to know, who am I? He say, "If you leave this house, don't come back." I didn't go to the show, because I have nowhere else to go.

After college Terry worked at a bank as a junior accountant for half a year, then took an examination and became an auditor. She kept telling herself she had to save her money and go back to Taiwan to find out who her family was. "I don't want to be here," she recalls. "I was here by force, because we didn't have money to buy food. My mother came because of the husband. That is the tradition." She saved two years vacation time and enough money for a trip to Taiwan, to find out who her natural parents were.

The woman who had told her about her "real" mother had mentioned the name of a bakery, which was all that Terry remembered of the conversation and the only clue of where to look. It was there she found the family who had given her up for adoption because they were too poor to keep another girl child. It was an exciting reunion with several siblings, her natural mother and numerous members of her extended family. Terry was relieved to know, at last, who her birth family was, but she was glad, also, to return to the mother who had raised her and to resume her life in America.

Terry joined a chorus composed of Chinese people, and there she met Charley. At first, he seemed to be good to her. But his mother was insulting to her and Terry was hurt that he either pretended not to notice or took his mother's side. They planned to marry, but Charley's mother interfered so much and he was so lacking in support of Terry, that she broke off the relationship. She was still in love with him, but she resisted his letters, phone calls and poetry. She had other people answer the phone at home and at work. She even dated a man her father had chosen for her, but she developed misgivings about his traditional ideas about women and they mutually ended the relationship. She called Charley and told him she still loved him. She said to her mother, "I thought about it, and I'm going to take a risk."

They were married in June and Charley's neglect became evident on their honeymoon. He kept telling her she was not as pretty, not as smart and not as good as his former girlfriends. When she asked him to use a condom, because birth control pills made her sick, he refused, saying it was "like wearing socks." Although he knew Terry was very conservative and that Chinese women were "supposed to be virgins" when they married, Charley ridiculed her inexperience. On one such occasion she lashed out at him verbally, and he hit her. Later, he apologized and said it would never happen again. When Terry complained about his insistence on keeping his former girlfriend's clothing and other items in their apartment, he again responded with violence.

He went to the kitchen and took out a very big knife. The watch that was given by his ex-girlfriend, he chopped it off. The clothes, he used scissors and cut it to pieces. Then he start hitting me. He was furious. I was so scared. He started going crazy and then he went back to bed. Then he start drinking beer again and got up and slapped my face. My ears, my face, were so hot. I was so shocked, I don't know what to do and he keeps hitting me.

I couldn't do anything because he is so strong. I could not stop him. I was in a state of shock. I said, "Nobody ever hit me like this in my life." He said, "Because your mother never hit you, that's why I have to do it now." My arm was bruised. I didn't know what happened, it happened so fast. He said, "I'm leaving, I'm not coming home tonight." I said, "Fine." I was married in June and this happened in August.

He came back and kneeled on his knees next to me and said, "Forgive me. I'll never do that again." I did not expect it to happen again. I tried to cover my bruises with band-aids, but people asked me, "What's wrong with your arm?" I was so ashamed to say that my husband did it. I just said, "I was robbed." My whole arm is numb. I can't work. I went to the hospital to have an x-ray. I could not wash, I could not cook. I had nothing to wear, and the laundry is two blocks away. He won't do it. He said, "You deserve to be beat. It's your fault."

He says I'm not good at this, not good at that, so I decided to take courses in computers and get a master's degree. After he injured my one arm I fell on the street and broke my left arm. I couldn't do my homework, but I still tried to make it to school. I have to rush home and do homework. I could use my fingers a little bit. One day I'm talking to myself and I say, "I can't understand this!" He swing around and he kick me from behind.

It was right on my spine. I had a spine injury once,

and he knew that. I was having my mid-term and I was furious. I said, "You told me you'd never hit me again. I believed you. Every time you told me something I believed every word you said." He warn me, "Don't come home tonight."

I have one friend I call and say, "Can I stay over with you?" She says, "Why? I thought you were married." I say, "Yeah, I'm married but I also have two broken arms." She says, "I cannot take you. Your husband will hate me." I cannot tell my mother, she'll be so upset. I walk the street for a while. I had no place to go. I went home and told him I was leaving. He said, "Give me another chance."

I didn't move out. I couldn't divorce yet. I thought maybe there was still a chance that it would work. We move to a new place, start all over again. I don't know what to do. It was like living in hell. I came home the day before Thanksgiving and saw a note. It said, "I went to bring my car to a body shop. I'll be home late tonight."

Charley didn't get home that night or the next, and a few days later he arrived to say he'd been gambling in Reno. He told Terry she "would not get a penny" from him if she divorced him and demanded to know if she was going to follow the custom of some divorcing Chinese women, putting an advertisement in the paper saying she was abused. He also tried to find out when her menstrual periods were, insinuating that she might be pregnant by someone else and would demand child support from him.

He said he wants to destroy me and that got me really scared. How can I take this? I fear every day for my life. My mother's begging me, "Don't divorce him." I went to my brother's for a few days. My brother said, "It's your fault. Why don't you leave here? Why don't you move out? You're over eighteen, you should be on your own. You're the only person who can solve the problem." I said, "Why do you hate me so much? Why are you doing this to me? I'm your sister."

I don't know what to do, and I tell my supervisor. She was divorced before and she says, "You can go to family court and get an order of protection." I left the end of December. It was just six months. I rented a room in a basement for a hundred and eighty dollars a month. So dark, no air, no lights, full of roaches. I lived there for four or five months. He tried to have people talk me out of it, and start all over again. In February we had Chinese New Year together. I said, "Wait! If I listen to you, I am the one to take whatever happen to me, not you."

Chinese people look down on woman if you're divorced. You're second-handed merchandise, second-class citizen. But I said, "When it comes to the point I want to save my life I don't care if you laugh." I did not know I had that courage to go through with it, but I had no choice. I carried a copy of the protection order all the time.

When we were together I tried to think maybe it would work, maybe it's going to get better. I believed him. It was so real. "I'll never do this again." He said that in front of other people. Before marriage I loved him, even when we argued. I cannot forget him. I don't know why I loved him. We talked and it seemed to me we have a lot of things in common. I thought he think the way I think, but that is not what he really thinks.

Was I ever tempted to go back to Charley? Are you crazy? When I saw *The Burning Bed* I regretted I did not ever do it. I could have killed him. Why didn't I do it? I didn't think of it when I was with him. The only thing I regret is that I did not kill him. If I don't kill him, he's going to do something like that to other woman. The only thing that would hold me back if I did have a choice to kill him, is I would think about my mother.

I feel like I just had an operation, a cyst and I cut it off and it's bleeding. It hurts but it's healing. But if you asked me if I'd get married, I don't know. I don't think I would trust a man that easily. I should use my head instead of my feelings. I have a decent job, not high paid, but it's secure. I work hard. I have a nice place to live, I don't feel like a gypsy. I have my own apartment, my own chair, my own desk, my own office. Maybe someday I get married, I don't know.

I just stay home now. I don't go out, because I'm afraid to bump into people I know. They ask, "How's your husband?" I did not tell many people, and I don't want to tell them in the street and in a restaurant. I could not tell them. I hide for two years already. If I stay with my mother for a few days and people ask, "How's your daughter?" she lies. She did feel shamed. A disgraceful thing. I feel that too. Later I say, "Hold on a second. I was abused. He should be the one ashamed. His mother should be the one ashamed."

Terry now volunteers at a service for battered women. When her mother coaxed her recently to go to a party Terry said, "I know lots of girls in their forties or fifties who are not married and who are happy. Marriage is not a necessity. You can have it or you don't. You don't just grab anyone. No. Never."

Terry lost friends, including one woman she had been close to who works in the same building but refuses to speak to her. "She is a very traditional girl," Terry says. "I am too, but how much can you take? All of a sudden I don't feel I have friends. How come nobody calls me? I'm dying for people to call me. But it's worth it, for my life. I tell myself if they don't care for me, that's it. I don't want to associate with them. I can make make new friends, and I do."

CHAPTER 28

Melissa

When I was a child, my mother had schizophrenic episodes. My father was in the navy and was gone nine months of the year, so he wasn't around to see my mother do weird things, like lock us all in the closet, or threaten to kill us if we didn't be quiet. She'd say things like, "You're going to die in an hour," and then just walk away. I was about six at the time, and that was the beginning of my thinking that I was supposed to be a victim. When I was about ten, the doctor finally gave her something that calmed her down.

When I was eighteen I was raped. I had been out with a friend, and she picked up these two guys and wanted to park with one of them. She wanted me to park behind them, so that if anything happened she could hit the horn and I could come running. So, *I* get stuck with this guy's brother in my car and he rapes me. I laid on the horn and screamed and yelled and nobody did a goddamned thing. Later, I called the police and they wouldn't do a thing. It took about three years for the anger to start coming out.

But just before I met Tom I felt pretty good. I'm manic-depressive, and I had been kind of confused, but I was beginning to calm down. I was working as a retail clerk, was writing a great deal and had just had my first public poetry reading.

I met Tom from some friends of mine who were in a band. I had been dating musicians mostly, and suddenly here was this manual laborer, this construction worker who was the opposite of what I was used to, totally ignorant of the arts and from an entirely different world. He embarrassed me sometimes, because I don't think that he was raised with the same kind of southern gentility that I was raised with. He was lacking in social graces. But there was something childlike that appealed to me. He was calm and almost shy, whereas I'm a total extrovert. He gave me a lot of attention, which my ego needed. He was charming, so nice to me, and at the time I thought he was gentle and he seemed open and caring. I felt marvelous when I was with him.

I had known him about a month and both our leases expired. We moved in together because I really loved him. I dropped out of college, more or less at his insistence, and there was a slow change. I was expected to be the housekeeper. I was a woman; it was my job. I had all these great dresses from the forties and fifties and Tom locked them in his car and refused to allow me to wear them. He took out his anger on inanimate objects, and I should have noticed that. I just thought he had a bad temper.

When he found out I had been raped, one of the worst things he did was to rape me himself. I was so sick afterwards, I vomited for three hours. He got a lot more physically abusive, and it got unbearable. He'd beat me because I wasn't making enough money, because I wasn't working hard enough or because I was "throwing my money away."

A therapist told me that a beater needs to get a reaction. If they don't get the effect they want from their action, then they do more. I was a pretty strong-willed person, and that's why things went as quickly as they did. Tom got worse very quickly when I stood up to him. I told him he didn't run my life and he ended up cracking my ribs.

He was an alcoholic and he beat me two or three times a week, whenever he was going through withdrawal. He would tense up and get this certain angle on his jaw, would pound his fist, and stalk around the house. And he would smoke my cigarettes, which he rarely did otherwise. That was a big warning. Twice, I promoted a beating, because it was building up and I knew I'd get hell in the morning, so I'd rather have him do it to me while he was drunk than when he was mean. But most of the time I'd try to be as nice and as pleasant as possible. It never worked.

He had me believing that I was fat, that I was a bitch, a whore. I felt like a prisoner at Auschwitz, not human. If I were beaten, so what? I would have been too embarrassed to discuss what was happening with my friends, and I was totally isolated from them anyway. It wasn't until later, when I found the missing screws, that I realized Tom had sabotaged my car, so he could make me sell it. The money went to him to pay for dope.

Before the car was sold I left him once and had nowhere to go, so I slept in the car all night. I went back, because I'd been laid off from my job and he had taken what money I had. By then I had developed so many nervous mannerisms that I knew no employer would hire me. Tom had taken away my drugs that I needed for my anxiety attacks. He wouldn't give me money for food and sometimes he would fix himself a steak and eat it in front of me while I had nothing. Sometimes I would go to the apartment manager, who would give me food.

Before I got so nervous I supported him during the times when there were no construction jobs. Once I was feeling sick and we got into a big fight over paying the rent. He slapped me and I just grabbed my things and ran out of the house. But by then he had convinced me that he was the only one that would love me. I was so afraid of losing him, I would do anything to hold on to him.

Once I told Tom to treat me better, or I would leave, and I ended up running after him and apologizing. This was after he had broken my nose, but the emotion was so powerful that I didn't care if he killed me, just so long as he loved me.

Melissa believes that once you reach the point at which you finally "see it all, then it's just as much your fault if you stay, as his." Several events led up to that point of realization for her. She was no longer working, had not been out of the house for four days and was "going crazy." Tom went out and she begged to go with him, but he wouldn't allow it. She found some change in his pockets, and went out to buy cigarettes and a candy bar, because she hadn't eaten in many hours and there was no food in the house.

People at the store were staring at her. Puzzled at first, she then saw her reflection in a store window and realized she was tearing her hair out. The strangers' reaction to her made her realize what a debilitated condition she was in. Not long after that, Tom hit her in the presence of his friends, which was a new kind of humiliation. Perhaps even then she would not have been able to leave, had it not been for the intervention of friends.

I was so grateful, because I had no money and nowhere to go, and it probably would have taken another three or four weeks to leave. I tried to stay with friends, but the man in the house told Tom where I was. I tried to get myself committed to a state hospital, but the nurse said I needed to go to a battered women's shelter.

I was frightened when I got there, but they were great, so supportive, and everyone helped everyone and shared stories about how they coped. Everyone had basically the same story. Everyone had been beaten and their men had made them feel that they were lesbians if they had any girlfriends. It still gives me goosebumps to remember the closeness and support I felt then.

I stayed in the shelter a week and then got my first disability check. The day I left, Tom came over to apologize and talk to me. Because a friend was in the car, I thought I'd be safe and got in. Tom started driving like a madman and hit three cars. I thought I was going to die, and that turned my life around. I realized I hadn't done what I wanted to do in life. I threw the car in park, got out and ran.

I thought that God had rejected me. I was beyond praying. All I could do was hope. I couldn't trust anyone except the two friends who helped move me out, who were there when I needed them and who understood. I stayed with them for a while and then I got a flat of my own. It feels good to have a place of my own to go to. I get lonely, but not as lonely as when I was with him. As far as going out and finding a man and having a relationship, it turns my stomach. I don't get turned on sexually, and even get nauseous after sex, but I do it, sometimes, because it's like a pat on the head.

After I left I had a repetitive nightmare that I was cutting up a chicken, but then it was really Tom, and I put a hatchet in his chest. I don't really think about killing him though, because I'd end up in jail.

I now have much more freedom and emotional and financial security. I'm with people Tom will never meet, and he doesn't have my phone number, so I feel safe. I had more friends when I was with him, but I have more true friends now. I'm still afraid of meeting people, of going places, of seeing people I knew in the past, but I'm a lot calmer. I'd like to go off tranquilizers, but I can't yet. I really enjoy solitude, as I never did before. Now I can read a book for hours. I don't worry as much as I did, and I'm looking at things differently. I'm not taking a vacation from life, but I'm looking at life as a vacation.

CHAPTER 29

Amanda

My father was out of the picture when I was two. We had lived in Iran where he was the head engineer for American interests for an oil company. At the end of two years my mom said, "We have no business being here. Screw this. I'm taking the kids," and she left him. They had a stormy, stormy, horrible relationship. He's a functioning alcoholic and he beat my brother severely, but not my mother or me. He was into psychological abuse, heavy duty, and is to this day. I only saw him once at eight years old and again at eighteen. He has a very, very low opinion of women. Women are "stupid," "inferior."

My mother didn't have any lovers. It was us and her together. She was a teacher so we always were together. Lots of security. Never had babysitters. There were a lot of tight bonds. We had a home where after-dinner discussions would go on for hours and hours and hours and we were always encouraged to be open. If you had a problem you could go either to the whole family with it or to one person you thought could help with it.

In my first relationship I think there might have been a lot of psychological abuse I wasn't aware of because I was so naive. I lived with Bill from the age of sixteen to just before my twentieth birthday and when I left him I felt like I was a bird flying out of a cage. I felt like chains were being ripped off me. But the next man, and Patrick, the one after that, were both very kind, loving, gentle people. There was never abuse of any kind. Not until Sam.

Before I met Sam I was very active and getting good grades in college, I was popular, had lots of friends, a nice place to live, a nice car. I was learning constitutional law from a dynamite teacher and writing my first research paper, which was just a real challenge for me. I had this real strong network of intelligent, hot, dynamite people. There were sixteen of us and we were just on all the time. We pulled together and I was real happy.

The man I'm with now, his name is Patrick. I met him when I was twenty-two. He's a diabetic and he wasn't taking care of his trip at all. He'd go into insulin shock and he was turning into a monster. I started playing the role of Mommy, pulling him out of shock. When Patrick and I had been together for about two years he became best friends with Sam. They're both writers.

Sam and I were definitely attracted and we couldn't keep our eyes off each other. We just had a few brief encounters, nothing sexual, just this strong urge. And then I went away for the weekend and I was just so in love it was overwhelming. All my logic went out the window.

We all went out one night and we were too drunk to drive home so we stayed at Sam's dorm. Patrick and I were on the bed and Sam pulled me down and I made love with him on the floor while Patrick was asleep on the bed above. It felt good. There was this urgency. When I think about it now, I just don't know! Where was I? What was I? I'm not that kind of person. I'm a very moral person, sexually.

One night Patrick wanted to make love and I said, "No." He coerced me into it. I gave in, and I just felt so sick, so ill. I got up and went into the bathroom and vomited. I just felt like I'd been raped. And I had. The next day I said, "I can't do this." I called Sam and I said, "You got me. I'm yours."

I had felt neglected and unappreciated by Patrick, sexually and intellectually. So Sam comes trotting into the picture just showering me with adoration and worshipping the ground I walked on. "My God, I'm so in love." And on and on and on. It felt so good. It felt great. Plus Sam was a big man on campus. Every girl was just hot after Sam Lewis. He was it. Mr. Wonderful. Mr. Exciting. Everyone wanted to be with Sam. And he turned his attention on me and I bought it hook, line and sinker.

One Fourth of July we were at a big party. I had sat on Patrick's lap and spent about a half hour with him. We had managed to salvage a friendship and I was glad to see him. I really loved him and cared about him as my friend. Later, as Sam and I were leaving in my pickup truck, I said something about the sorority scene at Western College and he said, "You know you amaze me how stupid you can be." I said, "What's that supposed to mean?" Out of nowhere he slammed on the brakes.

We were out on this deserted road in the countryside and he just turned on me, grabbed my neck and started choking me and just pounded me against the window of the car and I didn't know what was happening, because I couldn't get away. It was happening too fast. It was just bam! Like that! He just choked me and choked me and choked me, banging my head and then jumped out of the car and started running down the road. Just like that, he was gone.

I was choking and coughing and I didn't know what to do. I'd been just so sure I'd never let anyone do that to me. So I slid over behind the wheel and I was shaking and I saw him in the headlights and I just saw red. I wanted to kill him. I just wanted to drive right over him. I didn't even know what gear I was in, the brake was on, the car was really winding out, all this noise was going on, and I got up to him and he jumped out of the way. I don't think I was really going to run him over. Maybe I was. I got out of the car and ran up to him and grabbed him by the shirt and slapped him across the face and I just screamed, "Don't you ever do that to me again."

And then he just beat the shit out of me. He got me down and kicked me, slapped me, shoved me and threw me in the bushes. "You stupid bitch, you stupid slut!"

You this, you that. And he laid down in the grass and started crying. And then he picked me up and put me in the car and drove me home and put me to bed.

The next morning I just felt like I've never been so hopeless in my whole life. This couldn't be happening to me. I'm the kid that's got everything going for her. I'm smart, pretty, fun-loving, I've got a great personality, I love life, love people. This isn't happening to me. This isn't my script. I don't belong in this play. I was so embarrassed. He was beating me, so obviously I didn't have it together. I wanted everybody to think we were having such a great relationship, that everything was okay. "Look at Amanda and Sam, they're so in love!" That's the picture I painted and the one I wanted to hang on the wall. I didn't want anybody to look behind the frame.

I didn't think about if he would marry me or about staying with him for the rest of my life. I guess it was that whole outlaw, renegade thing. I saw him as a way of stirring me up or giving me more self-confidence. Through him I could learn to be really independent and not to be insecure. He could teach me. I was confident intellectually but insecure emotionally. And I knew that when I was with Sam he wouldn't hold me when I cried or was scared or insecure. See, this was his big strength he was going to give me. He was going to give me security in myself, instead of security externally.

Two weeks after the first beating we were coming home late at night and he punched me in the solar plexis. I fell down in the mud and he said, "Get up, pig." I don't think this second time it was jealousy. I think it was just pure disrespect for me as a human being. There was no confrontation. I would say something and it was bam! "You're stupid." After the second time I felt like all of a sudden I had a lot of problems. I never in my life was so confused or had so many problems. Everything started going—my dedication to my work, my loyalty to my old friends, because he couldn't get along with them —everything started to fall apart.

Sam was always drunk when he hit Amanda and he would apologize in the morning, but she thinks he rarely knew what he had done. Amanda had given up drinking for six weeks just before she met Sam, but started again when she became involved with him, and she was often drunk too, though less so than Sam.

The emotional abuse was the worst, especially the lack of respect, which often took the form of Sam's telling Amanda she was no good at anything she touched. She was hurt too by not being included in his social life, and by his declarations that he was tired of her "hanging around." In moments of desperation she turned to her friends for help, but she wouldn't listen to their entreaties to stop seeing Sam.

Amanda became pregnant and Sam was attentive, taking care of her, cooking and cleaning. In line with his idea of himself as a feminist, he accompanied her when she had an abortion. But later, on the way home, he struck quite a different attitude. Amanda was remembering "the Tom Robbins character who describes abortion as death holding a stag party in the most sacred room in her body." She felt sick, was complaining and perhaps, she says, looking for sympathy. But Sam's response was, "Oh, shut up. Quit your whining." The next night he insisted—over her strong objections—on having sex. She was afraid she'd get an infection and have to have a hysterectomy. Sam "reassured" her by saying he made love to his former girlfriend after she had an abortion and it had been all right.

Amanda was impressed with Sam's ability to hurt her where it wasn't visible, at least not unless she wore short sleeves. "I felt like a damned junkie trying to hide the tracks. I was a Sam junkie. I've been going through withdrawal ever since." One night he beat her up and dragged her into the yard where he continued to hit her, and neighbors called the police. No one had witnessed the violence before, and now, seeing herself reflected in the eyes of a kindly, fatherly police officer, she felt deeply shamed. That was almost the end.

Amanda left to stay with her mother, and Sam drove her to the airport, trying to cajole her into believing they'd work everything out when she returned. She said, "Okay, fine," but she knew it was different this time, because other people had seen him beating her, the police had come and the "picture was starting to get a little crinkled around the edges and it didn't look like it was going to get any better." She also knew he was seeing other women.

At her mother's house Amanda continued to see more flaws in the picture. She slept fourteen hours a day and realized she was "clinically depressed." When she returned, a woman friend drove her home from the airport and she discovered that Sam had been staying in her apartment while she was gone. He was there when she arrived, surrounded by a litter of beer bottles, filled ash trays, dirty dishes and empty pizza cartons. Then she discovered another woman's menstrual blood all over her sheets. Outraged, she began to yell at him, and he walked out. It was the only time he hadn't hit her when she screamed at him.

Amanda decided to start over; she packed everything up and Sam helped her move. She drove him to work and he said, "Well I guess this is it." She said, "You've got it," and that was it. She drove away and never went back. But she still loved him, she wanted him to stay, wanted to make him realize that what he had done was wrong. And she wanted him to love her.

Yet when he did pursue her, she knew she didn't dare respond to him in any way. He followed and harassed her when she tried to socialize with other people, creating such unpleasant scenes that some of her friends stopped inviting her to parties. He circulated rumors at her internship that she was "a lesbian, had weird sexual practices and was screwing every guy in town." Then he began to sit in front of her house revving his motorcycle at three in the morning. He called her in the middle of the night and at Christmas time he left her a gift of a sexy negligee.

Sometimes Amanda would feel sad and wish he'd call, not to be with him again, but to be reassured that he still thought about her. Once he did call when she was in that vulnerable state of mind and asked her to make curtains for his new house in exchange for taking her out to dinner. Fortunately she had a board meeting to attend, which helped her to say no. The harassment lasted from September to January, but

Amanda didn't give in. She loved him, but still felt so drained that it was easier to be lonely and insecure than to become reinvolved. Eventually she saw Sam at a party and agreed to talk to him.

He took my hand and gazed into me with all the strength he had, just poured into me all the loving he had. I said, "I'm empty, Sam. I don't have anything for you." And that's when I realized I didn't have anything for him any more. But I didn't have anything for anybody else either. I was empty, gone, finished. It scared me. That's when the long hard climb started on the road to recovery. That's when I started getting well. That was the final, final end of Sam.

Amanda sometimes feels afraid because she doesn't know how she got so deeply involved with Sam nor why she stayed nor why she left. She sees the experience as a "real quick brush with insanity." At other times it seems clear she got into the relationship because Sam was "sexy, and adoring and I was starved." After the first couple of beatings she thought, "I have to take responsibility for curing this man of his battering. I couldn't let him loose on other women, because I was afraid if he got someone weaker, he'd really destroy her." She was partially right. He started the beating of his new girl-friend at the level where he left off with Amanda, and it escalated quickly to broken bones. After Amanda left she was shocked at herself. "I'm not qualified to make him stop beating me," she says. "I have no idea how I was going to cure him. I guess I thought I'd love him to death, so that he'd never want to hit anybody again."

If I could have waved that magic wand I would have left after three months exactly. All the beatings occurred between July and September and they got worse and worse and more frequent toward the end, until I was out of there in October. After I left I'd start a project and then I'd ramble around my house talking to myself. I was bouncing off the walls. I had all this time to myself and I didn't know what to do with it. It was such a stark contrast to all the weird, bizarre things I had been going through. I sat in my rocking chair and just daydreamed, tried to figure out my goals. And I amused myself. The amusement was that I could do whatever I wanted. I'd go for walks by myself, just getting to know myself, getting comfortable with me. Not having a partner was a big part of my growing process. I liked the freedom of getting into my car with my sleeping bag and heading off to go camping without having to worry about anything. That freedom of choice. And never being afraid. That weight was lifted. I didn't know I'd been walking around with it on my back.

I came to the conclusion that if I let someone else take responsibility for my security or insecurity, then I was at the mercy of that person. I would be pretty much trapped, because they would know I was afraid. I made myself a security plan. I lock up the house real tight, I have a bell on my door and I know how to get out onto the roof and down to the ground if anyone is coming in.

Insecurity and loneliness were two things I was trying to escape when I went with Sam. When I'm alone now, I'm not afraid anymore, because I lived alone for nine months. I faced those fears and I don't have to go out to other people. I learned how to be my own companion, my own friend, how to hang out with myself and have a good time. I stopped drinking and that helped.

Patrick and I are back together and I'm probably going to get married next year. I feel real good and real calm about it. There's one hundred percent equality in the home. And he has his insulin trip together and I stopped drinking. I'm a special projects coordinator for a public corporation, which for me is an ideal situation, as my basic background has been community organizing and urban planning.

Every day it's gotten easier. I had this jumble of thoughts and emotions filling up this new environment and I just let it all go. After that, an order and a calmness came into my life and I never lost it. I have a place I go to and it's real still. I can go there just standing and waiting for the bus, if I need to get calm. I was one of those people who was always seeking and searching. I wasn't happy with the present. I always wanted to be five years down the road. I stopped searching externally and after a while I found that the thing was inside me all the time.

CHAPTER 30

Hope

Hope is a thirty-eight-year-old American Indian. She was in the sixth grade when her mother became ill with cancer, and as the eldest of seven children, she was enlisted to care for her three siblings who were still toddlers. She missed a great many classes and by the time her mother was able to handle the household again, Hope was embarrassed to be still in sixth grade while her friends had advanced to eighth. She dropped out of school. Her father was an alcoholic who sometimes hit her mother, but never assaulted the children. They were a close family and usually dealt with problems by talking them over.

When Hope met Barney he was driving a taxi and she was working as a maid. She was twenty years old and had moved away from her family, but weekend visits to them kept her from feeling lonely. Early in the relationship with Barney, the only sign of his controlling behavior was his refusal to go out with her friends, of whom he was hypercritical. She describes their relationship as "okay," noting that he would ask what she wanted to do and would generally be agreeable to whatever she suggested, and that he seemed interested in making her happy. They went together for four years, but once they were married things were different. She tried to avoid arguments by asking him what was wrong, but he refused to talk about what was bothering him.

I had the housework done and the dinner cooked and he worked overtime and I went next door to visit my girlfriend. I didn't know when to expect him and checked the house every so often. When I went home he was there and he said, "Where were you? When a man's married to a wife she should be home all the time." I resented that and I started saying, "You expect me to stay home twenty-four hours a day?" I was working too. He said, "Now that you're married you're not your own boss any more." He slapped me hard enough to hurt my feelings. I washed my face and calmed down and dished out the supper and just changed the subject. I still didn't know what I was getting into.

Usually Hope was slapped because she was speaking up for herself or because Barney disapproved of what she had done. His rage might be triggered by her cooking something in a way that was different from his family's cooking. Sometimes he would throw the dish of food at her. When Barney was five years old he had been adopted by an alcoholic aunt and uncle. Soon he was made responsible for chopping wood every morning, cooking the meals and generally running the household. Hope thought that as they lived together he would recover from his abusive childhood and become easier to live with. They hoped having a baby would solve some of their problems, but after she gave birth to a boy, Barney's tension and anger increased.

He would come home from the bars and I'd be upset and say, "Did you cash the check? We have to pay the rent." He would say, "Don't tell me what to do," and I would say, "We got a kid now and I'd appreciate it if you'd try to take more responsibility. I'm trying my best." He didn't like it when I spoke up for myself and my boy. Later on it got so that he could hit me and not hurt my feelings. It didn't bother me whether he hit me or socked me or pulled my hair or threw me down. He broke my partial and my front teeth, by socking me. He broke a ligament of my kneecap and I told the doctor I fell down. After he hit me he would watch TV and I'd go do what I had to do. After the baby was born it was more than twice a week. It was either the kid or me or he'd blame the job. There was always something wrong.

I told some of my friends, but it was hard for them to understand what kind of guy he is. They said I should leave. I said, "I can't go to my parents and working part time is not enough to support myself and my son." That was before the shelters came, and I didn't realize at that time that violence was all over.

I'd say to my boy, "Don't cry when Dad is home." I didn't know about being mentally battered. He mentally battered my boy. He was about five and he'd say, "Can I go play out with my cousin?" and my husband would say, "You're a big boy now. When I was your age I worked hard. You're too big to play out." I wanted to get him roller skates for his birthday, and my husband would say, "You're not a boy, you're a man. You don't need nothing for your birthday." I went out and got them anyway, but that made it harder on my boy.

I left and went to one of my old time friends from way back, someone he wouldn't think of. I stayed there for a week and he was all over town looking for me. Finally one of his friends saw the boy playing outside and told him, "that's where she is," and he came and got me. We left quite a bit and I was getting more scared, but after a few days I would go back home, because I didn't know where to go and was worried about my stuff and felt quite insecure. I would leave more than six times a month.

I would go to my friends, but their husbands would say, "You should either leave or you got to do something," so I stopped going to them for help. In the meantime I was working and I would cash a check and get a lot of groceries and I would hide money to go to a hotel. He always made me feel guilty. And I would think I had to go back for the boy's sake, because I figured a kid should have two parents. Even though he'd know how bad his dad was, he'd miss him. He'd say, "Maybe Dad will change now." I'd always go back home when he'd cry.

I called the police, but they didn't do very much. They would tell him to take a walk. I signed a complaint against him and they said, "He didn't really beat you up.

You're not in the hospital. You're still walking, aren't you?" I said, "Yes, but he's been hittting the boy and hurting me quite a bit and I want you to help me get out of here." They said, "It's not our job to do that."

I started worrying more about my boy. He would say, "We better get out, Mom. Let's go stay by Grandma." I went back because I felt sorry for Barney when I seen him cry and he said he'd change, he wouldn't drink any more and wouldn't hit us any more. He would even convince my mom and dad that things were going to be different. When I did go back home things were okay for a few weeks or months and he even quit drinking for a year. But that didn't help. He was more edgy and he didn't stop hitting me.

I took my boy to a clinic for his immunization shots and I seen the paper advertising the shelter. I called them and I was still scared to leave home, but I said to myself, "I got some people to help me now." I went to the shelter and asked a lot of questions. They said, "We're here to help and if he comes here we can call the police and they can throw him in jail." I said, "I called the police before and they didn't do nothin'." They said, "We're working with the police now and they have to do more cause we're helping the ladies and children that has these problems."

The shelter helped in a lot of ways. They counseled me on how to get a place to live and how to get welfare. I applied for assistance for my boy and they gave me a couple of months to start my new life. The shelter referred me to counselors. I'd tell them I still feel lost and I don't know what to do. They advised me, and that helped. Then I got a counselor for my boy for when he'd get upset.

At the shelter we would have something like a rap group. We talked about our feelings and our problems and that helped us feel better that we were not the only ones having the problems. And we started going out together and starting our new life together. We understood each other. It didn't seem so bad leaving home. There's other people that need help and you're not the only one. There's a lot of ladies that are still friends, just like families.

The first time Barney was nice I went back. Then later I knew he wouldn't change. My boy was happy and I had three part-time jobs as a maid, a housekeeper and kitchen helper. At first it was hard financially, but I started making money, gradually started buying clothes for the boy and getting my own place and it wasn't really that bad. It's just a matter of starting out. The boy started going to Headstart and he would go about nine o'clock and be home about three and I had two short jobs while he was gone. Then in the afternoon when he'd come home I'd have one from about four till seven or eight. He was next door playing out with the kids. I was a kitchen helper in a place for senior citizens. He would come in and I'd tell him it's suppertime and he'd eat and then he'd go play out.

I made about two and a quarter an hour for house-keeping, and was a teacher's aide for four dollars an hour and worked at the senior citizens for three seventy five. Then weekends at a hotel. I was doing pretty good until my husband came to where I worked and tried to get me back. I moved to Seattle by my sister for a while. It's been four years since I left him and he still follows me wherever I go, no matter if I stay in Seattle or anywhere.

I had full custody of the boy up 'til just last year. Barney had visitation on weekends and holidays and summers if he wanted it but he never did want it. He hired a private lawyer. I had legal aid. He gave them all the cash they need. I didn't have the money to fight him legally and legal aid can do just so much. What he had over me was that he had two jobs and money in the bank. He had enough money to fight in court no matter how long it took. During that time I quit work. I had arthritis real bad and they said he could take better care of my boy than I could. At that time I couldn't stand up because my ankles were swollen and my knee was swollen and I was on crutches. My boy is ten now and I have him for the summer and holidays in the winter. We're planning to go back to court and change that. I'm going to school now, taking office training to get my skills up.

For a while I thought all men were the same and I resented them. I wasn't interested and if they wanted to argue about going someplace I thought, "I don't want to start that again," and I'd drop them. I met my husband three years ago and I took a long time thinking before I married him. He has never hurt me in any way physically or mentally. If he gets mad he'll let me know right now and we'll straighten it out. He lets me see my friends, we go to dinner with friends, we're equal on everything. My boy found out that his stepfather is a lot different from his other father. They get along pretty good. I never thought I would be happy or get out of that other married life. I'm not talking about a bed of roses, but everything's good now.

It's not a very easy thing to talk about all this but it's like coming out of a bad nightmare. After you look back at all the things you went through you realize there was possible ways to get out of it. When you keep your problems to yourself you don't realize there's ladies out there. It's easy for you to communicate with other ladies that has the same problems and it helps them.

I never thought I'd make it on my own. I felt like I was the only person in the world who lost everything. It wasn't good, but that's all I had to lean on, just my marriage and my boy. During that stage you're afraid he's going to find you whenever you cross a street or turn a corner, but there's always ladies behind you or counselors that are giving you help. I never knew that there was people out there that was going to help me through my crisis. It makes you want to go on, that there's someone behind you. I've got my confidence back and my security. It was a real big thing that I made it out of there with my boy.

CHAPTER 31

Nicole

Nicole's father was in the armed services and later became a warehouse worker and delivery person for a pharmacy, often working two jobs. Her mother had a master's degree in business and was a certified public accountant. She worked nights as a juvenile center matron and during the day she ran a small business out of her home doing people's taxes. As a young child Nicole was aware of her father's violence toward her mother and recalls being frightened when he threatened her mother with a double-barrelled shotgun.

Her father had a long-standing relationship with a woman named Ethel, which Nicole sensed enough about to be upset when she saw the two of them together and watched them kissing each other goodbye.

My oldest brother is eleven years older than me. But he's not my natural brother. My mother had a son by another man and he would have lot of his friends to come over when my parents weren't home. I must have been about seven or eight and I don't know what led up to it, but I can remember he had me lay down on the floor and he would ejaculate on me. I was dressed, but he would pull my dress up. I can remember seeing his semen on my stomach, and his friends would stand around and laugh. I felt ashamed and dirty. He would say, "You'll never tell Momma what happened," and I was too frightened and I never told her. I never told my father to this day. After a while it just stopped.

I have a younger brother and we have a good relationship. I was spoiled by my mom and I wanted a lot of attention. I wanted people to like me and my mother to be proud of me. If I did something to disappoint her, I felt the hurt just like she did. I remember reading to my mother when she started to get sick. She had cataracts and she liked me to read the newspaper to her or different things from the Bible. It was like she sensed that she was dying, and she would talk to me and sing and I would brush her hair. Those are the good times I remember together. She always seemed to want what was best for me and my brother. She was a very brilliant woman and very elegant.

She died when I was ten. That was a real traumatic experience for me, because I loved her a lot and she spent a lot of time with me. It was real, real hard, because I couldn't understand why God would take my mother. She was the only one that I thought really loved me.

A year later my father got remarried to Ethel and brought that woman into the house. That was real hell for me. I felt like the love I had for my mother was all that I had. My father didn't love me, he was putting all his love on this woman. And she showed her dislike for me, always picked on me and she beat me. I was just like a little maid and my father never said anything about it.

When she was in high school Nicole sometimes confided in Len, her stepsister's husband. One night she was babysitting for them and Len came home unexpectedly early. He tried to rape her, but she scratched him and pushed him away. When she told her aunt what had happened she said, "What did you do to make him do that?" After that she kept it to herself, and "it was kind of like a sore." Her stepmother and aunt seemed to believe she had had an affair with Len, and her stepmother predicted she would be a prostitute.

In high school Nicole was outgoing and loved sports. But she wanted so badly to be liked that she allowed herself to be used by people. "I needed that," she says, "because I didn't have the love at home. I had a lot of friends, but they never came to my house because my stepmother was so nasty. I never got to go to parties. We had to go to church and Sunday school first and then we got to go to the movies."

Although she occasionally sneaked out to meet a boy, she didn't date until she was a senior in high school. She went to a white high school where she was one of about ten black students during the first year of bussing. "I really wanted to have more white friends," she says, "but at that time you just stayed with your black friends."

In her senior year of high school Nicole met Arnold, who was "really cute, funny and who loved to party." Although he was from a poor family, in contrast to Nicole's middle class background, he was a freshman at the university, which impressed Nicole. A year later they became sexually involved and after one quarter of being separated from him when she went to a college in the Midwest, Nicole wanted to be married. Now she realizes that at nineteen she was much too immature for such a commitment, but she wanted to escape the oppressive demands of her father and especially her stepmother. She wanted to be on her own.

In addition, she says, "I really loved him. He was my whole world. That's a fault of mine, making a man my whole world and forgetting about my identity. I just wanted to please this man, whoever it was, just to have him, not realizing Hey! I have potential too. Soon after she and Arnold decided to be married, she discovered she was pregnant, so the wedding took place rather quickly. Arnold quit school and went to work full time, but shortly before their baby girl was born he quit his job, which ushered in a long period for Nicole of being chronically dependent on welfare. Arnold is an artist and eventually earned some money from his sculpture, but it was never enough to support a family and he wasn't willing to work at anything else. Although there was no physical violence, Arnold controlled Nicole's friendships and the money and he was mentally abusive. They had a second child two years after the first and not long after that Arnold said, "I just can't deal with this any more. I got to get out. I can't be an artist and a husband and father. All I want to do is my art."

After the separation Nicole tried to relieve her resentment

at being left with the sole care of her children by using marijuana and alcohol and having sex with a variety of men. "The men were abusive mentally, because I allowed them to use me, letting them use my body. I was still trying to get this love from some man and the only way I knew how to do it was I gave my body to them. I would give them money and do little things for them like invite them over for dinner, without getting anything in return."

After Arnold left Nicole decided she just couldn't continue on welfare and she was able to find training in data entry and clerical work, but it never paid enough for her to support her children adequately. In addition she couldn't hold a job long because her children were often sick with asthma, bronchitis, hay fever or infections.

Nicole eventually decided to move to Washington D.C. She left her children with Arnold, but she had barely begun to get settled in her new home when he threatened to report her to child protective services if she didn't come back for the children. She went back to get them, but when she returned to Washington she found she had lost her job. Her stability began to slip away. "I wasn't taking care of my body," she says. "I was smoking a lot of weed, drinking, taking a lot of pills. For a while I was like a zombie, because I drank an awful lot. It was the pits."

A friend of Nicole's worked at a residential drug treatment center and suggested she go there. Nicole was desperate enough to try it and pleased that there was a place she could get help without leaving her children. Nicole had never used hard drugs and all of the other residents were heroin addicts, so it was a very restrictive program, which she felt was useful. For instance, having a sexual relationship was a privilege which had to be earned and such relationships were not allowed until the couple had known each other six months or more. She feels the sexual discipline was good for her.

After two years Nicole returned to her home town. She wanted to go to school, but her children were still young and it seemed too difficult. For a period she was more in control of her life, but whenever she had problems with her parents she found herself "sleeping around and drinking." After giving her number to a man when she was out drinking one night, Nicole realized the danger she had placed herself in and she felt she had better settle down with one man. She had previously turned down a man named Luke, but now she went to him and said she thought she'd like to become involved.

There was no violence and it was really nice. I could pick up that he was jealous, though. Then one day when I'd known him a couple of months I went out with my girlfriend and Luke grabbed me and choked me. He was upset and said, "Don't you know you're my woman and I love you?" I was scared. He left and when he came back I said, "I want you to pack up all your stuff or I'll call the police." So he packed up all his stuff.

My father said, "He's not right for you," but I wouldn't listen, because when Luke wasn't violent he had a gentle quality about him. He really loved me in his own kind of way. But he couldn't stand it if a man said hello to me. He was living with me and he would leave and come back and everything would be hunky dory for a while. Then the accusations would come. "Who you been sleeping with?" I think the first couple of times we split up I probably did sleep around, but after that I didn't. And if I did, so what? He wasn't my husband, and he had somebody. But he couldn't see that.

I said, "I'm moving and I'm going to live by myself." He said, "You mean you're going to move out and I don't have no money?" I said, "Here's five dollars and go get a hamburger. You're not moving with me." He left, but somehow or other I let him move back into the house. Things were pretty good for a while.

One time he was mad and I was pressing my hair and he was going to burn me with the pressing comb. He threw coffee on me and threw me up against the wall and started choking me. I called my girlfriend. She said, "Why don't you leave him?" and I said, "I don't know." I didn't know. I just knew that I loved him and I thought he would change. I was trying to convince myself that having him was better than having nobody. And I said maybe I am too flirty, maybe there is something wrong with me.

When times were good they were really good and the love-making was good, but it all boiled down to the fact that he hated women. He didn't know how to deal with them. I started going to a white church, and learning and reading the Bible, and getting some peace with myself. He used to hassle me about it, saying, "You think you're better than me." Then I wanted to get married. "Ain't I good enough to get married? It ain't right living together without being married." I just wanted to make things right. "If you don't marry me, you have to move."

He wasn't helping with the bills and wouldn't take me out. He wanted to keep me in the house. I did exactly what he said or I'd get beat up. I stopped going to my parents' house because he accused me of loving them more than him, and I stopped going to church and everything.

One day he started grabbing on me and he beat me for three and a half hours with a coat hanger. There was no way for me to get away. He was on top of me and he was a big man. When he got mad it seemed like he got inner strength from somewhere. I had bruises all over my thighs and arms and he had choked me. I still have a gash over my right eye where he put a fireplace poker. I felt this blood coming over my eye and I said, "Oh, God! You hit me in my eye." He saw the blood and immediately stopped and told me how sorry he was and started crying. I just told him to get away from me. He went to the store to get first aid cream, but he unplugged the phone and took it with him, so I wouldn't call the police.

The next day I called the police from my job and went down and made a report. They followed me to my house and they arrested him. He kept calling me from the jail and kept saying, "Please drop the charges." I had dropped the charges once before when he had said that he had been working for the Mafia and they would come and kill me and the kids. I believed him. But this time I said, "No, I'm not going to do it." I said to myself, "I still love him, but I have to stick to my guns." When I got home from work he kept calling me and begging me. Then he had another prisoner call me and say he was his lawyer. He told me Luke had buried this money in the yard and he wanted his money. I called the police department and said he was abusing me from the jail and another officer took a report and called the jail to say he couldn't make more phone calls.

When he got out of jail he came by and I should have never opened the door and listened to him. I let him spend the night and when my kids got up they were really upset with me. They were old enough to see all this shit going on. "Mom, why would you do this?" He was a real hard disciplinarian. Once we called child protection service, but they didn't do too much because he was my boyfriend. They took pictures of my kids' legs where he had beaten them with a coat hanger but nothing came of that. So he started coming around and he stayed around. After a while I said, "I can't take this no more. You have to go," and he did.

I did pretty good for a while. I got involved with my church and my kids were getting ready to go to Christian school and I was getting my life together and trying to find a job. But I got depressed again and then it was holiday time. I just like to have a family at Christmas, so I called him. He said how much he loved me and we made love and I said, "Maybe things will get better. Why don't you go to church with me?" He promised he'd never hit me and I believed again.

Some friends of his had told him I was sleeping with all these guys and he beat me up. I called the police and there were two police cars that stayed 'til he moved all of his stuff. I just wanted him out of the house.

He knew me pretty well physically, my sexual appetite. He knew just how long to stay away—just long enough—then he would come back, calm and cool. We'd start having sex again and he'd start giving the kids money and spending time with them and saying, "Why don't we get married?"—all these things that he knew I wanted him to do.

Sometimes we went out riding together and talked

about a lot of different things, what he wanted out of life. He was gentle and loving. Dr. Jekyll and Mr. Hyde. We had a good time with the kids. But the evil side. . . . The sex was good and I think I was still equating love with sex. That's how he would get me.

We hadn't seen each other for six months. My aunt died and that was traumatic for me and I felt really alone. I was living in the suburbs and there was no black folks there, and I was so alone and really wanted a man. I called him and he came out. I made up my mind that he wasn't going to stay but he did. Then he said he wanted to get married.

We got married December first. A week later he started saying that when I went into the city to work I was with this guy. He slapped me so hard that the whole side of my face was red, and I said, "What have I gotten myself into now?" I really wanted my marriage to work, I didn't want to leave. I started blaming myself, saying, "You shouldn't have married him. You knew what he was like, so you take it, you deserve whatever you get."

I didn't say anything, but I knew it wasn't going to last. When the kids came from school I gathered everything up and went to my dad's house. I stayed there 'til New Year's Eve and went back. I had talked to him on the phone and he said he would go to counseling if I would go back.

I still wondered if he was sincere, but we started going to counseling. He was telling the counselor how he wasn't going to hit me no more and I said, "I don't want to hear this. You always say this over and over." I just went off! I wanted him to leave me, because he wasn't doing anything, just talking. He didn't have any place to go, and the place we were staying in had a basement, and I said, "Stay in the basement, I don't give a shit, just get out of my house." I could tell that even though he wasn't being physically abusive to me then, it was just a matter of time. He did stay in the basement for a while and he'd knock on the door to use the ironing board or something and say, "It sure is cold down there." I'd say, "Go find you a place to stay then . . . ." Then after a while I let him come back upstairs and we did pretty good.

He jumped on me and choked me and then he left and said, "You better not call the police. When I come back tonight I'm going to beat your ass again because I'm not through with you." I put a chair to the door and called the police. They said they would call me and tell me when they arrested him and they did. I felt good, but I was still scared.

I said, "This is it. I have got to get some help for myself. It's four and a half years, and I cannot allow myself to go back." I called a woman who works with battered women and she told me about a group for black women. I called and started going and that's what really helped me.

But I started missing him. Don't ask me why. Nobody in the group told me not to go back. They said, "You have to do what you have to do." "I just want you to be careful." So Luke and I got together again and after a couple of weeks I saw the pattern, the mental abuse. He accused me of seeing some man and we got into a bitter fight. He slapped me.

I said, "I've made a mistake. I know I have to make a plan and get away." He left the house and it was pouring down rain. The telephone was dead and I knew he'd gone down to the basement and unhooked the telephone wires. I knew he'd come back the next morning when the kids were gone to school and beat the shit out of me, so I packed up my stuff and told my kids we were going. I called my friend, and she called a hotel that's affiliated with the Good Shepherd Mission, kind of a shelter, and we stayed there three days.

I called the police and the community service officers went with me to get my stuff out. He was there and really scared me. I wouldn't say anything to him. I took a few things and should have taken more. I came back the next day and I had my uncle change the locks and I stayed there a few days but I was scared. I went to my mom's house and when I went back to the house he had taken all of my clothes, all of my crystal, he broke the

TV, broke the lock on the front and back door.

I haven't been back since. Once I actually moved out he never came around or harassed me. I think he was afraid of what the police might do and of going back to jail. He might have thought if he left me alone long enough I would follow my pattern of getting in contact with him. He also figured I valued my crystal and my clothes—and I did—but I can replace all of that shit. All I want is my peace of mind.

What was different this time was I finally began to realize there was nothing else I could do to help him. And I felt so uneasy. It was the way he responded to me when I came back. Something wasn't right. I can't tell you how I knew, I can't put my finger on it, I just knew my life was in danger. I knew I got to get out of here.

The counselor made me realize if I'm not going to go back that I have to start thinking about me and valuing my life and the kind of person I am, and I can't help him. My kids started going to counseling and expressing their anger and hatred at Luke and how they were mad at me for allowing that man to beat me up and to abuse them and beat them.

The group was good particularly because it was a black women's group, because we're kind of private. We don't like to tell a lot of people what's going on in our lives. It was being around other black women, knowing I'm not out here alone. Even though I knew other women were getting beat up, I never figured I'd allow myself to go through that. Hearing their stories, women married sixteeen years, I said, "Am I going to be one of those, to continuously be there and never leave until one day I might be killed?" I didn't want to take that chance. I made good friends in the group.

The last couple of years I was in a pretty intense relationship and we lived together for two years. It was abusive, but not as badly. He grabbed me a couple of times and he slapped me. That's how I know that I still need more help. He has a very dominating personality. Everything has to go his way. It got to the point that I said, "I cannot be dominated by a man." So he decided he wanted to find him someone, a white woman in particular, which is what he has now. And the reason why he's with her now, he says is, "She will do what I tell her to do and you won't." I said, "That's fine."

I'm back in school and I'm going to get my degree. I got a 2.8 last quarter and I feel good about myself. I'm finally realizing, through the counseling, I'm worth something. Also going to school and taking women's studies, I have learned so much just from one quarter. I had to deal with the incest and the rape and the battering, a lot of things.

I am dating someone that I like and we have a lot in common. He has a bachelor's degree in black studies, he wants to get his master's in public administration and he's a corrections officer. He is really interested in me and impressed with me and what I've been doing in school. He's a gentleman and we have a good time together. I've only been seeing him three weeks and there's no sex involved and I'm not going to push it. I enjoy being treated like a lady. Some feminists might disagree with me, because a long time ago the term "lady" stood for an upper-class white woman. When I say "lady," I like the door opened for me, I like to be taken out to dinner, and to be courted, to be loved and shown affection. I'm still a feminist, I always will be. Those are just personal things I like and he treats me like that.

But now I know I don't need to have a man in my life to make me happy. I think about me now, for the first time in years. My advisor said, "Why don't you take women's studies?" I had never heard of it, but I did and I learned so much about myself. If I can tell my story and give another woman some insight I want to do that. I feel like I can counsel other women and help them, so I changed my major to women's studies. I'm taking a race and gender class and an Afro-American class. That's good because I didn't know that much about my history of being black and that will probably help in counseling black women.

I didn't have any power over my own life. I was always wanting the recognition of other people to make me feel good. I wanted to be special. Luke wanted to possess me. I think a lot of black women want so much to feel good and to feel special by their man, that if he batters them they say, "Well at least he loves me. He's concerned about me." Because we've been oppressed for so long, and after a while we start to believe that we should be oppressed. It's a sick way of thinking. Our man is being oppressed and he can't go out there and shoot at white folks, so he has to take it out on somebody and the person who is next to him is his woman. So we take that battering. I've heard women say, "He has to beat up on somebody and I'd rather he beat up on me, because he won't go to jail. If he beat up on a white man, they'd kill him." This is very sick reasoning. I was that way. There I was, his punching bag.

Black men have a tendency to say, "If you don't do it, a white woman will do it." Black women are afraid if they leave him, he'll go batter someone else or get a white woman and probably treat her better. I would tell a woman who said that, "You're your own woman, you're your own person. You deserve to be treated like a woman is supposed to be treated. You will find another man who will treat you better. You have to make that first step and say, 'I love me. I like me and the person that I am, therefore you cannot mistreat me.'" That's what I learned. I like me.

CHAPTER 32

Jennifer

Jennifer's first marriage lasted from her sophomore to her senior year in college, breaking up because of a difference in values and her husband's discomfort with her intellectual capacities. She has no regrets about the relationship. She graduated from college and started graduate school in a new city. She made friends easily, but she was lonely and looking for a relationship with a man when she met Bart. During the course of her relationship with him she prepared for her Ph.D. and earned a living as a teaching assistant and health agency administrator. Bart had just moved from the Midwest and had a bachelor's degree in accounting and political science, but was working in a shoe store.

During the five years they were together, Bart's prospects and status rose as he moved from the shoe store to owning a bar, to selling travel packages and eventually running a travel agency. But during the same period, while he was earning ten thousand dollars a year, Jennifer was making fifteen, and when his earnings rose to seventeen, hers rose to thirty thousand.

He was torn between being proud and pleased with my education, and feeling terribly threatened. Although he is bright and articulate, it seemed like he had a great stake in putting me down intellectually. If you think of it as a disease analogy, the symptoms of the relationship went from "sub-clinical" to "clinical" after about a year and a half. I think part of that came with my push for the relationship to take on a more committed character, and with his increasing frustration at not being able to get a job and do what he thought he ought to be able to do. I felt like we'd been together long enough to have some good solid commitments, so I was pushing for that, and he was feeling like, "Shit! I can't get a decent job, I'm just a flunky."

About then he had begun to get into the bar, but he always saw that as an interim thing. He wasn't actively looking for other work, but sort of feeling that it ought to be there. He has this destructive tendency to think in terms of miracles. Get rich quick.

In spite of their differences Jennifer and Bart had many good times, especially when they travelled together. Jennifer was intrigued by Bart's friends and the "late-night, long-party crowd" he introduced her to. And he was not only bright, articulate, sexy and playful, but was sometimes very caring. Jennifer expected that they would play a lot together, share many interests, live together and then get married, have children and live happily ever after. She also had the fantasy that at some point she might be supported by Bart, working as a "professional volunteer, doing the needed work that can't always be done inside the world of pay."

Jennifer and Bart did live together and at one point they were packing to move to a different house and she asked him to help her carry a heavy footlocker which she was struggling to move. He angrily refused and pushed her down the stairs, which resulted in ripped tendons and a sprained ankle. In retrospect, his refusal to take responsibility for what he'd done was the most significant aspect of that event for her. At the time, she was angry but she thought, "Jennifer, you're the one who wanted to move so bad. You shouldn't expect him to come home from work and help you move your stuff." She notes, now, that she didn't attend to the fact that she had worked all day herself.

The next incident occurred when, for no apparent reason, Bart threw something against the living room wall and then hurled a ladder through the kitchen window. Her first reaction this time was fear, but it soon turned to anger when he wouldn't help her repair the damage and she was faced with cold and rain in the house.

During one of their frequent separations, Jennifer visited Bart and they spent a comfortable evening together. As Jennifer was getting ready to leave, Bart suddenly picked her up and held her upside down over his head. "It couldn't have lasted long," she recalls, "but it seemed like forever. It was scary."

For a year or more there was no violence, but Jennifer wanted commitment and Bart didn't, though he wouldn't say so. He also was involved with other women, a fact he tried to keep from Jennifer. Her response to these problems was to keep working at finding solutions. The violence began again.

One night Bart came home two hours late, demanding dinner. Jennifer wanted to placate him, but was not able to curb her tongue. She told him to heat his dinner himself, and he took it out of the refrigerator and threw it all over the kitchen. Then he knocked her into a wall, broke a lamp and left the house. She locked the door, cleaned up the kitchen and said to herself, "Oh, Jennifer, you know he doesn't like you to give him a bad time about being late."

Arguments continued about Bart's staying out late, his other women and "his refusal to pull his own weight in the tasks of daily living." Jennifer felt she was doing it all. When Bart stayed out very late one night, she locked and chained the door.

He came home at three in the morning, kicked the door in, and snapped on the bedroom light. I woke up and said, "Would you please turn out the light?" He said, "Don't tell me what to do." The tone was, "Don't tell me I can't come into my own house. Don't tell me what time to be here. You don't have any say over my life. Who do you think you are? You don't control me." Those were all recurring phrases. He dragged me out of bed, and put my head through the wall. These were plaster walls, not stucco, but they weren't ticky-tacky. It takes a lot of force to put somebody's head through a wall. You break the wall with the back of your head and there you are, between the joists.

I was all of a sudden real still. I didn't want this to get worse, and my sense had been that if I were real quiet, completely compliant, he would quit. He pulled me out of the bedroom and into the living room and threw me against the lamp. It fell and broke, and I sort of was half on the floor and he dragged me up and threw me onto a big wooden chest. I fell, hurt my neck, hurt my back, hit my head and laid on the floor and pretended I was dead. I just laid there. He kicked me four times and I just tried to be limp. I'm sure it was clear to him I wasn't dead, but he could have thought I was unconscious.

After that we separated again, but I didn't get out. The violence bothered and scared me a lot, but I wasn't dealing with that. It was like an extra motivator, but it also wasn't public, and wasn't as humiliating as the the other women and the not showing up at public functions. I could handle anything, except someone making me look like a fool. At this point, I'm directing a goddamned social agency, and I have to be present at "affairs of state." We have our Mardi Gras night for all the bankers and business biggies to come and spend their money and contribute, and I'm expected to have my partner there to volunteer along with me, and the commitment's made, but he never shows up.

I remember feeling so tired, it was like slogging through mud in order to get up in the morning and walk to the door and then go to work. I needed somebody to say, "It's not your fault. You're not making him be this way and you can't make him not be this way." Nobody was saying that. One friend's response was, "Well, that's not really battering. It's not *that* serious. You didn't break any bones." As if it didn't quite count. It made me wonder, "Is this a figment of my imagination? Is this not really serious? Is this your excuse for wanting to get out of a difficult relationship? Are you trying to worm your way out, instead of hanging in there?" I still had this piece of me that thought I should be able to fix it.

"What's going on? Why can't you fix it?"

I, also, for a whole host of other strange and bizarre and twisted Freudian reasons, was—and in some ways *am*—in love with the guy. And I didn't want to start over again. Who wants to go on that market? That ugly singles scene? I didn't want all that pain and suffering you have in a new relationship. I was thinking, "This is real bad, but it could be worse." And who knew that there ever would *be* a new relationship?

I couldn't do my work as it should be done and if this relationship was going to take all this energy, I wasn't ever going to finish my Ph.D. I recognized that professionally I could never go anywhere so long as the bulk of my good, true energy was being consumed by dealing with the relationship. That was important. Another strong piece was fear. I'd finally arrived at the point I believed it was just luck that kept me from being killed or seriously wounded. I began to do some casual talking about battering and looking at an article here and there. I continued to stay with Bart, and to do a lot of self-talk, saying, "You've got to get out. This is no good," and finally talking to a couple of friends about it.

What got me out was work and fear, and finally I got so sick of telling myself, "You've got to get out, you've got to do something about this, this is how you're going to handle the next encounter, this is the kind of person you want to be" and then not doing it, that it was almost like vomiting myself out of the relationship. Fairly soon after the last violent incident, we quit going together and it was a mutual decision.

A consulting firm offered me a short-term job that included a lot of traveling. Being gone a lot helped. It was also dangerous, because when you're not in close proximity, everything else sort of pales, and when you see each other you can enjoy the good things without realizing the potential for strife in any situation that's beyond going to dinner and a movie.

After I left the last time, I was home visiting my parents, and Bart sent me eighteen red roses. Boy, am I sucker for red roses! I thought, "Oh, the sweetie. He loves me. It's all going to be all right." But that wasn't the film that was winning out. The one that was winning was, "I'm an independent person. I can take care of myself. I'm not ecstatic, but I'm reasonably satisfied. I can live by myself."

Jennifer had the support of friends who were encouraged by her change in attitude, and her parents provided unconditional love and approval. She also met a man in her travels, "a nice guy, ambitious, educated and solid," who was interested in her. Even though she knew she wouldn't become seriously involved with him, it was reassuring to realize that a good man cared for her and found her attractive, that there were alternatives after all.

Still, Jennifer waffled. When she heard Bart was talking about marrying another woman, her resolve to break off from him was strengthened. But then she heard that he had broken up with the new woman because he was still emotionally involved with Jennifer, and she considered trying again. A continuing business association with Bart necessitated contact with him, but also provided more proof that the relationship would not work. They had bought a piece of property together, but Jennifer found, on her return from a business trip, that he had failed to put her name on the deed, as agreed upon.

It was one more indication that he doesn't think of other people. The process for me was gradually adding one more piece of evidence that this would never work. If I believed it could work, I'd be in it today, no matter what it would take.

Even though I didn't talk about the relationship much, I was sure that everybody knew, and I was sure that everybody labeled me as committed to a loser. I got a job fifteen hundred miles away, because distance and a new beginning were critical. Here, no one knows about Bart. Finally, Bart realized the relationship was no good for me and I've got to give him some credit for supporting me in getting out of it.

Jennifer has been able to continue a friendship with Bart. She feels it's important to him to know there's someone who knows his worst traits and still cares, yet is not at all dependent on him and has no expectations of him. He visited her after she moved and it was the best time they ever had together, because, Jennifer says, "I wasn't *in* it any more. I really was finally *out*."

I'm glad it evolved that way, instead of me having to hate him. Oh, I hate parts of him. And if anybody were to raise a hand to me, it's probably a good thing I don't have a gun. I'd just shoot him. It's just utterly, completely unacceptable that anybody's going to use any kind of force against me, at all, for anything. I had to hate part of him, to get to that point.

Now, I can sleep at night. I enjoy listening to chamber music, taking ferry boat rides, giving parties, going out for coffee, seeing plays, everything everybody enjoys. Getting out is like cleaning out. It's like detoxification. It's like in a war, recapturing your own territory. "This is mine. This is mine. It's *all* mine." For me, it was getting it back a piece at a time. Now I think I own it all.

CHAPTER 33

Dianne

Dianne grew up on a farm, where she and her five siblings mostly looked after themselves, although her mother's three brothers lived with them and kept an eye on them while her parents worked. Her father worked in a steel mill and was affectionate and loving to his wife and the children. Her mother was a power machine operator who married at fourteen, had six children by the time she was nineteen, and for several years was left to raise them by herself while her husband was in the service.

I wouldn't say I was really abused by my mom, but I was told by her that I wasn't wanted, that she hated me. She stated to me when I was fourteen that she wished I would die, and from then on she kept saying it over and over. When my dad was home he would tell her to stop, so when he was there I would stay home. If he was gone, I would just stay long enough to do my chores and then I'd go to my uncle's and clean his house or to some of the neighbors' and do things for them. There was one lady who couldn't get up or anything because she was paralyzed. I would pick flowers for her or just sit with her for hours and talk because she was nice to me.

All the clothes went to my sister and I had to take her hand-me-downs, which was very embarrassing. I never got school lunches, so I'd wait 'til I got home to eat. After eighth grade I got a summer job babysitting and this lady was so nice to me, and paid good money, so I started buying clothes and stuff for myself. I had two bad teeth, and they were decayed down to the gums, so I asked my mom to have them fixed, but she wouldn't do it, so I paid for my own. When it was time to go back to school I just didn't do it. I kept on babysitting for about two years for twenty-five dollars a week and I thought that was really fantastic. No one else I knew dropped out, but neither of my parents said anything about it.

Dianne met Ian when she was sixteen. They were engaged a week after they met, married three weeks later and two months after that Dianne discovered she was pregnant. By December it was clear that Ian couldn't keep a job and Dianne was upset about his unwillingness to spend time at home. She tracked his movements, discovered his involvement with another woman, and when she confronted him he moved out. Dianne was convinced she was incompetent and stupid and that she'd be unable to manage on her own. "If I'd have looked, I'd have known I was managing, but I thought I needed someone to take care of me." She found an apartment and was able to get public assistance. She often took her baby, Jeff, for walks in the neighborhood and before long she began a friendship with Gerry, who who owned a neighborhood grocery store.

At first Gerry was real friendly, happy-go-lucky, had a good sense of humor, had money and was always doing things for me. He was kind to me and Jeff. He was nine years older than me and he had the same job and lived in the same house for ten years. That was neat to have somebody that was stable, compared to what I had just come from. In my first marriage we had owed everybody, but Gerry owned his store, his own car and a bike, and he didn't owe anybody. We were married two weeks after my divorce.

We had been married a year and two months and our daughter was five months old. We had gone to a wedding reception of one of his nieces. It was a big party and we were both dancing and having a good time. I danced two dances and came back to the table and he said, "Do you want to get next to him? You're trying to get his ____ in you." It hurt when he said that and I thought I'd just ignore it. So his brother walked up and asked me to dance and I said, "No," and Gerry goes, "Well, you want to, you know you do," and kept on and on, and finally I was really mad so I just got up and danced with his brother, and Gerry started saying all kinds of crude things.

He had never said that kind of stuff before, so I got up and started off to walk home, but he found me and dragged me back to the car and ripped my dress off. I mean the whole side was completely ripped, and he started hitting me and started slapping me and started using his fist on me and I was scared. I was really scared. I thought I was going to get killed. Finally he quit when his sister-in-law came to the car and asked me if I was okay. I was crying and Gerry said, "She's fine." She went on into the party and he said he was sorry and he'd never hit me again and told me that he loved me and it was just because he couldn't stand to see me with another man and that it would never, ever happen again.

So he went and found a needle and thread and we sewed my dress back up and he was just so sweet to me and so neat that night that I thought it would never happen again. It happened the second time about three months afterwards and then it just started into a pattern, and it didn't stop.

Looking back Dianne realizes there were some signs of trouble that she didn't recognize at first. Gerry was jealous of of anyone she talked to, including her son. After the first beating his jealousy and crude remarks took on a pattern. A friend of his would meet Dianne and say to Gerry something like, "How did you get such a young attractive gal?" Later Gerry would say, "You really want their cock in your cunt." (In recalling Gerry's language, sometimes Dianne was able to say the words, and sometimes not.) If a man smiled at her when they went shopping it would set him off, and if a woman smiled he would accuse Dianne of being a lesbian. She stopped smiling at everyone and pretended she didn't see anyone.

Dianne didn't think about the damage Gerry did to her, but tried to focus on the times he was loving and generous. Sometimes they had a good sexual relationship and sometimes he took her and the children camping or to the county fair. She would say to herself, "I have to stay, because when he is good to me, he is very good to me, and if he's mean to me it's because I *do* smile too much." She thought she was in love with him.

At first Gerry hit Dianne on her breasts and stomach. Later he hit her in the face, so she had to suffer the humiliation of having her bruises publicly exposed. After seven years he began to beat her up in public. Generally the beatings occured about every three months, but she never knew for sure when another one was coming, and there were periods when they occured once a week. Gerry drank heavily and sometimes he'd be gone from the house four or five days. He also started seeing other women, which was the last straw for Dianne.

I told him, "If you're going to mess around on me, let me show you what it feels like." I threatened and threatened. So my next door neighbor and I went out and I met a guy and started seeing him. He would take me to dinner and be nice to me. He called me one day and Gerry answered the phone and handed it to me. I talked to him and when I put the phone down he asked who it was. "Is that your boyfriend?" Normally I'd just say, "You know I don't do that." This time I just said, "Yes." I was truthful. I should have made a lie up, I should have done anything, because the next thing I knew he threw me against the wall, he was ready to kill me, he was choking me, and started ripping my clothes off and he started pulling on my ring and when he finally got it off—I thought he wanted it—he ripped my pants off and put my wedding band inside my vagina. My nose was bleeding, my lips were bleeding, I was a mess and he just stomped out. But he called about every ten minutes to make sure I was in the house.

When he beat me up, I'd say, "You'll never beat me up again. You'll never get the chance. I'm leaving." And he would say, "What do you think you can do? You were on welfare when I met you and you've never worked a day in your life. You don't know how to do anything." And then when he would go to work I'd start thinking, "How am I going to take care of my kids?" and I'd start thinking about the security of this home and that at least he worked and at least my kids were fed and what I should do is stay here. "I'll just be nicer and try not to get hit."

It got worse each time he hit me. Afterwards he would drive off or go to work and the next day he'd be sorry. I was ready to make up, because I was scared. I didn't have any place to go, I didn't want to live with my parents, and I was scared to be out in the cold with two kids. So I would do anything for peace.

In a desperate attempt to establish some independence, Dianne worked up her courage and applied for work as a nurse's aide. She was pleased to be hired, but had been on the job for just a month when her mother became seriously ill and soon it became apparent that she was dying. Dianne felt that she should be available to her and she left the job. During one visit, observing Dianne's black eye, her mother startled her by saying, "I never, ever figured you'd put up with that. You never put up with that from me. You always mouthed off at me. I always thought you had more spunk than that."

After her mother died Dianne began to think that perhaps she didn't have to put up with Gerry's violence. Watching her mother die at the age of fifty gave her a new perspective on her own life and she began to ask new questions. "Am I going to let myself be beat? Is this what I'm going to look forward to the rest of my life? Is this what I want from my life? Will I make it to forty?"

After my mom died we went East for the funeral. My aunts and uncles are as young as I and my uncles are real good looking. At the funeral home everybody was hugging and kissing. Gerry went off mad and came back drunk, saying "You want your uncle's _____ in you." He grabs me and calls me a slut. "I'm going to tell your uncles you're out here waiting with your legs wide open." He said he was going to pack up the kids and take them back home. I promised I would do anything, not to have to leave before my mother's burial the next day. "I won't talk to them, won't even look at them." So the next day I had to ignore them. I hadn't seen them for thirteen years and I couldn't even look at them.

A year later he hit me across the face for some reason I can't even remember. I told him that was it. Never again. I called the shelter and they set me up with an attorney. For exactly one year, the fact that he did what he did to me on the day my mom was buried was eating away at me. And *everything* was eating away at me. The funny part of it is, this slap was nothing compared to other ones that year. I wasn't mad, I did it so calm, so cool, so collected, I just took the ring off and handed it over and told him it was over and he'd never hit me again. And he hasn't.

I didn't know where I was going to go, I didn't know anything. He quit his job and left for Oregon to get into construction and left me with fifty dollars. I thought, "Fifty dollars! That ought to last me a long time!" The day he left here I went out and looked for a job.

I went to a few places and I was scared stiff, but I kept telling myself, "I can get a job. I know I can." I went to a nursing home and walked around it about four times before I got the courage to walk in the door. They said, "No openings," but I just happened to see a friend whose husband was in the home and she said to the guy, "If you need a good worker, she's a good worker." So from her saying that they had me fill out an application.

A week went by and then three weeks went by and I kept calling and they didn't have any openings. I tried to look other places. I would go and I'd try to say that I wanted a job; I was so nervous and scared 'cause I thought, "Why would anyone want to hire me?" The doubt was there, but yet I knew I had to try, because if I didn't get the job I would have to go back to him and I would have to take the abuse and I'd have to put my kids through all this again.

I had no other choice. I went down to welfare. It was a big hassle, and when I came back home there was a phone call from the nursing home and they said I could start tomorrow morning. I told welfare I wouldn't need them after my first check, but the lady showed me with all my debts and everything else that I'd still need assistance.

The first day, they put me on ward five, which is mental. It has locks on it and I didn't know it was for mental. I went in there to take this tray to a room and the door shut. These people were moaning and groaning and screaming and yelling to let them out and I'm just standing there with this tray in my hand 'cause I didn't know what I was doing there. I was so scared I ran to the door and started beating on it. "Let me out, let me out!" But there was those other people standing around yelling the same thing. I was standing in a corner crying and I just knew I was going to die right there. There was nobody ever going to find me. Finally a nurse came in and found me and took me out. She gave me some coffee and calmed me down and I was just shaking.

I wasn't going to do it. I didn't think I could do it. I was going to go home right then. But the nurse talked to me and then put me on another ward and I made it through that shift and then a week went by and I still was working and I still was making it. Just that week gave me the encouragement I needed, that I could do it. I didn't want welfare, I wanted to make it, because so many years he had put me down. So many years he told me that I couldn't do it, that behind this was the determination to prove to him that I could do it. I could do the house payments, I could do the light bills, I could do the groceries, I could do the things that he said all those years I could not do.

They gave me a full-time position and exactly one month after that my boss says, "I want to make you supervisor of the area," and I go, "Supervising what?" I couldn't believe it. That was my wing, I was to take care of it and train other girls. I was so proud of myself. I mean I really felt like I was somebody. Then I started thinking, "You're not so dumb. You're uneducated, but you're not stupid. You can do things."

The next thing was, "I'm going to get a car," and my kids going, "Yeah, sure, Mom, sure." Okay, earning four hundred and fifty a month was not very much. I had a hundred and fifty dollars in savings. This girlfriend knew somebody who had a car for three hundred and I got a loan from a credit union and a neighbor taught me how to drive.

A friend who was starting a job at a home for retarded adults tried to persuade Dianne to apply for work there too, but she insisted she couldn't do it. The friend persisted, accompanied her when she handed the application in and soon Dianne was called for an attendant counselor position. "That sounds important, right? All the way there I'm saying, 'I'm too dumb. I'm a nurse's aide, not an attendant counselor.'" She was hired in spite of herself and on the first day was as shaky and scared as she had been the first day at the nursing home. But within a week she was told that her employer liked her work and she was able to relax somewhat.

Dianne was doing well until nine months after the separation, when Gerry started calling. Then the "old depressed Dianne" started talking to herself again. Once more a friend came to her aid by lending her self-help books. Dianne doubted at first whether she would be able to use them, since her education had stopped at eighth grade and she had persuaded herself that she couldn't read. But she picked up one of the books and one more time proved to herself that she could do what she had thought impossible. "It was really fantastic. I read a whole book all by myself." Now a stack of self-help books are always by her favorite chair, and she considers them indispensable.

Although the books helped give her strength, they were not always enough. More than once Dianne walked in her door after work to find Gerry sitting in a chair waiting for her. She never knew how he got in. On one of those occasions, about a year after she had sued for divorce, she let him stay. He never hit her, but the crude remarks began again, and Dianne thought, "I'm not going to have to build myself back up. I'm not going to do it again." After four weeks, without warning, she packed his clothes and put them on the porch and locked the door.

It's taken me a long time to bring myself up as far as I have and I don't want to go back down. I want to continue going up. Thirty-five years is old to wake up. That day he slapped me I said, "I'm thirty-five years old. Here I'm going to be living the rest of my life with a man slapping me around? When I'm forty, fifty, sixty, and when I'm an old lady? I'm going to be living like this, afraid to move out of the house, afraid to smile?"

Sometimes I'll be at the store and all of a sudden I'll just smile at anybody that walks by. It's mainly because of all those years I was afraid to smile. My kids are away and for the last three weeks I've been living by myself. I have never been by myself for any length of time. I guess I thought I would die from loneliness, but I really don't need somebody to keep me entertained or to keep me from being lonely. I've got my books, I've got my stereo. Before I had to have somebody to protect me, somebody to feed me, pay my bills. But I don't need that, because I'm doing that myself.

CHAPTER 34

Lessons From the Women Who Got Away

Some of the women interviewed for this book had specific advice for other women who are in relationships with dangerous partners. There are also aspects of their lives which offer implicit examples of what to do and what to avoid. In this chapter I'll summarize the hard-learned lessons they wanted to tell other women about.

LOOK OUT FOR WARNING SIGNS

Some of the women had little or no warning that they would be battered until they were married or otherwise entrenched in the relationship. Although many partners tried to dominate the women by requests or demands that they confine themselves to household tasks, drop out of school or quit work, the women tried to please the partners and didn't recognize these attempts to isolate them as omens of potential control, which would later be backed up by threats and abuse.

Many of the women had no experience that would alert them to the dangers of their partners' efforts to control them, especially when those efforts were disguised as loving protection. Most women either ignored them or shrugged them away. In some instances they allowed their partners to "explain" that an angry outburst or unreasonable demand was "only because of stress . . . or alcohol . . . or an unhappy childhood or . . . ." Sometimes the abusive partner persuaded the woman it was her fault, or she blamed herself for being too selfish or too thoughtless.

When George got drunk at a party and smashed a window, Madlyn comforted herself that he hadn't hit her. When she learned that he had beaten his first wife she was sure it didn't matter because she would never "run around on him." Like many other women she assumed his treatment of his first wife was brought about by the wife's behavior, and that it would never happen to her.

Some women ignored signs of alcoholism, drug abuse and other addictive behavior such as gambling and habitual stealing, which didn't necessarily indicate battering, but which typically have adverse effects on intimate relationships. Denial and minimization of the potential danger usually began soon after the relationship started. The women whose stories appear in this book hope to save other women from repeating the mistakes they made, and they were adamant about the importance of noticing everything about a potential partner and staying alert for signs of trouble.

If they drink too much or call you names or hit you even once, don't stay. Listen carefully to what they say to you and other people. Watch how they are with you, alone and in groups. See how they treat animals. Watch how they treat other people, whether they're responsible, on time, pay their bills. These are practical things, but can be emotional.

There's always going to be a sign of battering. It may not be physical, but when you feel like your human rights as a woman are being stepped upon and you're being mistreated, stop and think about it and say, "This may not be the best for me." When they are very argumentative, protective, possessive, want you with them every minute, you have to get away.

TELL OTHER PEOPLE

You may not want to tell anyone your partner has abused

you, especially if there have been apologies and promises not to repeat the behavior. It's hard to admit out loud that you've been mistreated by someone you love or "need," but it's also the beginning of your best protection. The women in this book say, "Don't be isolated" and "Find caring people." That means talk to people. Tell them what's been done to you. Before it even gets to that point educate your friends about abuse. Then, if you're feeling weak because you love a person who's violent or you're enduring abuse because you're lonely, they can remind you that you deserve better.

I know it's embarrassing, but don't be afraid to tell somebody. If someone turns you down, go to another person. The main thing is don't give up.

It was good for me to tell other women friends, "This is what I've done. I've been talked into believing it won't happen again. Help me stop myself from doing that again." It's embarrassing to have people know that you allowed this to happen to yourself, but if you're going to get help you you've got to admit it.

NOTICE WHEN YOU'RE VULNERABLE

Although some of the women became involved with the abusive partners when their lives were going well, others were particularly vulnerable. Any condition that makes you feel weak or alone or needy can cause you to be less discriminating about a potential partner than you ordinarily would. If you're living in a strange city and wishing you had friends or people of your own sort to spend time with, you can easily overlook signs of trouble.

Lynn was isolated as a black woman in a new city, new school and new job when she met Warren. When his extended family took her in, she was so glad to have something like a substitute home that she ignored signs of trouble. May was in a similar position the first time she was away from Chinatown and her family. She wasn't feeling good about herself either, because for the first time in her life she wasn't performing well. Janine was recovering from an emotionally abusive relationship and her bruised ego finally succumbed to the adoring attentions of a young man she didn't even care for.

Other women had been subjected to longstanding disabilities or abuse as children of adults, and became vulnerable to partners who either repeated familiar patterns or seemed to provide protection which was badly needed. The abuse Dee's mother subjected her to made it difficult to recognize the same pattern in Pete. Her mental illness caused her to be chronically disabled and hospitalized. She knew her condition would be used against her in court if she left her husband and tried to take the children. Grace was so ill when she met Del that he was surprised she had survived at all. All of her adult life she suffered damage from polio and could only work part-time, which would not provide her with enough money to support her six children.

> Be especially careful if you're sick, depressed or just feeling down about the way things are going in your life. If you're lonely, try to connect with women friends instead of looking for a lover right away. Look out for boredom. It's a warning sign.

TEEN INVOLVEMENTS

Quite a few of the women first became involved with the abuser when they were vulnerable teenagers. Chris' family life was disrupted, she had been molested by her stepfather and neglected by her father. She was bored with school and had no goals. Moving in with a man seemed like a way out of all of it.

Lucia, Maria, Margaret, Maddie, Gloria, Dianne, Dee, Allie and Lou all were teenagers when they became involved with the people who battered them. Nearly all of them lived in chaotic or abusive families and were eager for independence and hungry for love. They didn't realize that the partners they chose would demand much more obedience and dependence than their parents had, and would subject them to at least as much abuse. Several of those women were involved with partners quite a few years older than they, which lent an aura of glamor to the relationship. It also gave the abusive partner an extra edge of power. Many teenagers are at special risk because their home lives are unsatisfying or dangerous and their options are limited. The implicit advice for young women in confining or abusive homes is that there may be choices you haven't thought of:

> Wait! Give it a year or two. Take time to find someone with whom you can develop a healthy, nurturing relationship, rather than jumping blindly into something even worse than what you have now. Even though you may feel you can't endure your situation, you have some flexibility now or can develop it, but a relationship with a violent, controlling partner may last for many years before you're able to leave.

If you're a teenager and you're being abused, emotionally, physically or sexually you can call your local child protective services office or the police. Child abuse is against the law and you can ask them to either insist that your parents change or help you find a foster home. That won't be an ideal situation, but in a few years you'll be old enough to control your own life. Two or three years may seem forever now, but remember that it took Margaret, Maddie, Gloria, Dianne, Dee and Allie between ten and twenty years to leave their partners. While you're waiting for your freedom you can concentrate on making good friends who appreciate you and learning skills that will help you be independent.

DON'T TRY TO RESCUE

Some women believed they could rescue the partner. It was especially appealing if the partner had had a difficult childhood, had been left by other women, was unemployed or vulnerable because of personal or societal mistreatment. Joe's greatest appeal to Kate was that she had never seen anyone in so much pain and she thought she could take it away.

The lesson here is that great pain and compulsive behavior require tremendous will and professional help to overcome. A lover is not the person to act as therapist.

Sue faced a difficult ethical dilemma when her boyfriend tried to kill himself after she left him. Her decision wasn't as simple as her therapist saw it, and perhaps she never would have forgiven herself if she hadn't gone back for one more try at a good relationship. But when it became clear that she couldn't rescue someone who wasn't trying to rescue himself, she left right away.

> He started telling me things about how his mother used to get beat up by men and then I felt like, "I can change him. I can rescue him. He's had a hard life . . . "

You can get wrapped up in believing it's your role to be supportive of his insanity, but don't.

RESPECT YOURSELF

It's extremely difficult to build your self-esteem and to develop some self-respect yourself when you're involved with someone who consistently tries to tear down your self-concept. If I hadn't talked to so many women who were able to do it in spite of their abusive partners, I wouldn't believe it possible. Many of the women were demoralized, brainwashed and physically and emotionally depleted, yet when it was clearly necessary, they garnered the strength to act with decisiveness and courage. Their ability to do that in the face of such obstacles is the most puzzling aspect of their lives.

Some of the women felt extremely weak when they left. Dianne had "hit bottom" and had been so isolated from the world that she didn't even know fifty dollars was a drop in the bucket of her needed support for herself and her two children. But soon she was supporting herself and had found a core of strength she didn't know she had. Madlyn said that at some point she simply lost her will and Ruth distinctly remembered the moment her will was broken, but when their lives were clearly threatened they both were able to act in time to save themselves. Against all odds, some of the women felt stronger when they were preparing to leave than when they had entered the relationship.

> You have to learn self-respect. The idea is to get it into your head you are worth it. The first thing I want to tell an abused woman is don't blame yourself for what the abuser does. If any psychiatrist says, "You're wrong, it's your responsibility to make this marriage work," I'd leave immediately. If anyone tells you you're to blame, run! Just turn around and go.
>
> If any therapist implied I wasn't abused, like the one that said I was "supposedly," abused I'd confront her right there. I would check it out. "What do you mean 'supposedly' abused?"

GET OUT NOW

All of the above presupposes that you aren't going to be ready to leave the first time you are hit or threatened or emotionally abused. But it's much safer to act immediately after the first sign of abuse even if it seems minor.

Women who have struggled to free themselves, to rebuild their self-esteem and make radical changes in their lives have this advice for women still in dangerous relationships: "get out as quickly as possible." Some put it bluntly, while others speak sadly of their regrets and their hopes that you can be saved from making the same mistakes.

> Promises to change are just a bunch of bullshit. When you stop kidding yourself that things are going to get better and realize they're going to get worse, you really want out. Things won't change. Maybe it's smoothed over for a little while, but even if you're not physically harmed again, it's going to be the same mind trip.
>
> I look back and I'd never put my children through that. I feel like my fifteen-year-old was robbed and I resent it. Get out when they're small.

If you're a Latina woman and you're afraid you'll be ostracized if you leave, check it out. It's not so likely to be true any more. Other women have left abusive men and have been accepted by many people in their own culture. If you're an undocumented woman, don't give up. Find out what the law is and whether you really are in danger of being deported. How can he have you deported if you go to a shelter and he doesn't know where you are? There are lots of people who can help you. See if there's a Latina hotline or safe home or shelter in your community.

If you're an Asian undocumented woman, find out if there is an Asian organization that can help you. If there isn't one in your city, try the nearest city with a large Asian population. Get information about what you need to do to get your own permanent residency established. Try to have your papers available, in case you have to leave suddenly.

If you're a lesbian try to find a lesbian counselor who understands that lesbians batter and who takes your problem seriously. Call a shelter to find out what they can do for you and whether they are knowledgeable about lesbian battering. If it comes down to whether I'm going to live, I'd be in the closet if necessary. I'd just say "he's" doing it and be vague about "him." Then when I got in the shelter I'd find somebody to support me. If it came to the legal stuff I'd come out of the closet.

Don't think you can't be battered just because you're a lesbian. I didn't realize I was raped because I defined it as penetration. And don't think there is something wrong with you because you're a lesbian who's battered.

If I was on the streets as a prostitute again I'd get information and support. If I'd had information that I had a right not to be beaten, I might have made a different choice. A prostitute can exert her rights there just the same as I can. I'd work on getting a support system with other women. And I'd want to work on getting legal rights in the system the same way I want legal rights as a lesbian.

Once you've left, don't for any reason go back. You can make it. You're better off without somebody telling you that you can't do it.

My saving grace was that this time I just did not listen to him. All the other times I had talked to him and listened to what he had to say.

I had always thought every time that happened, I was going to leave. And I would go in the bedroom and take one last look and he would smile at me and say, "Are you still mad at me?" This time I was just sitting there thinking, "I cannot stop him, and I have to face this every night, even when the children are all married and gone? . . . I don't want that."

CREATE YOUR OWN NETWORK

Some women left before they had an opportunity to create a helpful network. Jennifer moved several hundred miles away and had to develop new friends, but she was far safer doing that than staying close to Bart. After she left, Sue wanted to start over with an entirely new group of friends, which took time to find. Nicole kept in touch with women in the group for black women. Each woman found some way to develop the kinds of relationships that could be relied on.

Get involved in activities. The first time I went to a Parents Without Partners meeting I was petrified. But I wasn't expected to do anything, and I could just sit and observe, so I felt safe. I stayed for the discussion, but afterwards I hurried home. Then I met another woman and we decided to go together to dance. We sat on the edges and watched, but the "shuffle" just looked so neat

out there, I said, "We've got to learn that." So we got on
either side of this guy who was very friendly, safe, older,
and we learned that shuffle.

At first it's like a void. Nobody asks you out, nothing
happens to you, you walk around like a zombie, and day
by day, little by little, things start filtering in . . . maybe
because you let them. At first you're just numb, and you
won't let in any good feelings. Then you realize, "Oh, a
week has passed and I didn't feel so bad." Next time it's
a month, then six months.

When you're in pain it's just excruciating, but the
depressed times get shorter and shorter.

Don't look back. Don't think you're alone. Seek help
wherever you can find it. If you don't have a reliable
friend yet, see a counselor or go to a group. Go to a social worker or a church. First look someone in the eye.
Then smile at them. Begin with women. Find other
women, whether in a shelter, a formal group, in new
friendships or through confiding in trusted old friends.
The world is full of women who are lonely, depressed
and poor too, and you can help each other. Find women
to live with, communally.

You need some intelligent, experienced women. It
would be good if they're single and doing all right,
somebody you respect, that you can call when you're
feeling weak. A support group should never say, when
you go back, "Well, you've been here three times, we
don't want to see you again." No matter how many times
you try to get out and fail, the group should always be
there until you don't need it. And one day you won't
need it.

When you feel lonely, instead of looking for a man,
you can go with some women to hear music. If no one
asks me to dance, I'm not going to worry. Three of us
might get up and dance, where before that was a symbol
of failure. If I hadn't of left I wouldn't have known all
these great women. I'm feeling really good about that.

You need somebody that's definitely not going to look down on you or say it's your fault, you're not strong or you made a bad choice. You need someone who says, "I understand. I know it's rough, it's hard." Whether men or women, stay away from people who won't listen or won't be involved. Find caring people.

CREATE YOUR OWN ENVIRONMENT

The women who stayed away took responsibility for moving to new houses, new cities, choosing jobs and making important decisions about where and how they'd live, often for the first time in their lives. Whether they went to school or to work or stayed home or moved to another city or developed an entirely new set of friends, it was their decision, not someone else's, and they were willing to take responsibility for the consequences. When things didn't work out they tried something different.

Any city is better than a small town for singles. You can find free concerts, museums, walking tours and parks. There are coffee shops where you can sit for three hours and hear piano. You can go up in hotels and look down at the city, wander the wharf, take the bus to the beach, go to poetry readings, pay two bucks for the theater or nothing for street theater, jugglers, puppet shows, etc.

Move to Timbuktu. Live in another state for a while. Read everything on being single and being lonely. Don't let yourself feel like a failure. You have to begin with little tiny steps.

Don't dwell on the negative, dwell on the positive. When I was feeling enraged because I was still paying the bills from letting him charge expensive items on my cards, I learned to say to myself, "This is just another installment in the school of hard knocks."

ADVICE ABOUT NEW POTENTIAL PARTNERS

The women were most vocal about the need for women friends and about the things to look out for in potential new partners. Their advice includes negative traits to be wary of as well as positive things to look for. You need to rely on your intuitive feelings to tell you when someone you're with is acting in a way that may be dangerous for you. Even if you can't articulate what is wrong, if you're uneasy, trust yourself.

Pay special attention to stomach upsets, tense muscles or anxiety. When your body is trying to give you a message, think about whether there is any reason at all that you might not trust the person you're with, even if it seems like "no big deal." In fact be especially watchful if you hear yourself excusing some behavior as unimportant, as "just" the result of stress, alcohol, an unhappy childhood, a misunderstanding, etc. Notice how many times you say to yourself that it's just this or that, that it's not important or that after all you have faults too.

You'll find it much easier to be aware of problem areas if you've allowed yourself a period without an intimate partner, so that you know you can get along well witout having to attach yourself to the first potential partner that comes your way. You'll be in a better position to evaluate a new person's negative as well as positive traits. When you begin to become involved with someone new, pay special attention to the person's reactions when you disagree; express your feelings, say what you want or just say, "No." It may be that your potential lover is nice or fun, but ultimately wants to be the one who decides how you will be together. So it's a good idea to take the time to put the new relationship in perspective.

Be real leery of people who want to have a lot of power. The ones who want the fast, hot cars or motorcycles can't seem to feel enough power, and that feeds their ego. I'd look out for them.

They want to win your confidence and at first they appear passive, but eventually under stress, they change. Particularly if you're in a hurry or something, how do they respond? And watch whether they're putting you down subtly.

Look out for their reactions to frustrations. Notice whether they feel that they're better than you and if they want to listen to your experiences or if they're impatient with your pain.

If they drink, stay away. Stay away from those who don't know who you are or who are hostile about the world. People who do a comraderie thing of pushing, shoving and horseplay have some kind of retarded development. They're back in the twelve to fourteen age group.

Watch for extremely hostile relationships with previous lovers, and look out for obsessive talk about previous relationships. Watch for whether the partners try to come between you and your girlfriends. See how your friends react to your new lover.

Don't trust people who don't express emotions. If they can talk, they won't need to hit.

Don't meet them in bars. If you're looking for someone for real, you're going to have to be a little bit pickier about it. Next time I'm in a new relationship I'm going to see a counselor even if I'm just dating, because I don't trust myself with reading the messages. Sure I'm better at it, but....

But don't think that dating is such a big deal. I was just setting myself up to be lonely, waiting for calls.

If you're looking for a man, find one who cares about women and who's interested in the women's movement, who says that women matter, that we're important. We need to spot chauvinists.

If you're beginning to fall for somebody ask yourself questions about them. How much control do they have? Do they decide where you're going to go or do they ask your opinion? Are they willing to say, "I'm afraid?" like

"I'm afraid to drive when I've had too much to drink?" Do they listen to you as much as you listen to them? Can you trust each other? Do you like each other? Can you laugh together? What are their insecurities? Can you share, be yourself, laugh, cry, be angry, be up, down, sick, well—and still be accepted? Are they, and are you, totally accepting? Can you be quiet, spend time by yourself? Can you be friends?

Know yourself and know your limits. Get the emotional compatibility first. It takes time to develop. Lots of communicating. Know what you're looking for. Give yourself time. Plenty of time. Try different ones. Look for the opposite of the one you were with.

I tested my husband, deliberately getting him angry. And I tested myself. Could I leave him for a week to visit friends? I said to myself, "don't be afraid of losing him; if he doesn't like you because of this it's just as well to find out now."

Aside from "Get out now," the clearest, most emphatic message the women expressed is to talk to other people, especially other women, and to keep talking until you find someone who understands what your situation is and what you need. It may seem that there is no one in your life right now who would understand, and that may be true. But remember the women like Pauline and Terry who thought they had no one to turn to, until the moment of desperation came. Then a friend, co-worker, relative, or professional helper was remembered and came through with housing or transportation or a connection with someone else who could help. When it was clear that taking the initiative was absolutely necessary, most women were willing to take the risk of being turned down and often they found help where it hadn't been expected.

Although there are common themes in the women's advice, as there are in their personal stories, each woman found her own way of being strong. Each of you will find your individual way of developing a life of peace and freedom. You may think of those words as too lofty to apply to you. Maybe they seem like Fourth of July speech material, or part of the political rhetoric. But they can be applied to you and your most intimate relationship as well. Peace, freedom and justice, like charity, begin at home. Or at least they can if women continue to work together to make it happen. In the next chapter I'll discuss the reasons the women left their abusive partners and the things that helped them stay away.

CHAPTER 35

Leaving and Staying Away

GETTING AWAY

As I have re-read these stories, what stands out to me is the complexity of each woman's reasons for staying, leaving and remaining free. The women are markedly different from each other in personality, character, class, ethnicity, age and occupation—even in sexual orientation. Yet their experiences with their violent partners are similar, as are many of their reactions and even their language in describing the partners and the ways they behaved. Phrases like "Jekyll and Hyde" and "walking on eggshells," for instance, are used over and over.

In this chapter I'll discuss the most common reasons the women gave for breaking away and the aspects of their lives that enabled them to do so. I also want to look at the difficulties of trying to name a single cause of each woman's decision to leave. One incident sometimes appears to cause a woman to make the final break from the abuser, but it is often just the last link in a long chain of events.

Few women gave only one reason for finally leaving, and even those who did usually also mentioned background factors that had some influence. There were an average of more than five explicit reasons for each woman's final exit and for some women there were as many as nine, in addition to the earlier events that appeared to open the way for change and eventual separation.

There is nothing surprising about these multiple causes. If we asked people why they made almost any change in their lives—stopped smoking, got married, dropped out of school or changed careers—they would probably not give definitive, simple answers. Many of us respond, even to relatively easy questions, with explanations of a process which may include more than one immediate cause as well as background factors and the pros and cons of various options. Leaving a partner you're committed to, perhaps married to, or with whom you have raised children requires a far more complex decision.

In deciding to leave abusive partners, some women seem to experience a sudden breakthrough similar to the "snapping out" phenomenon in which people "suddenly" come out of a trance-like state induced by some religious cults. A new perspective surfaces and the abused person says emphatically, "That's it. No more!" She leaves and never returns. But it may not be as abrupt as it looks. "Snapping out" has been compared to a geological theory of catastrophe, which describes how earthquakes and other natural events, which we experience as sudden, have been invisibly inching their way toward the final dramatic eruption for years or even centuries.[1] The theory offers an apt analogy to human decision-making processes.

The precipitating cause for the final break may be an escalation of the violence, a newly perceived threat to the children, the partner's interest in another woman, increased support or special attention from others, a period of respite from the abuse or a host of other events. On a first reading of a story a single event appears to be crucial to the women's decision to leave, but a more careful review often reveals that preparatory emotional and psychological "rumblings" have been hidden under the surface for a long time before the obvious eruption.

Fear of Staying

Several women left when they realized they couldn't count on any limit to the amount of violence they endured and the damage it could do. They believed their partners might kill them or do permanent physical damage. Melissa's sudden understanding that she might die made her acutely aware that she hadn't done what she wanted to do in life. She knew she would have to leave Tom if she was to live long enough to do the things that were important to her.

There are subtle differences in the women's reactions to the threat of death. When Maria's husband said he was going to kill her, she had a single-minded reaction. "I'm afraid. I don't care where I'm going. I close my eyes." She left for the United States at the first possible moment. When Margaret saw Roy's gun on the floor she acted to save her life, though later she didn't remember doing it.

The threat to Pauline's life was less dramatic, but every bit as real. Her health had deteriorated, she had been hospitalized and she was too weak to feed herself. On two occasions when she left the hospital Pauline was certain she had no choice but to return to Matthew. Yet when he beat her the last time she realized he could kill her. She found a woman friend to stay with and then arranged an extended stay with her aunt.

Fear for the children was a major motivator for several women to leave, though it wasn't always the only reason. For instance, it may have been fairly easy for Janine to act on her fear for her daughter because she didn't love Raul and she had never really expected the marriage to be permanent. In addition, Raul's absence during most of the week gave her an opportunity to explore her ability to run the household alone and to build her self-confidence. Madlyn left when George threw her daughter on the floor, but she did not leave during an earlier period when he abused her son.

Some women first developed the courage to leave and then made plans to actually do it. The women who left suddenly after a specific frightening incident often had no plans at all. After they left they had to find resources and develop the capacity to persevere in the face of the ex-partner's harassment or attempts at seduction or both.

Loss of Hope for Change

Although Lynn's fear of being killed was a strong motivator in her decision to leave, another important factor was her certainty that that there was nothing she could do to change her situation. She and Warren had been to counseling together. She had called the police and Warren had been to court numerous times. He had even been to an anger management group. None of it made a difference and she had run out of things to try.

Some women lost hope when they realized their partners were involved with other women. Sue had believed her boyfriend was trying to change his life and that he needed her. When she saw him with his arm around another woman, she said to herself, "This is the guy who is going to kill himself over me?" She knew, then, that he didn't care for her enough to change. She also realized that she didn't have to assume responsibility for his potential suicide. She was free to leave without guilt.

Hitting "Rock Bottom"

Dianne said, "You have to hit rock bottom, like an alcoholic." She left when Gerry slapped her face, but she had known the time was coming since her mother's death a year earlier. The humiliation she experienced at the funeral appeared to be the "bottom" for her. Even though that wasn't the moment she chose to leave she knew then that she wouldn't stay long. As she nursed her mother through her last illness a new awareness of her own mortality contributed to her eventual decision to leave. In addition, comments her mother had made about her "taking" the battering had caused a shift in her perspective.

"Rock bottom" was experienced by each woman in a different way. Shame when she was observed being beaten caused Amanda to leave, but it isn't clear whether she would have remained separated had not Sam flaunted his affair with another woman. It was her outrage at the other woman's menstrual blood on her sheets that propelled her out of the relationship.

When Robin threw Ruth out of the house without any clothes on Ruth said, "She broke me. There was still fear and terror, but it was sort of like she was beating a dead person." Yet when Robin beat her again she was able to leave. It's not clear whether feeling "dead," or hitting bottom, kept her from leaving then or contributed at a later time to her ability to leave. Perhaps it was both.

Hope for a Better Life Without the Abuser

Many women had stayed as long as they did because they

felt hopeless about either finding a more satisfactory partner or of creating a life of their own. Some were able to consider leaving when they saw a small sign that someone else cared for them. They began to think that separation from the violent partner didn't necessarily mean a life alone. A romance helped Grace realize she could respond to a man and was not "this shriveled up, frigid discard in the corner." The approval of a man she wasn't even interested in gave Maddie hope for a new life.

A few of the women had hit their lowest point long before they left and their lives had actually improved at the time they made the final break. Gloria, who thought she was "just a dumb Indian," had experienced no physical abuse and even developed a somewhat compatible relationship with Hal for several years before he reverted to his previous pattern of heavy drinking. It was the first time in her life she lived in relative peace, and the contrast may have made Hal's renewed verbal abuse and heavy drinking intolerable, even though it was not yet nearly as abusive as it had been in the past. She had learned what it was like to live a fairly companionable life without the threat of violence and perhaps she realized it would be possible to experience it with someone else.

Some women benefited by temporary separations. Janine's husband traveled on his job and whenever he was gone she gained strength. Jennifer and Sandy were blessed with jobs that took them on the road; they could gradually become used to the separation and begin to regain self-esteem. Chris and Dianne each gave the relationship one more try after having left "for the last time." But each insisted her husband leave after a short period and relatively minor indications that the men had not significantly changed. Chris' husband had not gotten work as promised and Dianne was unwilling to accept the renewed verbal abuse. She knew she didn't want to have to build herself up again. The brief separations seem to have given each of these women enough autonomy to believe they could live alone if that became necessary.

Positive External Influences
Shelters offered some women an opportunity to gain a new

perspective on the relationship and to see their lives reflected in the reactions of other women. Paid staff and volunteers, some of whom had survived battering and forged successful new lives, provided emotional support. Gloria stayed in a shelter twice, the first time using it as a safe base from which to persuade Hal to move out and leave the house to her and the children. Although Nicole returned to Luke one more time after she joined the group for black women, their support helped her make the final break.

Professionals, work colleagues, friends and family sometimes offered strong, positive messages of hope that a comfortable life could be found without the abusive partner. A few of the women benefited from family members' or friends' direct intervention. Maria might never have gotten away had it not been for the cooperation of the shelter in her home country and the one in the U.S. She was given the necessary money for the plane trip by her mother and sister. Although Joan's therapist sabotaged her moves toward freedom at one important point, he also contributed to her feeling that she could attract another man and exercise some personal power. Later that confidence played a role in her decision to leave. Several women found therapists who helped them see it was not their fault they were being abused. Lou said of her one visit to a psychiatrist, "That was the first time I thought it was something Barry was doing." Nicole's counselor helped her build her self-confidence.

Work was an important factor for some women. Jennifer talked to herself for a long time about the need to separate, and much of her "self-talk" was about the importance of her career. Lou's long hours and increasing responsibilities on the job absorbed her attention and helped her through the period of transition.

Events Beyond the Women's Control

For some women, events that were out of their control accelerated their leaving. When Sandy's husband said their child was probably not even his, she left. But she didn't expect him to be packed up and gone upon her return. Once that happened she maintained the separation and didn't give in when he entreated her to come back to him. Clearly she had been getting ready to leave, but we don't know how long it would have taken if he hadn't left first.

Some events were dramatic and definitive. For Margaret, as we have already seen, the unexpected appearance of her husband's gun instantly limited her options. Gwen's husband finally took himself out of her life forever by killing himself.

Tipping the Scales of Hope and Fear

There are common themes to these stories. The reasons for leaving can be summarized this way: increased fear following an intolerable escalation of abuse or a heightened awareness of its danger; loss of hope that the partner would change; increased hope for a good life without the partner; diminished fear of life without the partner. In other words, during the course of the relationship the women had made decisions by balancing their fear of staying against the hope for an improved relationship without the partner, or weighing the hope for change in the relationship with their fear of living alone. Although they didn't necessarily state it that way, many left when there was a shift in the balance of fear or hope.

For some women the scales tipped very gradually, with no perceptible point that made the crucial difference until the end. For others there was an event that caused a change in the woman's view of her situation, then another in the same direction, and then another. When Sandy's husband was verbally abusive to his son, she saw it as the "rebirth" of her father's treatment of her and realized it was an assault on her self-esteem, just as her father's words had been. That was an important moment, but not the first event to move her toward separation, since she had been working with a psychiatrist for a long time before that. The therapy had begun when she heard a child crying—a child who turned out to be herself. As mentioned above the time she spent on the road singing had also contributed to an improved sense of her self-worth and her abilities. Even earlier, her brief affair with a man at her friend's wedding taught her that there were people who could form nurturing, gentle, loving relationships.

Kate consciously created the events that would eventually

set her free even while she was attending couples therapy and supporting her husband's work in his group for batterers. She gradually spent less and less time with him, made new friends, found a job and just before she left, found an inexpensive communal home. May waited until a natural time to move away after college graduation; once she had established herself in a new city she broke off the relationship. She was able to move at this leisurely pace partly because she didn't recognize the danger she was in until long after she left.

If you are now in an abusive relationship, the message here is to attend to whatever barely perceptible rumblings are under the surface of your consciousness—so you can be ready when they "suddenly" erupt. If there aren't yet any signs of an opening in what seems like a hopeless trap, it's good to keep searching and stay active, meeting new people and doing new things as much as possible, even if this doesn't result in obvious or immediate changes. Just as it is difficult, even after the fact, to tell what deciding factor was most important to these women, no one can be sure what series of actions will turn out to be the combination that unlocks the way to freedom for you.

STAYING AWAY

Each of the women described had her own reason or reasons for feeling finished with her relationship. But some had felt that way before and yet had a difficult time staying away. They had to continually talk themselves out of going back. The last time they left they developed methods of strengthening themselves and were helped by friends, family and professionals. In this section we'll look at what seemed to make the difference in the women's ability to stay safe.

Relatively Easy Situations

Some women are both clear and convincing about never having considered going back to the men who abused them. As you read their stories you might have been surprised at the ease with which they remained safe. They are the nes who had broken the attachment, whether of dependency or love, some time before they actually left. It is equally important that their partners were willing, at a fairly early point, to stop threatening them. Joan lost all positive feelings for Randy when he kidnapped her child, and once she left she never looked back. May had gradually become less interested in Ross and more became independent before she told him the relationship was over.

Even though these women weren't tempted to go back, life wasn't necessarily easy. Some were lonely, depressed, exhausted and anxious about the future. Like those who remained in love, addicted to their partners or dependent on them, they too had to cope with limited social supports or the reality-based fear of the former partners' harassment and violence, until they had proof it had stopped.

The intervention of outside forces such as the justice system helped Pauline stay away. However, the external aid was by itself no guarantee of safety. Pauline had patiently waited for Matthew when he went to jail the first time, as had Chris when Wes was in jail. Some of the women who still cared for the ex-partner put thousands of miles between them to minimize the temptations to return.

Practical Supports

Although the essential elements in staying safe were not always concrete items like housing or financial support, those were crucial for some women, especially in the first weeks away. They were provided by public assistance, shelters, friends or relatives.

Public assistance provided a safety net for several women. Along with low rent housing, it has helped Maria survive until she improves her English enough to earn a living for herself and her children. For Dianne it was a stop-gap for the short period before she was paid an adequate wage at her new job. Melissa's mental condition and Pauline's physical illness enabled them to get temporary disability payments, which allowed them to pay their basic expenses until they were able to work. Chris used her vocational rehabilitation program to further her education in a field that would ensure her economic independence and adequate support of her two children.

After she had separated, Gloria stayed in a shelter just one night when she felt threatened by Hal's anger. Janine was in a shelter a longer time, and listening to a woman recount her years of beatings made her realize Raul would never stop. Hope was provided with counseling at a shelter and even worked there for a period. She and the other shelter residents went out together and started their new lives together. Knowing there were "ladies behind her" gave her the courage to go on. A short while after Lucia left she began work at a shelter and was reassured at the acceptance she experienced. Having been battered was an asset on the job, rather than something to be ashamed of.

Other people provided temporary housing for short or long periods. Janine is free to live in her grandmother's house indefinitely, which is an important addition to the sparse stipend allowed by public assistance. Pauline's aunt provided her with a healthy new environment and an opportunity to regain her health.

Lynn was given a guard dog and Jane was encouraged to use her housemate's dog to provide her with a sense of security. Joan found that her friends at work referred her to auto mechanics and gave her rides and advice on her income tax. Terry's employer told her how she could get a temporary restraining order.

Those Who Helped And Those Who Hindered

Women's groups were important for several women. At a community based group for abused women, Joan could count on the support she often couldn't get from her therapist. Sandy found the company of other women who had been "down some of the same roads" important for understanding. In a group for formerly battered women Barb was encouraged to remember the battering and to confront her fears. Ruth found a group that helped her sort out her feelings about being in a lesbian battering relationship and the residue of racism she had left with.

It was fortunate that there were people to lend moral support because many of the women were disppointed by the reactions of friends and relatives. Jennifer's friend said the battering "wasn't that bad." Jane felt betrayed when her father listened to Gerald after they had separated and "didn't remember" that he had been told about the beating and stranglings.

Although financial assistance of some kind was a necessity for many of the women, their morale was also affected by the professionals they encountered as they sought practical and emotional support. Lynn, Margaret and Jane were angry or bitter about the lack of appropriate response of police or prosecutors. Allie's isolation with her secret was more extreme for her than for some other women because of the homophobia she encountered in hotline counselors, who were not prepared to help lesbians. It was compounded by lesbian counselors' resistance to taking lesbian battering seriously.

Had she listened to the social worker who first offered to "help" her, Chris would have given up her second child for adoption and might have abandoned hope of improving her life. Her vocational rehabilitation counselor, on the other hand, encouraged her efforts to be an independent, responsible parent. Dianne and her children would have been deprived of basic needs, had not her welfare worker explained that she would still need assistance even after she started her first part-time job. Several women benefited from the advice and support of counselors who helped them identify the problem, resist the temptation to return to the destructive relationship and to rebuild their lives.

Dee found a stay at a mental hospital useful. She had been hospitalized many times, but her reluctance to stay away from her children had always caused her to leave before treatment could be effective. After leaving Pete she decided to stay at the hospital until she was well.

The women who had children found life without a partner to be difficult economically and in other important ways. Adequate affordable housing in safe neighborhoods was out of reach for some of the women and they weren't free to take advantage of community activities because of childcare responsibilities. But many of them found their children to be comforting and encouraging.

Work, Organizations and Classes
Though some of the women didn't take advantage of such

activities right away, work and classes were important sources of self-confidence and direction for nearly all the women. In addition there were a range of activities which included volunteer work in the Epilepsy League for Chris and working with children for Sandy, as well as jogging, hiking, music, writing and sewing for several others. These involvements kept the women busy and distracted them from romanticized memories of the partners who had beaten them and whom in many instances they still cared for.

Organizations such as Al-Anon and Parents Without Partners were helpful to Dianne and Joan. Joan found that after an initial period of "sampling" too many men at Parents Without Partners, she could go to the dances to simply enjoy herself. Usually now she chooses to leave the dances with the woman friend she came with.

Nicole was gratified at her ability to do college work and her women's studies courses have given her a new, optimistic perspective about herself. Hillary gained confidence as she wrote about her experiences as an incest survivor, a prostitute and a battered woman and gradually spoke out to more people about them.

Self Help

Several women discovered ways to talk to themselves or think about their lives that helped them combat loneliness, discouragement and depression. Sue and Barb each found that limited goals and small steps were important to keep from becoming overwhelmed by the tasks of building new lives. Amanda devised a safety routine, complete with escape route from her bedroom, to alleviate her fear. Dianne found that she could read well enough to use self-help books.

Some activities were useful in enduring frightening and lonely periods, especially right after separation, but they weren't constructive in the long run. Several women drank too much, although it usually didn't last too long. Some went to bed with a series of partners they weren't emotionally involved with, just to be held or to have the momentary illusion of being cared for. A round of frantic activity, whether work, school or other distractions were useful for a time, but most women found that it was eventually necessary to slow down and take a good look at what they had been through.

New Partners

Several women found that men were helpful, either as dates, sexual partners, friends or new partners. Most of the women who had formed new relationships were able to find partners who treated them well, or they quickly left anyone who emotionally abused them. Both Ruth and Allie were helped through difficult times by their new lovers. Quite a few of the women had left the abusive partner some years before the interview and had had plenty of time to form new relationships, yet only a few had had a second relationship in which there was battering, and all but one of those had been short-lived.

Hillary became involved with an emotionally abusive partner after leaving the man who battered her. This time it was a woman, and it only took about two months to realize that her self-concept was affected and that she felt powerless. She immediately broke off the relationship.

May has formed a relationship with a man whom she recognizes as "a bit sexist," but he is also a fair person who will discuss issues with her and she is not afraid to point out to him the things that upset her. She's determined to finish her schooling before she makes a permanent liaison. Allie went directly into a new relationship before she was completely separated from Jane. She and her lover are working on their problems together. Pauline is remarried and has a truly equal partnership with a peace-loving, lively man. Several other women have married and established satisfying relationships with nonviolent men.

Not all of the women found or wanted another relationship. Some wanted to wait quite a while in order to recover from the abusive relationship and establish their own autonomy. A few women still felt that they would never have a serious relationship. They thought they couldn't trust their judgment. After being in an emotionally abusive relationship Hillary said, "I just have this fear that if I let go a little bit, I'm going to lose it all, and the person's going to take me over."

Some believe there are few people who are worthy of their trust.

A few of the women who didn't have partners and wanted them were lonely and far from satisfied with their lives. Edith, who "always wanted to be someone's wife and someone's mother," had a great number of adjustments to make after she left Jack. Her youngest child moved out and she finds it hard to come home to an empty house. She also lost a great deal of money by paying off her husband's debts during the marriage and through a costly divorce settlement. She thinks much of her depression is due to the fact that she's fifty-four years old and "not bouncing back" the way she did when she was younger. Even so she finds that there are pleasures in being alone. She can get up in the middle of the night without anyone questioning her and can sing with the radio. She has a rewarding job which pays enough to boost her ego. She has a "much better feeling of self-worth" than she had with Jack.

Terry also feels low sometimes and regrets that she has lost friends in her Chinese community. Yet she finds satisfaction in her job, in her volunteer work and in the knowledge that she is safe. She is definite about the rightness of her decision to leave her husband and to live alone if she doesn't find a man she can trust. "I know lots of girls in their forties or fifties who are not married and who are happy... You don't just grab anyone. No. Never."

Joan and Barb, among others, are enjoying seeing different men and eventually may settle down with one. Meanwhile they grow stronger and more certain of what they want and what their limits are and each have a good time enjoying a variety of activities. Chris has turned down proposals and is more interested in her studies and preparing herself to be financially independent than in romance. Dianne is contented with her self-help books and music and enjoys her own company. Jane recognizes that she is not suited to marriage and is enjoying the cosmopolitan life of a single woman.

It has been said that battered women learn to be helpless about changing their situations and there is some truth to that. After trying everything they could think of to placate and change their partners, with no success, most of the women went through periods of despair and hopelessness.

But far more significant is their courage to rise above those feelings at crucial moments. Far more important is their ability, in spite of enormous obstacles, to make radical changes in their lives. Developing the capacity and the confidence to fix the washing machine, take care of the car or earn an adequate living were great morale boosters.

Collectively the women illustrate many alternatives to living with violent, controlling partners. Some of those who thought they could never find a partner who would treat them well, did so. Others who thought they couldn't survive without a partner are learning to like it or are discovering that they can cope with it even though it isn't what they want. None have any regrets about leaving. No matter how lonely they may get, how poor, or how great the responsibilities they shoulder, all of them know they are better off solving their problems without the interference of an abusive partner.

Researchers, therapists and the general public are given to speaking of "the" battered woman, as if "she" were all of a piece. It is my hope that such assumptions will be less easy to make after reading this book. The women are strikingly different from each other, yet similar in certain reactions to abusive partners and in many ways like women who have not been battered. Nearly all women have felt abuse of some kind or its threat, have tried to rescue someone they've loved, have been reluctant to give up a relationship, even though it was necessary.

Most of us make dramatic changes at more than one stage of our lives. We take or give up jobs outside the home or in it. We raise children or decide not to, form families whether of blood or chosen relationships, and we sever those ties. Whatever our pattern and whether or not we have been physically battered, we share many of the fears and satisfactions that the women in this book experienced.

If all women who had been battered spoke with a collective voice it would sound something like this:

I am a Latina, white, black, Indian woman who grew up in a stable, poor, chaotic, middle class, alcoholic, wealthy, professional, violent, working class, distant, rigid, warm, close, dependable family. As a child I was outgoing, shy, athletic, a bookworm, molested, protected, living in a fairy land, trying out new adventures on a daily basis.

When I met my future partner I was feeling depressed, happy with myself, sick, upset about being alone, looking forward to living alone. I was unhappy at home, a widow in my middle years, at the prime of life and my career, a teenager. At first everything seemed glamorous, romantic, a little dangerous, I didn't like this person at first, but I got used to being loved, I could hardly wait to get married, I didn't know how to get out of it because everyone expected it, the sex was great, I felt secure, I was scared but I thought it would be good for me to be tested.

After the first hit I was so shocked, so stunned, so horrified at what I had gotten into. The warning signs had all been there. There hadn't been any clues to what to expect until our honeymoon, until a month after we were married, for the first year. There were clues, but I thought it was just the alcohol, the stress, the unhappy childhood, that I could fix it, could rescue my lover, could be the "psychiatrist," if I just had enough love.

I used to envision myself laying on the ground like a murdered woman I saw a picture of once. I was like a varmint in a trap. I was depressed and all I wanted was to stay in bed. I felt like I was a prisoner at Auschwitz, not human. It was excruciating coming to grips with what's real and what's not real. I forced myself to eat, to get up and go on about my day.

After the second, fourth, fifteenth, five hundredth hit, beating, verbal assault, rape, humiliation I finally knew that I had to get out or I would be dead, or my children would be dead, or there would be nothing left of who I was. I was empty, depleted, brainwashed, finished, angry, drained, furious, determined, desperate. I left for the last time and now I have a different life. I am a different person now and I'm the same person now.

I felt a lot of sadness, letting go of the dream, the fantasy that we would be able to work things out. But I was letting go, letting the grief come through that this relationship was over. I was real confused. I can't say where the transition was, but the happier periods got longer and the slumps got shorter. I never looked back. It seemed forever at first, but it's worth it.

The only thing I would do differently is somehow or other be able to gain more sense of myself earlier. It's all a growing thing. I should have left years ago. It was okay to give it three years of my life, but no more. It was what I had to do, and I gave it the years it needed. It crippled me forever. I am a better person than I ever could have been had I not gone through it.

I don't surrender much of my autonomy any more. I'm really looking at myself as a fully independent functioning person. I vacillate between wanting to be part of someone's life, to share things, to have a companion and at the same time wanting to expand myself, to know myself better. But look how lucky I am, I'm married now to a good person. In the past two years I'm finding out who I am and I'm on the way up now. I love living alone. I still would like to be someone's wife, but I'm a person who wants to grow and wants to go and if it gets to be dull or routine I'll look for something different.

I feel like there's something I'm going to be and that's why I'm alive. Sometimes I'll be at the store and I'll just smile at anybody that walks by. Life is marvelous now. I enjoy everything because I don't have this cloud hanging over me. I go for a ride and look at tulips. Now I'm free. I really love the freedom. I can do the things I want. The freedom is great. At last I'm free. No one is looking over my shoulder. I'm free, I'm free, I'm free, I'm free.

Notes

INTRODUCTION

1. For a sample recent year, see "Circumstances by Relationship," U.S. Federal Bureau of Investigation, Uniform Crime Report (Washington, D.C.: FBI, U.S. Dept. of Justice, 1985), 9. The total number of female victims in 1985 was 2,773. Of those, 2,517 were killed by men. Of the 2,773, 30% (or approximately 832 women) were killed by men with whom they were having intimate relationships. (Only 6% of male murder victims were slain by wives or girlfriends.)
2. See M'Liss Switzer and Katherine Hale, *Called To Account* (Seattle: Seal Press, 1987). This is the personal account of a woman who called the police after a mandatory arrest law had been passed in her state: her husband later attended a group for men who batter and continues to involve himself in treatment groups, knowing he is not "cured," even though he is no longer violent.
3. See Lee Bowker, *Ending The Violence: A Guidebook Based on the Experience of 1,000 Battered Wives* (Holmes Beach, Florida: Learning Publications, Inc., 1986). Bowker reports on the successful and unsuccessful techniques women used in trying to stop their partners' violence.
4. Some researchers are convinced battering is transmitted from one generation to the next by a battering parent. Pagelow summarizes and analyzes the literature and indicates there is little basis for such conclusions, though there is some evidence that a disproportionate number of

boys who were abused by their fathers grow up to batter. See Mildred Pagelow, *Family Violence* (New York: Praeger, 1984), 244–257, and Lenore E. Walker, *The Battered Woman Syndrome* (New York: Springer, 1984), 19.

5. Lenore E. Walker, ibid., 21.

6. Diana E. H. Russell, *Sexual Exploitation* (Beverly Hills: Sage Library of Social Research 1984), vol. 155: 183.

7. Pagelow, *Woman-Battering: Victims and Their Experiences* (Beverly Hills: Sage Publications, 1981), Vol. 129: 59.

8. Pagelow, *Family Violence*, 89.

9. R. Emerson Dobash and Russell Dobash, *Violence Against Wives: A Case Against the Patriarchy* (New York: Free Press, 1979), 27–30.

10. Dobash and Dobash, ibid., 24. See also Walker, *Battered Woman Syndrome*, 36.

11. Walker, ibid., 109.

12. Please see the following books for discussion of the issues mentioned:

Sexism: Murray A. Straus, "A sociological perspective on the Prevention and Treatment of Wifebeating" in Maria Roy, *Battered Women* (New York: Van Nostrand Reinhold Co., 1977), 194–238.

Fear: Mildred Pagelow, *Family Violence*, 306.

Helplessness: Lenore E. Walker, *The Battered Woman Syndrome*, 86–94.

Brainwashing: Ginny NiCarthy, *Getting Free: A Handbook for Women in Abusive Relationships* (Seattle: Seal Press, 1986), 285–291.

Guilt: Pagelow, ibid., 309.

Addictive love: Ginny NiCarthy, *Getting Free: A Handbook for Women in Abusive Relationships* (Seattle: Seal Press, 1986), 51–53.

Childhood bonding: D. Dutton and S. Painter, "Traumatic Bonding: The Development of Emotional Attachments in Battered Women and Other Relationships in Intermittent Abuse," in *Victimology: An International Journal*, 6(1–4): 139–55.

Religious Beliefs: Dobash and Dobash, *Violence Against Wives*, 51–56.

Traditional ideas: Ginny NiCarthy, Addei Fuller and Nan Stoops, "Abuse of Women in Intimate Relationships," in Diane Burden and Naomi Gottlieb, *The Woman Client* (New York: Tavistock Publications, 1987), 209–222.

Lack of resources: Lewis Okun, *Woman Abuse: Facts Replacing Myths* (New York: State University of New York Press, 1986), 225.

Hope for change: Beverly Wigen Gravdal, "Battered Women: Learned Helplessness or Learned Hopefulness in Abusive Relationships," paper delivered at Association of Women in Psychology (AWP) conference, Seattle, Washington, 1983.

13. Pagelow, *Family Violence,* 306–308.

14. See Kerry Lobel, *Naming the Violence* (Seattle: Seal Press, 1986), for lesbians' descriptions of the reasons they stayed.

15. See Robin Norwood, *Women Who Love Too Much* (New York: Pocket Books, 1985), and Anne Wilson Schaef, *Co-Dependence* (San Francisco: Harper & Row, 1986).

16. Stanton Peele with Archie Brodsky, *Love and Addiction,* (New American Library, 1976), and G. Alan Marlatt and Judith R. Gordon, *Relapse Prevention* (New York: The Guilford Press, 1985), 9–19.

17. Felicity Barringer, "A Dissident in Moscow is Anxious," *New York Times,* Oct. 2, 1986, p. 5.

18. "Emigres in U.S. Opt for Soviet Union," *Seattle Times,* Nov. 5, 1986.

19. Sandra Blakeslee, "Fear of Big Quake Assessed in West," *New York Times,* July 30, 1986, p. 9.

20. Joan Mower, "Personal Reasons Bind U.S. Citizens to Stormy Country," *Seattle Times/Post Intelligencer,* November 23, 1986, p. 3.

21. Diana E. H. Russell, *Rape In Marriage* (New York: Macmillan Publishing Co., 1982), 282–285.

CHAPTER 35

1. Flo Conway and Jim Siegelman, *Snapping* (New York: Delta, 1978), 134–151, 146.

About the Author:

Ginny NiCarthy is widely recognized for her extensive work in the battered women's movement. A professional therapist with the Women's Counseling Group in Seattle, she has led groups for abused women for over a decade. She is the author of the well-known book, *Getting Free: A Handbook for Women in Abusive Relationships* and the co-author of *Talking It Out: A Guide to Groups for Abused Women.*